Anxious Appetites

Contemporary Food Studies: Economy, Culture and Politics

Series Editors: David Goodman and Michael K. Goodman

ISSN: 2058–1807

This interdisciplinary series represents a significant step towards unifying the study, teaching and research of food studies across the social sciences. The series features authoritative appraisals of core themes, debates and emerging research, written by leading scholars in the field. Each title offers a jargon-free introduction to upper-level undergraduate and postgraduate students in the social sciences and humanities.

Kate Cairns and Josée Johnston, *Food and Femininity*

Peter Jackson, *Anxious Appetites: Food and Consumer Culture*

Further titles forthcoming

Anxious Appetites

Food and consumer culture

Peter Jackson

Bloomsbury Academic
An imprint of Bloomsbury Publishing Plc

B L O O M S B U R Y
LONDON • NEW DELHI • NEW YORK • SYDNEY

Bloomsbury Academic
An imprint of Bloomsbury Publishing Plc

50 Bedford Square   1385 Broadway
London   New York
WC1B 3DP   NY 10018
UK   USA

www.bloomsbury.com

BLOOMSBURY and the Diana logo are trademarks of Bloomsbury Publishing Plc

First published 2015

© Peter Jackson, 2015

Pater Jackson has asserted his right under the Copyright, Designs and Patents Act, 1988, to be identified as Author of this work.

British Library Cataloguing-in-Publication Data
A catalogue record for this book is available from the British Library.

ISBN: HB: 978-1-4725-8814-2
        PB: 978-1-4725-8813-5
        ePDF: 978-1-4725-8815-9
        ePub: 978-1-4725-8816-6

Library of Congress Cataloging-in-Publication Data
Jackson, Peter, 1955-
Anxious appetites : food and consumer culture / by Peter Jackson.
pages cm
Includes bibliographical references and index.
ISBN 978-1-4725-8814-2 (hardback) – ISBN 978-1-4725-8813-5 (pbk.)
1. Food habits–Social aspects. 2. Food–Quality–Social aspects.
3. Food contamination–Social aspects. 4. Consumers. 5. Anxiety–Social aspects. I. Title.
GT2855.J33 2015
394.1'2–dc23
2015006534

Series: Contemporary Food Studies: Economy, Culture and Politics, Vol. 2

Typeset by Newgen Knowledge Works (P) Ltd., Chennai, India
Printed and bound in India

Dedicated to
Deb, Sam and Martha

Contents

Figures and tables

Figures

Tables

Preface

Around 15 years ago, the *Chronicle of Higher Education* charted the emergence of food studies as an academic field, noting a recent 'publishing bonanza' that had turned this formerly disdained field into what it called a 'hot commodity' (Ruark 1999). While mostly celebratory in tone, the article worried about the populist tendencies within some areas of food studies that the author characterized as 'scholarship lite', undermining more serious attempts to gain food studies a legitimate place at the academic table. More recently, the *New York Times* ran a similar article (Spiegel 2012), reiterating the *Chronicle*'s anxiety about whether food is a worthy subject of academic study. 'Food studies' is much less established as a distinctive research area in the UK (where I live and work) than in the United States, although one British author recently described it as a 'burgeoning field' (Murcott 2013).

Having been trained in human geography and social anthropology, I was attracted by the wide horizons and inherent interdisciplinary of food studies. But I have also been repeatedly drawn back to the comparative perspective of my disciplinary training, feeling compelled to make the case that 'geography matters' in terms of the contextual specificities of time and place, as well as being wedded to the relativizing impulses of social anthropology, with its characteristic suspicion of anything that is claimed to be absolute or universal. In what follows I attempt to show the value of this twin perspective, emphasizing the general and the specific, the disciplinary and the interdisciplinary. The book focuses on the pervasiveness of consumer anxieties about food in contemporary Western societies, tracing the rise and fall of specific food-related anxieties and seeking to understand their spatial and temporal variation. The distinctive insights of an ethnographic perspective are also brought to bear as a critique of over-hasty generalizations and, especially, the pervasive tendency to moralize food and eating.

The research project on which this book is based (the funding for which is acknowledged below) addressed the nature of consumer culture in an 'age of anxiety' through an analysis of the moral and political economies of food. While many historical periods have been described as an age of anxiety, this book seeks to understand why we, in modern Western societies, are currently so anxious about food when governments and other official bodies assure us that it is safer than ever before. Charting the rise and fall of specific food anxieties and exploring their social geographies, the book seeks to understand our vexed relationship with food, exploring how food serves as a powerful lens on society, acknowledging its richly symbolic value while not losing sight of food's insistent and irreducible materiality.

As will become apparent, the book's focus is on the *social* nature of contemporary food anxieties rather than on the way they are experienced psychologically by individual members of society. But it is often hard to separate the personal from the political or the local from the global, for food has a unique ability to bridge such conventional distinctions, transcending the psycho-social, the here-and-now and the there-and-then. As Warren Belasco asserts in *Appetite for Change*, 'Food is a strong "edible dynamic", binding present and past, individual and society, private household and world economy, palate and power' (2007: 5).

Before taking up my argument in more detail, I want to acknowledge some intellectual debts and offer some personal thanks. One of the great pleasures of academic life is the opportunity to work with other people who share your interests and enthusiasms but who are not afraid to offer challenge and critique. While this is, in one sense, a sole-authored book, it would not have been possible without the help and support of many friends and colleagues. First among these, I would like to acknowledge the team who worked alongside me on the CONANX project (*Consumer culture in an 'age of anxiety'*). Helene Brembeck and Matt Watson were my co-investigators; Ben Coles, Maria Fuentes, Qian Gong, Richard Lee, Angela Meah, Richard Milne and Jakob Wenzer worked as research associates; Nick Piper was our PhD student and Daphne Lai provided administrative support. Qian and Angela's work features strongly in Chapters 6, 8 and 9 and Nick's research underpins the argument in Chapter 7 (and their contribution is formally acknowledged at the start of these chapters). It was a very productive and highly enjoyable project that culminated in a jointly authored book (Jackson and the CONANX group 2013) and a series of other publications (details of which are available on the project website: http://www/sheffield.ac.uk/conanx).

Second, I would like to acknowledge the generous funding of the CONANX project, provided via an Advanced Investigator Grant from the European Research Council (2009–12) and a subsequent Proof of Concept award (2013–14) to explore the potential practical application of this work. I have since embarked on an ERA-Net project (2014–17), focusing on food, convenience and sustainability and I would like to acknowledge my co-investigators on this new venture:

Helene Brembeck, Bente Halkier and Jonathan Everts. Jonathan was previously a postdoctoral fellow in Sheffield where we co-authored the original version of the theory of social anxiety that is elaborated here in Chapter 3.

Third, I would like to thank my colleagues in the Department of Geography at the University of Sheffield who have supported my work in many ways over the years and the wider cross-Faculty sustainable food group (SheFF), which has provided an invigorating interdisciplinary forum in which to develop my research. The Faculty of Social Sciences at Sheffield awarded me a Senior Research Fellowship in 2013–14, coinciding with a year-long study leave granted by my Department, which provided the opportunity to complete this book, together with continuing financial support for Angela Meah whose energy and enthusiasm, wit and wisdom, I have come to rely on. I am grateful to everyone at Sheffield, including both academic and professional services staff, for their collegiality and practical support. It is a great place to work. I would also like to pay tribute to an exceptional group of food-related PhD students including Lauren Blake, Jonas House, Ian Humphrey, Beth Kamunge, Anna Ludvigsen, Hannah Lambie-Mumford, Nick Piper, Ava Shackleford, Vincent Song, Roza Tchoukaleyksa, Bel Townsend and Sarah Wrathmell.

Colleagues in numerous other places have contributed to the thinking behind this project though they are not responsible for any of its shortfalls. Among them I would particularly like to acknowledge Anne Murcott with whom I have worked on several projects including the *Changing Families, Changing Food* programme for which she served as a critical friend (Jackson 2009). Anne was kind enough to read final drafts of two key chapters, offering sound advice and encouragement at a crucial time. I have also enjoyed working alongside Anne at the UK Food Standards Agency (FSA) where we both serve on their General Advisory Committee on Science. This also provides an opportunity to thank Sian Thomas and her colleagues at the FSA for supporting me in my role as chair of the Agency's Social Science Research Committee from which I have learned a great deal about current UK food policy (as reflected in Chapter 5). I have also benefitted from the friendship and support of Richard Le Heron in the School of Environment at the University of Auckland, Harry West in the Food Studies Centre at SOAS, David Evans at the University of Manchester and Monica Truninger at the Institute of Social Sciences in Lisbon. Also deserving special mention is Polly Russell who has collaborated with me on numerous projects, providing valuable insights into the commercial world of food as well as helping me to communicate my research to a wider public.

As part of their series on Contemporary Food Studies, Michael Goodman and David Goodman encouraged me to write this book and saw it through to publication, offering critical advice and generous support at key moments. Thanks also to an anonymous reader who provided constructive criticism of an earlier draft and to Jennifer Schmidt and her editorial team at Bloomsbury. The maps in Chapter 2 were drawn by Jeremy Ely and the one in Chapter 5 was drawn by David McCutcheon. The index was compiled by Angela Meah.

Last but not least, I would like to thank my family, starting with my mother, Nancy Jackson, who has always been there for me and whose advice to 'slow down a bit, you're not getting any younger' I promise to take to heart one day soon. But most of all it is my partner Deborah Lee and our children, Sam and Martha, who deserve my most heart-felt thanks. They sustain me in everything I do, keeping me grounded and putting my academic life into perspective. Deborah also provided the artwork for the cover design. There is no adequate way of thanking them – but I dedicate this book to them as a token of my love and gratitude.

Abbreviations

BAFTA	British Academy of Film and Television Arts
BOC	British Oxygen Company
BSE	Bovine spongiform encephalopathy
CSA	Community supported agriculture
DAFM	Department of Agriculture, Food and the Marine
DEFRA	Department for Environment, Food and Rural Affairs
DFA	Drug and Food Administration
DSM	Desinewed meat
EFRA	Environment, Food and Rural Affairs
EFSA	European Food Safety Authority
FBO	Food Business Operators
FMD	Foot-and-Mouth Disease
FSA	Food Standards Agency
FSAI	Food Safety Authority of Ireland
GM	genetically modified
HACCP	Hazard Analysis and Critical Control Point
IME	Institute of Mechanical Engineers
MRM	mechanically recovered meat
NFA	Swedish National Food Authority
NFU	National Farmers' Union
RSPCA	Royal Society for the Prevention of Cruelty to Animals
WRAP	Waste and Resources Action Programme

Chapter 1

Introduction: The roots of contemporary food anxieties

This book examines the nature and extent of consumer anxieties about food in modern Western societies. It does so by exploring a series of specific events such as the European horsemeat incident in 2013 and the infant formula scandal in China in 2008, also including longer-term issues such as the social impact of technological change in the food industry and the rise of 'celebrity chefs', which have influenced consumer attitudes to food in more diffuse ways. It uses a variety of evidence from official documents and government enquiries to social surveys and more qualitative evidence including interviews and focus groups, as well as ethnographic observation at the household level. Combining these sources reveals some significant issues about food-related anxiety including the gap between high levels of reported anxiety in surveys and other expressions of public opinion and the day-to-day experience of food where consumers are shown to have negotiated their anxieties into routinized practices which allow them to go about their daily lives in a relatively untroubled manner.

One of the key arguments of this book is that food-related anxieties should not be understood at a purely individual level. To do so is to neglect the irreducibly social dimensions of contemporary consumer anxieties about food. While individuals may have personal anxieties about food (such as food allergies or concerns about the health implications of what they eat), the incidence of food issues also has an intrinsically social aspect, varying by class and gender, for example, as well as historically and geographically. The book seeks to trace the contours of specific social anxieties about food, charting the way they rise and fall at different times and in different places. Addressed in this historical, geographical and sociological manner, the book seeks to understand the causes of this variable social condition (tracing the 'roots' of contemporary anxieties about food) and to follow the course of specific anxieties as they wax and wane, moving between social groups and morphing from one issue to another (mapping their 'routes'). When approached in this way, consumer anxieties about food can be seen to have a wider sociological significance, acting as a vehicle for the expression of a range of other issues including concerns about social class and regional identity, gender relations and changes in family life.

As well as examining specific issues such as concerns about food safety, revealed in periodic 'food scares' such as the horsemeat incident or the infant formula scandal, the book also explores the impact of consumer anxieties on more systemic issues such as the environmental and health implications of the rise of 'convenience' food and the way that everyday domestic practices contribute to the generation of food waste at the household level. Besides its academic interest, this way of understanding consumer anxieties has practical value in terms of its relevance for food policy, addressing the gap that often exists between official advice (based on the best-available scientific knowledge) and everyday practice (based on lay understandings). The book advocates an assets-based approach to public understanding, emphasizing the stocks of knowledge which consumers use to make sense of their world rather than a deficit approach where consumers are assumed to lack essential knowledge or to wilfully ignore well-intentioned advice. The book ends with a critique of 'consumer choice', arguing that this concept forms a questionable basis for policy interventions, overemphasizing the role of individuals and neglecting the social character and wider context of dietary decisions such as those that are examined here in terms of consumer anxieties about food.

Writing about contemporary food anxieties can be a hazardous undertaking and it is sensible at the outset to clarify the book's specific focus, including some necessary caveats and cautions. Despite its concern with appetite and anxiety, this book does not focus on individual food pathologies such as bulimia or anorexia, except insofar as such 'disorders' can be seen as symptoms of wider social anxieties about food. It should also be clearly stated that the book focuses mainly on experiences of food anxiety in modern Western societies in the Global North rather than on issues of hunger and malnutrition in the Global South. These issues are, however, ultimately inextricable and the current food security agenda shows how questions of 'over-consumption' in some parts of the world are intimately connected to questions of chronic malnutrition and periodic famine in other parts of the world. These issues surface at various places in the book, notably in relation to questions of food waste and related ethical dilemmas (in Chapters 8 and 9) but they are not its principal focus.

Nor, despite my title, is the focus exclusively on anxiety (as a psycho-social condition), ignoring the positive emotions that are frequently associated with eating and drinking. Rather, the book attempts to show how pleasure and anxiety are deeply interwoven as food has an almost unique ability to elicit feelings of desire and dread, provoking fear and fascination to varying degrees, sometimes simultaneously.[1] The book will, however, argue that anxiety, in the way it is approached here, is a neglected issue in the academic study of food. Compared to all the recent interest by food scholars in concepts of trust and risk, for example, anxiety has received much less academic discussion, beyond its extensive treatment in the psychoanalytic tradition.[2] This book aims to address these issues head-on, seeking to identify the roots of present-day consumer anxieties about food and to trace their effects in contemporary Western societies.

The paradox of contemporary food anxieties

There is a paradox at the heart of contemporary anxieties about food which centres on the question of why Western consumers report such high levels of food anxiety in public opinion surveys when food is, arguably, safer today than at virtually any time in human history.[3] Harvey Levenstein (1993) identifies a similar 'paradox of plenty' in his history of American diet since the Great Depression where 'the best fed people the world has ever seen' have been subject to recurrent anxieties about weight, nutrition and processed food. Claude Fischler makes a more general claim that 'societies of abundance' tend to be 'impassioned over cuisine and obsessed with dieting' (1990: 219). What, then, is the nature of these anxieties and how might they be explained?

Some contemporary concerns about food are truly global in nature, such as the daunting challenge of feeding an anticipated 9 billion people by 2050 with limited or diminishing resources. Western consumers express high levels of concern about global food security but they report equally high if not greater concerns about domestic food safety and a range of other issues.[4] Western concerns about food security peaked in 2007–8 following the 'price shocks' that affected many agricultural commodities, leading to food riots in many parts of the world.[5] Such concerns have been reinforced by the experience of food shortages in even the most affluent economies, as demonstrated by the rapid increase in demand for food banks and other forms of emergency relief (Cooper & Dumpleton 2013, Lambie-Mumford et al. 2014).

Notwithstanding their concerns about future food security, consumers in the more privileged parts of the world also express anxieties about a range of other issues such as food safety, authenticity and provenance. Why, then, are there such high levels of public anxiety about food, given its relative abundance, alleged safety and general affordability, compared to many other times and places? The book does not seek to establish whether such anxieties are rational or proportionate to the actual risks (however they might be measured). Instead, the argument follows the sociological imperative of seeking to understand why such concerns arise, how they circulate within society and what 'work' they accomplish, whether or not they are judged to be logical or merited by external criteria.

The book also explores the apparent gap between reported anxieties about food (based on social surveys and similar evidence) and consumers' everyday experience, where observational and ethnographic data show that consumers are not constantly paralysed by fear or rendered incapable of making mundane dietary decisions. Rather, the book proposes, consumers have negotiated their anxieties into everyday practices that are, for the most part, routine and relatively unconsidered at a conscious level. Consumers may not be able to resolve all of the ethical dilemmas that surround their daily actions, including complex trade-offs between cost and quality, health and indulgence or any of the other potentially conflicting issues that Warde (1997) describes as 'culinary antinomies'.[6] But the evidence presented here (particularly in Chapters 7–9) suggests that most consumers have reached some kind of compromise that enables them to carry on their daily lives without having to confront insuperable moral dilemmas at every turn. How consumers traverse this potentially troubling terrain is at the heart of the book. It also seeks to trace how we (in modern Western societies such as the UK) have got to where we are today in terms of the development of our highly industrialized agri-food system and how various 'alternative' forms of provisioning have emerged. These 'alternative' systems can, of course, introduce new anxieties of their own (such as whether organic farming can provide sufficient food at a low enough price to feed the world's rapidly increasing, highly urbanized, population – or whether the reduction of 'food miles' through the consumption of local food might impose higher costs in terms of energy and other environmental demands than imported food grown at greater distance from the point of consumption under more energy-efficient conditions).

As already mentioned, it is important to remember that, for most Western consumers, most of the time, food is a source of pleasure rather than being a cause of constant anxiety.[7] As most readers know from personal experience, there are few more satisfying moments in life than sharing a meal with family and friends, where conviviality goes hand in hand with commensality.[8] But, as many would also concede, meal-times can be tense occasions and kitchens can be crowded, sometimes violent, spaces within the 'heart of the home' (Jackson & Meah 2013, Meah 2013a). These conflicting emotions arise because food has such powerful material and symbolic properties. It is vital to our health and well-being, and closely bound up with our embodied identities (when ingested, food literally becomes part of our selves). It has strong metaphorical force as well as being a necessity for sustaining life and well-being.

Contemporary agri-food systems have evolved to try and ensure that our appetites are fed, with constant year-round availability and a sometimes-bewildering choice of things to eat. Many Western consumers experience the anxieties associated with abundance and choice rather than the risks associated with a scarcity or lack of food. They experience what food scholars refer to as the 'omnivore's dilemma', where feeding our apparently insatiable appetites propels a constant search for novelty which poses inherent risks, especially for those whose culinary tastes go beyond the tried and tested.[9] Besides these basic drives, the use of food in identity formation may also be a source of anxiety, though the routinized nature of 'consumer choice', as well as processes of group identification and social regulation, arguably reduces the risks associated with exercising such choices in practice (cf. Warde 1994).

To reiterate the book's core concerns and essential caveats, the argument focuses on the food anxieties of modern Western consumers with some reference (particularly in Chapter 6) to the experience of consumers in the world's 'emerging economies'. It does not deal directly with the more than one billion people (mainly in the Global South) who face a different kind of food anxiety, characterized by chronic undernourishment and long-term food insecurity. Nor does it focus specifically on the so-called obesity epidemic that is affecting an approximately equivalent number of people (mainly in the Global North) who can be considered chronically 'over-nourished'. That the world is simultaneously 'stuffed and starved', in Raj Patel's (2007) graphic phrase, is an important context for the following discussion of modern Western consumer anxieties about food but it is not its central thread. The focus is, instead, on the prevalence and persistence of consumer anxieties about food among those who normally have sufficient to eat and who do not face imminent shortages. It seeks to understand how particular food-related anxieties rise and fall, why they peak in particular times and in particular places, how they circulate within society, how they are promulgated, regulated and controlled, whose interests they serve and how they might be abated. This is, then, an account of *social anxieties about food* at an aggregate (collective) level, not an analysis of psychological concerns at a purely individual level. This distinction is central to the theory of social anxiety outlined in Chapter 3.

Anxiety as an explanatory term

A further characteristic of the book is that it sees the social occurrence of anxiety as an issue to be explained rather than employing anxiety as an explanatory term. This is a crucial issue which can best be illustrated through a reading of how the term is deployed in several recent books that focus on food and which include the word 'anxiety' in their titles or sub-titles. For example, Sian Griffiths and Jennifer Wallace's edited book *Consuming Passions* (1998) refers to 'food in the age of anxiety', Susanne Freidberg's study of *French Beans and Food Scares* (2004) is subtitled 'culture and commerce in an anxious age' while John Coveney's *Food, Morals and Meaning* (2006) refers to 'the pleasure and anxiety of eating'. But none of these books makes any sustained attempt to define the nature of anxiety, using it instead as a kind of catch-all for contemporary fears and concerns about food.[10] Even a book called *Appetites and Anxieties* which examines the representation of food in film manages to avoid any systematic discussion of the nature of anxiety, besides a generalized reference to 'the aspirations and . . . anxieties of people in consumer society who live with the promise and threat of industrialized food production' (Baron et al. 2013: 7–8).[11]

Chad Lavin's recent book *Eating Anxiety* (2013) is a major exception, going significantly further in defining its terms while insisting that food anxieties are best approached as a metaphor for more fundamental concerns within American society. As a political theorist, Lavin examines the current saturation of America food discourse with anxieties about diet and obesity, often expressed in the neoliberal vocabulary of individual choice, anxieties which he interprets as a response to perceived threats to individual and national sovereignty (ibid.: xiii–xxxii). While the materiality of food is sometimes submerged in the discussion of food's metaphorical and symbolic power, Lavin takes anxiety seriously, looking at food through the lens of political theory and moral philosophy, arguing that 'the physical act of eating offers a distilled and intensified terrain for thinking about the more generalized questions of ethics, aesthetics, ecology [and] politics' (2013: xi). In Lavin's suggestive account, food is a subject of anxiety because it threatens the integrity of the borders between the self and the world, between public and private, and between the human and non-human. The saturation of food discourse with fear and anxiety, Lavin argues, is symptomatic of broader concerns about economic power, self-determination and the reliability of government institutions and the scientific establishment (ibid.: xiii).

However, there are also limitations to Lavin's analysis as an account of current food anxieties. For, if discourses of food 'are often not about food at all' but about our existential condition then food is reduced to little more than a cipher or 'structural metaphor' (2013: xvi–xvii). This issue then runs through the remainder of Lavin's book, where the abundance of food metaphors in contemporary political discourse is described as 'no mere coincidence' or as a 'reflection' of wider concerns about national sovereignty, international immigration or personal privacy (threatening the borders of self, space and species). While Lavin makes a valuable distinction between psychological and political anxiety (focusing on the latter), his analysis hinges on the identification of a series of historical parallels, temporal coincidences and elective affinities. He argues, for example, that 'The application of thermodynamics to digestion was *entirely consistent with* the demands of a growing capitalist economy' (p. 51), that 'the ingestion and accumulation of food energy *directly parallels* the process through which Marx describes industrial production and capitalist exchange' (p. 61), that 'the digestive turn in German political thought *mirrors* the revolutionary politics and industrial development in Germany in and around 1848' (p. 67) and so on – with the italics added in each case to show the operative terms in this way of thinking.

Lavin's analysis recalls Alan Hunt's cautionary remarks about the use of anxiety as an explanatory concept by sociologists and social historians who invoke some ill-defined, unconscious, collective psychological force in accounting for social phenomena. Hunt refers to the way anxiety often works as a 'submerged middle term' in sociohistorical thought (1999: 511), where causal mechanisms may be lacking to link the occurrence of collective anxiety with some putative social force. Hunt suggests that inferential connections should be substantiated empirically and that specific agents (or 'moral entrepreneurs') should be identified before such explanations can be validated. This is particularly important, he argues, when a cause is identified which does not form part of the consciousness or discourse of contemporary participants and where historians claim to be able to identify 'what was really going on', even when it may not have been apparent to those directly involved in the phenomenon being examined. So, for example, historians might argue that anxieties over prostitution in nineteenth-century North America can be explained in terms of underlying social anxieties about nation-building, racial 'degeneration' or urban decay, which themselves involve the repression of deeper anxieties about gender, race and class. In such cases, Hunt urges historians to go beyond the principles of convergence, where several phenomena converge on a particular focal point, to specify the causal processes that are thought to underlie what otherwise are merely inferential connections. Historians, he suggests, should be particularly careful in applying the attributes of individuals to social aggregates or in using the logic of displacement to indicate where the 'true' source of social anxieties actually lies. Hunt asks what kind of evidence should count towards the substantiation of an 'anxiety analysis', suggesting that notions of 'discursive affinity' and 'configuration' may be helpful in articulating such arguments, moving explanations beyond the speculative and conjunctural towards the identification of necessary or causal links. These are admonitions which are taken to heart in the rest of this book, especially when the argument moves beyond the contingent towards the causal.

Ambiguous appetites

'Appetite' is, of course, no less complex and ambiguous a word than anxiety, encompassing medical, biological, social and cultural aspects (Jackson 2013: 23). Like 'taste' (Korsmeyer 1999, 2005), appetite involves both physiological and socio-cultural dimensions. Platonic philosophy sought to distinguish between reason and appetite, comparable to the distinction that Descartes drew between mind and body, the latter having to be satisfied before the former can be set free. So, too, in his meditation on appetite does Brillat-Savarin draw attention to its physiological, imaginary and dreamlike qualities, evoking matters of the heart and soul as well as involving the 'whole digestive machine' of stomach and gastric juices. According to Brillat-Savarin (1825/2009: 67), 'Appetite declares itself by a vague languor in one's stomach and a slight feeling of fatigue'. M. F. K. Fisher's translation continues:

> At the same time one's soul concerns itself with things connected with its own needs; memory recalls dishes that have pleased the taste; imagination pretends to see them; there is something dreamlike about the whole process. This state is not without its charms, and a thousand times we have heard its devotees exclaim with a full heart: 'How wonderful to have a good appetite, when we are sure of enjoying an excellent dinner before long!' However, one's whole digestive machine soon takes part in the action: the stomach becomes sensitive to the touch; gastric juices flow freely; interior gases move about noisily; one's mouth waters, and every part of the machine stands at attention. (Ibid.: 67)[12]

The human appetite for food is what makes it such a strong vehicle for carrying psycho-social meaning. Human appetites are profoundly embodied and culturally embedded, making the appropriate choice of food a highly charged issue where much is at stake beyond the satiation of bodily needs. ('Much depends on dinner', in Byron's famous phrase.) While some aspects of our culinary appetites appear to be hard-wired into the human brain, many others are subject to the disciplines of social convention, such as eating times and the structure of what is generally agreed to constitute a meal (Douglas 1971).[13] Studying human appetites and their associated anxieties therefore leads back to some of the most fundamental questions of social science, distinguishing 'nature' from 'culture', the material from the symbolic, self from Other.

Culinary appetites can also be compared with sexual appetites, both forms of carnal desire providing pleasure and provoking psycho-social anxiety, calling forth a range of regulatory regimes (Probyn 2000).[14] In each case, the satisfaction of raw appetite is commonly distinguished from more cultivated tastes and discerning behaviour. Gluttony and sexual excess are both culturally deplored though both are common sources of fantasy and guilty pleasure. Philosophers have therefore sought to elaborate a more considered approach to food as 'thoughtful practice' (Heldke 1992), encouraging a breaching of the separation of knowing from doing, treating thinking as a form of embodied practice and eating as an opportunity for reflective thought.

These ideas are also relevant beyond the world of academic philosophy. In his book on *Appetite*, for example, British food writer Nigel Slater contrasts a formulaic approach to cooking, where recipes, ingredients and quantities are 'laid down in tablets of stone', with a more spontaneous approach whereby Slater encourages his readers to 'break the rules' and 'follow your appetite' (2000: 10). Slater wants his readers to trust their taste and develop a feeling for food rather than being hide-bound by convention or awed by the admonishments of professional chefs. But this approach to cooking by instinct and cultivating the taste-buds, based on an appreciation of the integrity of ingredients – their freshness, quality and provenance – requires a level of skill and confidence that can generate its own anxieties.

The pleasures and anxieties of food and sex are also, of course, a staple of contemporary advertising and other forms of popular culture (Parasecoli 2008). Susanne Freidberg explores these ideas in her 'perishable history' of freshness where notions of what is considered natural and healthy, pure and fresh, refer simultaneously to the physical or material qualities of food and to ideals for living and eating well (2010: 478). Food and sex share a common vocabulary as witnessed by the visual and verbal conventions of what has come to be called 'food porn' and in the sexualized language with which food-related anxieties circulate within society (discussed in more detail in Chapter 7 and in the Conclusion).

Consumer anxieties about food

It should by now have been acknowledged that referring to 'consumers' and their anxieties, as opposed to other designations such as 'citizen' or 'public', frames the subject in distinctive ways. As Frank Trentmann argues in *The Making of the*

Consumer (2006), consumers were 'made' through specific historical (social, political and economic) processes and the word is a reflection of modern market economies, not a neutral analytical term. The decision to refer to 'consumer anxieties' is an attempt to capture the contemporary Western public's predominant relationship to food (through acts of buying, preparing, eating and disposing of food) but this distinctive positioning should be constantly borne in mind. Where necessary, a range of other terms is employed, referring specifically to 'parents' in Chapter 6, to 'audiences' in Chapter 7 and, more generally, to different constructions of the 'public'.

Several recent books have touched on the social analysis of food anxiety, two of which merit particular consideration at this point. In *Fear of Food* (2012), an entertaining and informative history of what he calls America's 'fraught relationship' with food (ibid.: vii), Harvey Levenstein shows how markedly scientific understanding and nutritional advice about food have shifted over time. Reviewing the historical evidence, Levenstein concludes:

> Chemical preservatives went from being triumphs of modern science to poisons. Whole milk swung back and forth like a pendulum. Yogurt experienced boom, bust, and revival. Processed foods went from bringing healthy variety to the table to being devoid of nutrients. Prime rib of beef was transformed from the pride of the American table into a one-way ticket to the cardiac ward. Margarine went form 'heart-healthy' to artery-clogging, [while today] salt, historically regarded as absolutely essential to human existence, is swinging the grim reaper's scythe. (2012: 161)

It is no surprise, then, that the 'shifting sands of nutritional advice' have contributed to American anxieties about food, to the point where, Levenstein feels, fear of food in now 'akin to a permanent condition of middle-class life' (ibid.: 161–62).

Less focused on dietary and nutritional issues, Alison Blay-Palmer's *Food Fears* (2008) adopts a geographical perspective to explore how today's pervasive anxieties about food in North America can be attributed to the growing physical, social and intellectual distance between consumers and their food. Blay-Palmer argues that the experience of recent 'food scares' demonstrates how contemporary agri-food systems have privileged quantity over quality, treating food as a commodity rather than a source of nourishment and pleasure. Although her distinction between industrial and sustainable food systems may be a little overdrawn at times, Blay-Palmer offers a convincing account of how a variety of 'alternative' food initiatives (from organic farming and community-supported agriculture to farmers' markets and Fair Trade initiatives) have arisen in reaction to the industrialization of agri-food systems. Less attention is paid to how 'main-stream' food producers are appropriating the discourses of the 'alternative' food sector or how such alternatives may give rise to their own anxieties.[15]

Several authors refer to the present as an 'anxious age' or claim that Western consumers are living in an 'age of anxiety'. Such assertions should be treated with caution. The characterization of our present times as uniquely anxious is highly contentious and such claims should be closely examined.[16] For all such 'anxieties' are socially, spatially and historically specific and what constitutes 'anxiety' in one place or time may be very different from similar emotions experienced in other times and places. Many commentators, however, seem untroubled by such doubts. In an early account of the meaning of anxiety, for example, Rollo May concludes that 'The evidence is overwhelming . . . that men and women of today live in an "age of anxiety", characterized by a state of "nameless and formless uneasiness"' (1950: v). More recently, Iain Wilkinson confidently asserts that 'It is now a matter of sociological common sense to identify ourselves as living through a period of acute insecurity and high anxiety' (2001: 42). Similarly, for British newspaper journalist Madeleine Bunting, fear is now 'the dominant currency of public life': 'Despite the unprecedented security of life in the west', she argues, where 'we live for longer and are less vulnerable to absolute poverty than any previous generation of human beings – we seem more anxious, and fearful than ever' (*The Guardian*, 25 October 2004).

Social theorist Zygmunt Bauman offers an even bleaker assessment of the current Western condition, arising from the global insecurities associated with the 'war on terror' as well as from more localized concerns such as the fear of unemployment and the corrosive effects of prolonged recession. According to Bauman, anxiety has become a normal, everyday condition, whereby modern citizens are living in a state of constant anxiety. The darkness and fear that characterized premodern Europe has, according to Bauman, been replaced by new kinds of fear that threaten the human body, the social order and our very survival as a species. Bauman identifies a terrifying 'grey zone' of contemporary anxiety that he characterizes at length:

> A sense-numbing and mind-chafing grey zone, as yet unnamed, from which ever more dense and sinister fears seep, threatening to destroy our homes, workplaces and bodies through disasters – natural but not quite, human but not completely, natural and human at the same time though unlike either of them. The zone of which some over-ambitious yet hapless accident-and-calamity-prone sorcerer's apprentice, or a malicious genie imprudently let out of the bottle, must have taken charge. The zone where power grids go bust, petrol

taps run dry, stock exchanges collapse, all-powerful companies disappear altogether with dozens of services one used to take for granted and thousands of jobs one used to believe to be rock-solid, where jets crash together with their thousand-and-one safety gadgets and hundreds of passengers, market caprices make worthless the most precious and coveted of assets, and any other imaginable or unimaginable catastrophes brew (or perhaps are brewed?) ready to overwhelm the prudent and the imprudent alike.

Bauman concludes:

Day in, day out we learn that the inventory of dangers is far from complete: new dangers are discovered and announced almost daily, and there is no knowing how many more of them and of what kind have managed to escape our (and the experts!) attention – getting ready to strike without warning. (2006: 5)

It is a chilling vision but not dissimilar from the anxieties outlined in Ulrich Beck's influential account of the 'risk society' where he warns of the invisible risks associated with air pollution, radiological hazards and food contamination, the 'stowaways of normal consumption' that 'travel on the wind and in the water':

They can be in anything and everything, along with the absolute necessities of life – air to breathe, food, clothing, home furnishings – they pass through all the otherwise strictly controlled protective areas of modernity. (1992: 40–41)

For Beck, Western society's response to risk has been predominantly technocratic, involving expert systems of risk management such as the Hazard Analysis and Critical Control Point (HACCP) measures that are now adopted as the industry standard across many modern agri-food systems. But, according to Beck, contemporary society's response to risk also involves the elaboration of symbolic systems that provide 'magical' resolution to the fundamental contradictions of modern life. Through our increasingly individualized lives, Beck argues, we have escaped the shackles of tradition but at the cost of greater uncertainty, anxiety and risk (ibid.: 32). In place of established social roles and stable institutions, new forms of 'constructed certitude' have emerged to provide a guide to human conduct in an uncertain world – and there are innumerable examples of these constructions in the commercial world of contemporary food advertising, where ideas of authenticity and tradition, provenance and heritage, are a common stock in trade.

Reflecting on Beck's *Risk Society*, Sheldon Ungar (2001) attempts to identify the specific sites of social anxiety associated with environmental, nuclear, chemical and medical threats. He sees anxiety as a response to uncertainty and ambivalence where concerns about public safety lead to an extreme response akin to a contemporary 'moral panic'. Commenting on Ungar's argument, Sean Hier (2003) suggests that sites of social anxiety are converging with discourses of risk, frequently containing a strong moral dimension. The moralization of risk, Hier argues, often works through an exaggerated conception of individual human agency (as when government food policy, through its emphasis on individual choice, ends up blaming consumers for their lack of knowledge and skills, exonerating wider and more powerful institutional actors from blame for people's unhealthy diets and unsustainable behaviours). Hier identifies a growing tension between the 'techno-scientific rationalities' of the expert world (including food scientists and health professionals in the current context) and what he calls the 'social rationalities' of everyday living (experienced by 'ordinary consumers'). The gap between expert and lay knowledge is a key feature of the theory of social anxiety outlined in Chapter 3. The social significance of the increasing gap between food producers and consumers is explored in more detail in Chapter 4, while the problematic framing of 'consumer choice' is further explored in Chapter 10.

The roots of contemporary food anxieties

The roots of contemporary food anxieties might, then, be sought in the increasing gap between food producers and consumers. Most consumers, in modern Western societies, now live at considerable distances from the main sites of agricultural production, giving rise to the potential for consumer distrust and anxiety of the kind that was evinced during the recent horsemeat 'incident' (explored in Chapter 5). Lengthening supply chains clearly give rise to major challenges for the food industry and for those who seek to regulate them. Sources in the food industry and some food educators are keen to emphasize the ignorance that they attribute to modern, urbanized consumers. One of the chicken producers who will be encountered in Chapter 4, for example, complains about 'the British housewife' whose alleged lack of basic cooking skills she decries, while a chicken hatchery manager is quoted in the same chapter, deploring the fact that today's young people apparently don't know that milk comes from cows (rather than in plastic bottles from the supermarket) or that eggs come from chickens (rather than in cardboard boxes from the grocery store). But it is too easy to blame 'consumers' for modern food anxieties and previous research on the UK poultry industry (Jackson et al. 2010) shows that teenagers in some urban areas have a better understanding of modern food production methods than some of their rural counterparts who were physically closer to the site of agricultural production but less socially and politically aware.

Nor can all of the blame for contemporary food anxieties be laid at the door of the modern food industry and its avatar, the major supermarkets, tempting though it can be to make such an association. Retail power is highly concentrated in many Western countries such as the UK, where over 70 per cent of groceries are bought from the 'big four' supermarkets (Asda-Walmart, Morrisons, Sainsbury's and Tesco). But even their fiercest critics might be forced to admit that the supermarkets have provided reasonably priced food for the great majority of consumers. They might even agree that 'alternative' food producers would struggle to match the level of output of more intensive farming methods, even if a more level playing field were provided that recognized the true costs of food production under different systems of provision. Small-scale producers may be able to achieve higher yields per hectare than more industrialized modes of production but they cannot currently match the overall volume of output achieved by more intensive agricultural regimes.

The metaphor of tracing the 'roots' of contemporary food anxieties (as in arguments about the growing distance between producers and consumers) implies a normative agenda of how things could and should be done differently. While the implications of the disproportionate power of food retailers and corporate agri-business is examined in Chapters 4, 5 and 6, including arguments about the overextension of supply chains and the failures of food regulation, the book's argument also moves in another direction, tracing the paths through which food anxieties are transmitted and the connections that consumers make between apparently unrelated processes and events, showing how anxieties about food spill over into other issues (concerning class, gender and place, for example). Indeed, the final chapter explores the 'routes' of contemporary food anxieties to signal this manoeuvre more clearly, distinguishing it from an analysis of the underlying causes or 'roots' of these anxieties.[17]

Outline of the argument

Chapter 2 reviews recent evidence of the pervasiveness and persistence of reported consumer anxieties about food, drawing on data from the Eurobarometer social surveys. While there are some discernible patterns within these data, with food anxieties most prevalent in eastern and southern Europe and in the European Union's new accession states, there are also some unexplained paradoxes. Comparisons are drawn with Kjaernes et al.'s work on *Trust in Food* (2007), which suggests that explaining varying levels of distrust across Europe requires a comparative analysis at the institutional level rather than trying to relate variations in consumer trust to any objective variations in food risk. The chapter also examines the epistemological issues involved in analysing survey data (which rely on respondents' verbal accounts and reported behaviour rather than more direct observation of their actual behaviour in practice).

Chapter 3 outlines a novel theory of social anxiety which has been deployed in recent studies of food anxiety in the UK and Sweden (Jackson & Everts 2010, Milne et al. 2011, Jackson et al. 2013). The approach aims to explain how and why anxieties peak in particular times and places and how an underlying level of anxiety persists. The theory demonstrates how anxieties are 'framed' in different ways, how they spread and/or are contained and why anxieties about food are so intense (because of their intimate, embodied nature and because of the way they disrupt the established routines and rhythms of everyday life).

Chapter 4 provides greater historical depth to the study of contemporary food anxieties, tracing the origins and development of a particular form of food-related technology, the 'cold chain', which enabled Western consumers to eat fresh as opposed to frozen food (notably chicken). Pioneered by British retailers such as Marks & Spencer and Sainsbury's, the 'cold chain' increased consumer choice, expanding access to a wider range of fresh foods. But it also had a number of unintended consequences in terms of lengthening supply chains and disrupting food's seasonality and local provenance. The chapter draws on oral history interviews with key players in the food industry and focus groups with consumers concerning their current anxieties about preparing and cooking food including their apparent 'squeamishness' about touching raw meat. The chapter also explores how these ideas apply to varying degrees in relation to different animal species and levels of processing (with greater consumer anxieties about the provenance of whole chickens compared to chicken portions or processed chicken, for example).

Chapter 5 takes a recent food 'incident' – the adulteration of a number of beef products with horsemeat in the UK and across Europe – to explore the loss of control over contemporary food supply chains.[18] The incident raises questions about the regulation of extended supply chains; the role of science in food emergencies; and the ability of fragmented national agencies to exercise control over food-related issues whose operation clearly exceeds national borders. The chapter draws on documentary research from newspapers and government reports as well as insights from my own involvement in the work of the UK Food Standards Agency (FSA).

Chapter 6 focuses on the recent history of 'food scares' in China, including consumer reactions to the 2008 contamination of infant formula. It draws on focus groups with parents in the city of Chengdu and on analysis of television advertising campaigns. Emerging themes include the shifting popularity of domestic and foreign brands; the significance of 'scientific motherhood' and other parenting ideologies involving the medicalization of pregnancy and childbirth; the intergenerational implications of increased female participation in the labour force; and the mediation of 'science' and 'nature' in TV advertising. The chapter also raises wider issues about the growth of middle-class consumption patterns in China and the implications for future food security of the so-called nutrition transition in emerging economies.

Chapter 7 examines the role of 'celebrity chefs' in the mediation of consumer anxieties about food, tracing their increasing influence on wider debates about food and society. It focuses on a British TV series (*Jamie's Ministry of Food*) and the way audiences responded to the series in Rotherham, where the series was filmed, and elsewhere in the UK. The chapter examines the circulation of consumer anxieties about food and how food acts as a vehicle for the mediation of other issues including stereotypes of place, class and gender. The chapter also reflects on the role of food in collective memory (including the legacy of war-time rationing in Britain under the auspices of the original Ministry of Food) and on the role of TV chefs as cultural intermediaries and moral entrepreneurs. The chapter draws on documentary research and on focus groups with media audiences and the wider public.

Chapter 8 is based on the ethnographic observation of consumer practice and focuses on the way consumers negotiate their reported anxieties into everyday practice, drawing on household-level observational and interview-based studies. Taking inspiration from the work of Theodore Schatzki, including his analysis of the 'doings' and 'sayings' that comprise contemporary social practice, the chapter addresses the paradox of high levels of reported anxiety in survey-based studies such as those discussed in Chapter 2 and the significantly lower levels of observed anxiety found in the ethnographic studies reported here. The chapter considers the kind of embodied, tacit and practical knowledge that consumers employ in their routine domestic practices, compared to the more abstract, formal and explicit knowledge espoused by food experts and government authorities. The chapter also explores the multiple trade-offs that consumers routinely make between different practical and ethical claims on their attention, such as quality and price, taste and value, convenience and sustainability. Comparisons are drawn with Daniel Miller's (2001) work on everyday consumer ethics which attempts to explain how the immediate claims of family and friends generally trump the more abstract claims of farmers and food producers located at greater distances, often overseas.

Chapter 9 provides ethnographic evidence to challenge conventional ideas about the nature of 'convenience' food and the supposed profligacy of consumer attitudes towards food waste. The chapter shows how basing an understanding of consumption on the observation of everyday practice at the household level leads to radically different conclusions from conventional ways of framing 'consumer choice' in terms of individual behaviour and personal responsibility.

The implications of such a reframing are taken up in the Conclusion which contrasts the Introduction's emphasis on the historical 'roots' of contemporary food anxieties with a more nuanced understanding of the 'routes' through which consumers make sense of how their food is provided. The chapter draws out three key arguments: about the moral and political economies of food; the methodological and theoretical challenges of combining different kinds of evidence; and the disputed 'locus of responsibility' for contemporary food issues. While the book explores the way food can serve as a vehicle for a range of other social, political and ethical issues, it insists on food's materiality as well as its symbolic and imaginative potential. It is this combination of the metaphorical and the material that gives food such a powerful role in consumers' everyday lives, with a force that operates at all geographical scales from the personal to the planetary.

Notes

1. See, for example, Carolyn Korsmeyer's essay, 'Delightful, delicious, disgusting' (Korsmeyer 2002) and her extended treatment of these and related ideas in her book, *Savoring Disgust* (2011), where she explores the interweaving of foul and fair in aesthetic theory including the paradoxical nature of 'attractive aversions'.
2. For a summary of recent work on food, risk and trust, see Kjaernes (2013).
3. Sources such as Eurobarometer (2010) report high levels of public concern about food (examined more closely in Chapter 2), while national governments simultaneously insist that food 'is safer than it has ever been' (Cabinet Office 2008: iii).
4. Data from Eurobarometer (2012), examined in more detail in Chapter 2, report that 31 per cent of European citizens are very concerned about global food security (when asked if there is 'sufficient food . . . to meet the needs of the population in the world') with a further 45 per cent reporting that they are fairly concerned. More than three-quarters (79%) are reported to be concerned about food safety (Eurobarometer 2010).

5. The prospect of food-related civil unrest in many parts of the world attracted wide-spread media attention. For example, *The Guardian* reported on pasta protests in Italy, tortilla rallies in Mexico and demonstrations about the cost of onions in India ('Riots and hunger feared as demand for grain sends food costs soaring', 4 December 2007).

6. Warde (1997) identifies four such antinomies that structure everyday consumption practices involving tensions between novelty and tradition, health and indulgence, economy and extravagance, convenience and care. It is important to note that these are not dichotomies, representing mutually incompatible alternatives. As discussed in Chapter 9, for example, so-called convenience food can be used to express care for friends and family members rather than always being seen as a sign of neglect or carelessness.

7. Survey evidence from Eurobarometer (2010: 13) confirms that the majority of Europeans associate food and eating with pleasure, with 94 per cent reporting their enjoyment of fresh and tasty food and 91 per cent reporting that they enjoy having a meal with friends or family. By contrast, 48 per cent report being concerned that food may damage their health and 53 per cent report dietary concerns (such as putting on weight or diet-related diseases).

8. With his interest in group affiliation and patterns of sociality, Georg Simmel wrote about the 'tremendous socializing power' of meals taken together (1910/1994: 346).

9. The omnivore's dilemma was expounded by Paul Rozin (1976), developed by Claude Fischler (1988) and popularized by Michael Pollan (2006). Lisa Heldke (2003) provides a critical examination of the risks encountered in satisfying the 'exotic appetites' of those she calls food adventurers.

10. In a separate paper on 'ambiguous appetites', Freidberg (2010) argues that a history of taste would tell us much about the anxieties and social hierarchies of different eras.

11. There is a later and more specific reference to 'the promise and anxiety surrounding desire, seduction, and sexuality' (Baron et al. 2013: 23).

12. The self-styled professor of transcendental gastronomy provides a similar commentary on the nature of thirst, which he describes as the inner consciousness of the need for drink, identifying three kinds of thirst (latent, artificial and burning) which he associates respectively with natural need, factitious enjoyment and imperious desire (Brillat-Savarin 1825/2009: 142–43).

13. See, for example, recent studies of changing meal-times across Europe which chart significant transformations in everyday life over recent decades (e.g. Warde et al. 2007). Longer-term changes, over centuries rather than decades, are reported by Tannahill (1973) and Mennell (1996) among others.

14. Probyn suggests that sex and eating are both carnal pleasures that benefit from a sense of touch and timing, arguing that 'the sensual nature of eating now constitutes a privileged optic through which to consider how . . . the relations between sex, gender and power are being renegotiated' (2000: 5–7). She explores how food and

sex can elicit powerful emotions of shame and disgust as well as an overriding sense of pleasure and desire.

15. For a compelling account of the 'mainstreaming' of organic farming in the United States and its attendant anxieties, see Guthman (2004).

16. Even a cursory bibliographic search confirms that many previous historical periods have been regarded as no less anxious than the present day. For example, Dodds (1991) refers to an 'age of anxiety' in his analysis of religious experience in late antiquity; American historians characterize the Cold War as a period of intense anxiety, tracing the prevalence of anxiety from McCarthyism to the current 'war on terror' (Cuordileone 2000, Johnson 2006); while contemporary criminologists use the term to contrast the 'true risks' of crime with much higher levels of social concern about its perceived prevalence (Hollway & Jefferson 1997, Lee & Farrell 2008).

17. The intellectual conceit of contrasting 'roots' and 'routes' has a long history in the social sciences and humanities and is described in more detail in the Conclusion.

18. The reasons for writing 'incident' (in quotation marks) are explored in Chapter 5, which argues that such events are framed very differently when construed as an 'incident', a 'scare' or a 'crisis' (among the many other terms used to describe such episodes).

Chapter 2

Mapping contemporary food anxieties

This chapter provides an overview of consumers' reported anxieties about food, based on an analysis of social survey data from Eurobarometer (a representative sample of EU citizens). The chapter includes both a literal mapping of the data and a consideration of the geographical imaginations that inform them. The data record high levels of consumer anxiety about food across a range of issues from food safety and pesticide use to animal welfare and genetically modified (GM) food, and from food security to concerns about health and diet. The chapter questions the epistemological basis of these data, asking what respondents mean when they report high levels of concern about food safety and related issues, and how social and spatial variations in the data might be explained. The data provide a statistical baseline against which other kinds of evidence concerning consumer anxieties about food can be assessed including the ethnographic data presented in Chapters 7, 8 and 9. As will become clear, anxiety is not a topic that is easily addressed through social surveys and the meaning of the data is not easily amenable to statistical analysis.

The Eurobarometer surveys

In 2010, the European Commission published the results of a survey of European citizens probing their concerns about food-related risks. The report was undertaken on behalf of the European Food Safety Authority (EFSA) and was based on a representative sample of over 26,000 citizens from all 27 member states. The headline findings were quite positive, confirming that the majority of Europeans associate food and eating with enjoyment and pleasure, and that most Europeans have confidence in national and European food safety agencies as reliable sources of information on possible risks associated with food. But high levels of anxiety about food safety and related issues were reported across Europe, particularly in terms of pesticide residues in fruit, vegetables and cereals (of concern to nearly three-quarters of survey respondents) and in relation to a range of other issues.

The survey results are summarized in Table 2.1. They show that 79 per cent of respondents had concerns about food safety, while almost half (48%) were concerned that food was likely to damage their health and around two-thirds (68%) were concerned about the quality and freshness of food. Little more than one-third (36%) had confidence in supermarkets as a reliable source of information about food safety and around two-thirds (66%) had concerns about genetically modified organisms in food and drink. Of particular note was the finding that only a minority of respondents (42%) felt that food was safer now than ten years ago, despite the intense efforts of EFSA and national food authorities over the intervening years to improve food safety and reduce the risks of food-borne illness.

An earlier report on European attitudes to risk (Eurobarometer 2006), based on data collected in 2005, allows some exploration of the trends in these data – though not all of the same questions were posed in each survey and the 2005–6 survey reports on a slightly smaller geographical area (25 member-states, compared to 27 in 2010). In 2005, 42 per cent of respondents were concerned that the food they eat may damage their health, slightly lower than in 2010 (48%). Concerns about avian influenza ('bird flu') had decreased (from 66 to 60%), while concerns about genetically modified organisms in food and drink had risen (from 62 to 66%) and concerns about the welfare of farmed animals had also risen (from 60 to 64%). Concerns about pesticide residues remained at approximately the same level (at just over 70%), while concerns about BSE ('mad cow' disease) had decreased from 54 to 46 per cent and concerns about food poisoning from bacteria such as Salmonella and Listeria had decreased from 65 to 62 per cent. The summary figure regarding consumer perceptions of changes in food safety over time showed that those who felt that food was safer compared to ten years ago had risen from 38 per cent in 2005 to 42 per cent in 2010. In the earlier survey 29 per cent felt that the safety of food was 'about the same' while the 2010 survey made respondents choose whether they 'tend to agree' (33%) or 'tend to disagree' (33%) that food safety had improved over the period.

The 2006 report provided information on the socioeconomic characteristics of respondents, allowing some further analysis of the aggregate data. For example, health concerns (that the food you eat may damage your health) were higher among women (44%) than among men (41%) and higher among those living in towns and cities (45%) than among those living in rural areas

Table 2.1 European attitudes to food-related risks

Percentage of respondents who:	EU 27	Highest	Lowest
Are concerned about the *safety of food*	79	97 (Cyprus)	59 (Netherlands)
Are concerned about *pesticide residues* in fruit, vegetables and cereals	72	91 (Spain)	53 (UK/ Netherlands)
Are concerned about the *quality and freshness* of food	68	94 (Lithuania)	37 (Netherlands)
Are concerned about *GM* in food or drink	66	81 (Latvia/Spain)	46 (Greece)
Are concerned about *welfare of farmed animals*	64	81 (Luxembourg)	44 (Hungary)
Have confidence in national/European *food safety agencies*	64	84 (Finland)	52 (Latvia)
Are concerned about *food poisoning* (Salmonella, Listeriosis, etc.)	62	85 (Cyprus)	23 (Sweden)
Are concerned about new viruses found in animals like *avian/bird flu*	60	81 (Spain)	36 (Sweden)
Have *'dietary concerns'* (diet-related disease, putting on weight etc.)	53	71 (Cyprus)	31 (Sweden/ Netherlands)
Are concerned about eating a *healthy/ balanced diet*	52	78 (Spain)	22 (Netherlands)
Are concerned that food is likely to *damage their health*	48	81 (Spain)	23 (Austria)
Are concerned about *BSE* ('mad cow disease')	46	69 (Italy)	16 (Sweden)
Think that food is *safer than 10 years ago*	42	67 (Malta)	9 (Bulgaria)
Have *confidence in supermarkets* as a source of information about food risks	36	67 (France)	6 (Spain)

Source: Eurobarometer (2010).

or villages (39%). There was a general pattern in terms of age and sex, with women and older people reporting higher levels of concern about a range of food-related issues. This was true for those who felt that food safety had worsened over the last ten years; those with concerns about BSE and GM; those who were worried about pesticide residues; and those who were concerned about avian influenza (see Table 2.2).

A more recent report, based on fieldwork in July 2012, explored European citizens' attitudes towards food security, food quality and the countryside (Eurobarometer 2012). Here it was reported that 96 per cent of respondents were concerned about food quality and 71 per cent about the geographical origin or provenance of food; 76 per cent of EU citizens were concerned about global food security (defined as sufficient food being produced to meet the

Table 2.2 Demographic variations in European attitudes to food

Percentage who:	Are concerned that food may damage your health	Feel that food safety is worse than ten years ago	Are concerned about BSE	Are concerned about GM in food or drink	Are concerned about pesticide residues in food	Are concerned about new viruses such as 'bird flu'	Are concerned about the welfare of farmed animals
EU 25	61	28	54	62	71	66	60
Male	59	25	49	64	67	63	55
Female	63	31	58	63	74	69	65
Age							
15–24	60	23	48	64	62	62	56
25–39	64	25	51	66	70	64	60
40–54	63	29	57	59	73	69	62
55+	58	32	56	58	73	68	60

Source: Eurobarometer (2006).

needs of the world's population) and 91 per cent were concerned about the price of food (rising to 97% among those who had difficulty paying their bills most of the time). These survey data also showed significant variation among member-states, with those having concerns about the geographical origin of food, for example, varying from 90 per cent in Greece to just 47 per cent in the Netherlands.

Mapping European anxieties about food

Overall, the Eurobarometer data indicate high levels of food-related anxiety across Europe (expressed in the survey's terms as 'worry' or 'concern'). The data also demonstrate considerable geographical variation across Europe. While 16 different member-states appear in the list of countries with 'highest' or 'lowest' levels of concern about specific issues in Table 2.1, some general patterns can be discerned, with new accession states (those countries who joined the European Union since 2004) and countries from southern and eastern Europe generally having highest levels of concern and those from northern and western Europe having least concerns about food-related issues.

Looking at the data in more detail, however, reveals few consistent trends, although people in the Netherlands and Sweden appear to have the least concerns about several measures while those in Spain and Cyrus report high levels of concern on a number of different issues. For example, concerns about food safety (averaging 79%) are highest in Cyprus, Finland and France (all above 90%) and lowest in the Netherlands, Austria and Germany. But high levels of concern (above 80%) also occur in Sweden and the UK, in some Mediterranean countries (Spain, Portugal and Italy) and in eastern Europe (in Bulgaria, Romania and Latvia) (see Figure 2.1).[1] Concerns about the quality and freshness of food are less intense that concerns about food safety, averaging 68 per cent across the European Union, but all countries registered rates above 50 per cent, except for the Netherlands (37%) and Sweden (39%). The highest rates of concern about food quality and freshness are not confined to countries with high summer temperatures where concerns about food spoilage may be high (such as Spain, Portugal, Italy, Malta and Cyprus) also occurring in France, Hungary, Bulgaria, Poland and Latvia (see Figure 2.2).

Concerns about potential health risks (that food may damage your health) averaged 48 per cent. They were highest in southern and eastern Europe (in Portugal, Spain and Italy, and in Latvia, Lithuania, Romania and Bulgaria) and lowest in northern Europe (in the UK, Sweden, Finland, Denmark and the Netherlands) and also in Austria and Greece (see Figure 2.3). Another measure of the relationship between food and health focused on concerns about

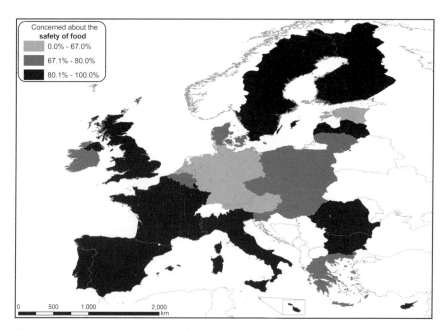

Figure 2.1 European concerns about food safety.
Source: Eurobarometer (2010).

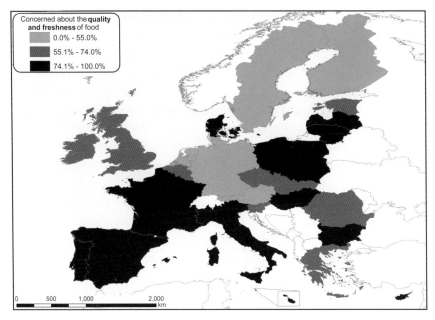

Figure 2.2 European concerns about food quality and freshness.
Source: Eurobarometer (2010).

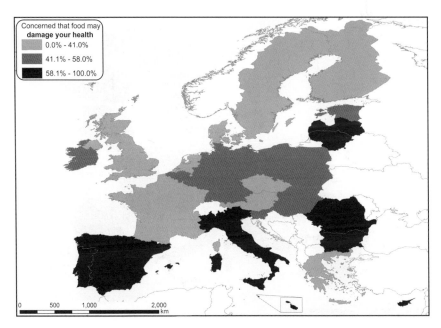

Figure 2.3 European concerns that food may damage your health.
Source: Eurobarometer (2010).

not having a healthy or balanced diet. Nutritional concerns potentially affect all European consumers from the most affluent to the most impoverished, including those experiencing both under- and overconsumption. All but two countries reported more than 40 per cent of respondents experiencing such concerns (the exceptions being the Netherlands at 22% and Sweden at 25%). Those with the highest levels of dietary concern included Cyprus (73%) and Malta (64%) whose 'Mediterranean diet' is usually celebrated as a marker of good nutritional health, though Greece had below-average concerns about diet and health (at 41%) while Spain and Portugal had relatively high levels of concern, at 78 per cent and 69 per cent respectively (see Figure 2.4).

Turning to more specific food-related anxieties, Figure 2.5 shows variations in levels of concern about pesticide residues in food. Averaging 72 per cent across the European Union, the highest levels were reported in Spain, Italy, Cyprus, Bulgaria, Latvia, Hungary and Luxembourg (all above 80%), with the lowest levels (53%) in the Netherlands and the UK.

Somewhat lower levels of concern were expressed about genetically modified organisms in food and drink, averaging 66 per cent. The distribution shows no clear pattern (see Figure 2.6), with all member-states reporting levels of concern above 50 per cent except for Malta, Sweden and the UK (all at 48%) and Greece at 46 per cent. Concerns about viruses such as avian

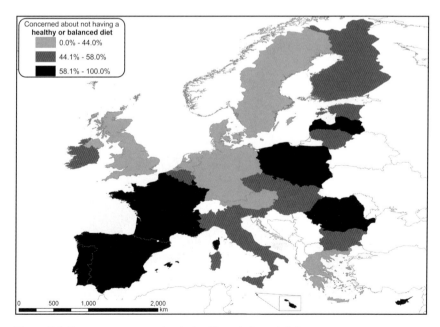

Figure 2.4 European concerns about a healthy or balanced diet.
Source: Eurobarometer (2010).

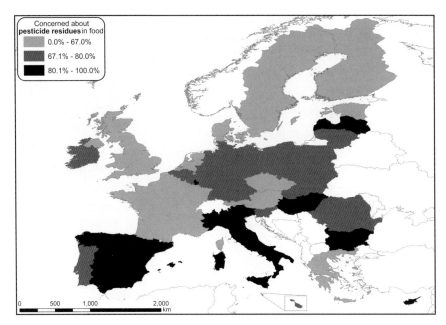

Figure 2.5 European concerns about pesticide residues.
Source: Eurobarometer (2010).

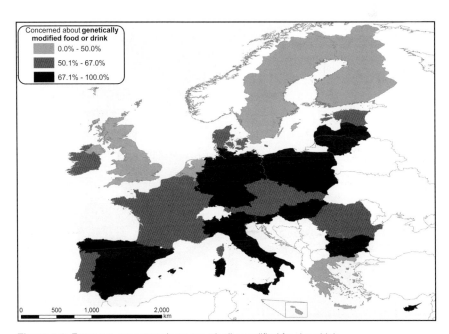

Figure 2.6 European concerns about genetically modified food or drink.
Source: Eurobarometer (2010).

influenza averaged 60 per cent and were more pronounced in southern and eastern Europe, with the highest levels reported in Spain, Italy and Bulgaria (see Figure 2.7), while concerns about the welfare of farmed animals (see Figure 2.8) averaged 64 per cent and were highest in Luxembourg (81%), Denmark and Portugal (76%), Italy (75%) and Sweden (74%).

Less than half of those who responded to the Eurobarometer survey (43%) agreed that food was safer now than ten years ago, with a very wide variation from just 9 per cent in Bulgaria to 67 per cent in Malta (see Figure 2.9). Only eight countries reported a majority who felt that food was safer now than ten years ago, including Austria, Belgium, Finland, the Netherlands, Sweden and the UK – plus Greece and Malta. These concerns will be of interest to national food safety authorities and to European agencies such as EFSA, in whom survey respondents reported relatively high levels of confidence (averaging 64%). Levels of trust in national and European food agencies varied considerably, however, from a low of 52 per cent in Latvia to a high of 84 per cent in Finland (see Figure 2.10). Much lower levels of public trust were reported in relation to the retail industry, with only 36 per cent of respondents having confidence in supermarkets and shops in the event of a food safety issue arising (see Figure 2.11). Most countries (19 out of 27) reported confidence levels

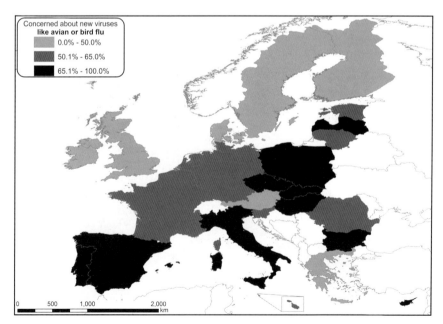

Figure 2.7 European concerns about avian influenza.
Source: Eurobarometer (2010).

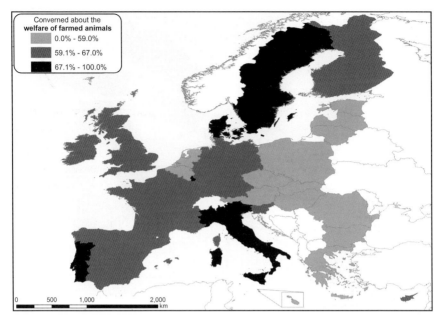

Figure 2.8 European concerns about animal welfare.
Source: Eurobarometer (2010).

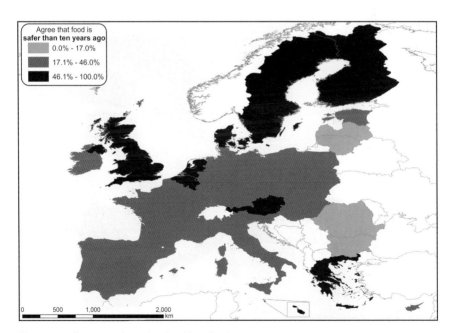

Figure 2.9 European views that food is safer than ten years ago.
Source: Eurobarometer (2010).

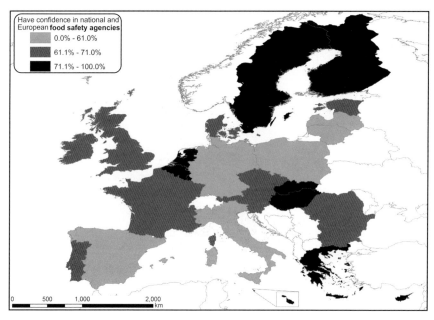

Figure 2.10 Confidence in European food safety authorities.
Source: Eurobarometer (2010).

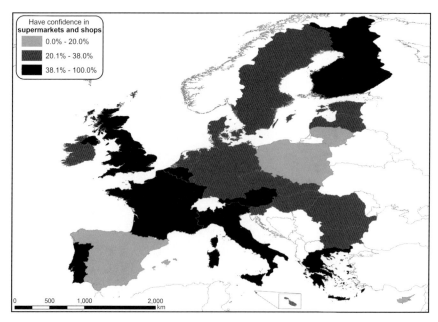

Figure 2.11 Confidence in European supermarkets and shops.
Source: Eurobarometer (2010).

below 40 per cent, with the lowest levels in Spain (6%), Poland (15%), Cyprus (16%) and Lithuania (20%).

How, then, should these data be interpreted and *whose anxieties do they represent?*[2] At one level, the data might be taken at face value as expressing variable levels of consumer concern across Europe. But it is also possible that asking these kinds of questions in the context of a survey about food-related risks, commissioned by EFSA, actively shaped the answers given. Respondents to official surveys about food-related concerns may feel that certain answers are expected in terms of contemporary discourses about 'feeding the family', for example. Statisticians refer to 'social desirability' biases (where certain kinds of answers can be anticipated as a culturally appropriate response) and the precise wording of survey questions can, of course, influence the outcome. Respondents may feel that it is 'right' for responsible parents to express concerns about the healthiness of their children's diet. Answers to questions about food potentially damaging one's health (or those of one's family members) could also be inter-preted in this light.

The decision to use 'closed' as opposed to 'open' questions raises similar issues as does the request to rank a number of pre-selected options as opposed to voluntarily raising concerns of one's own. Different responses are likely when respondents are given a free choice to name any issues of concern to them, answering questions in their own words, compared to when they are asked to choose between a list of pre-given options (including some they might not even have considered unprompted) or where they might have framed their answers in significantly different ways compared to the categories they are asked to choose between.

The stability of attitudinal data over time can also be questioned, particu-larly when significant events occur between successive survey rounds (such as a major 'food scare') or when other circumstances change (with the onset of recession, for example). All of these issues, including the broader context in which survey data are collected and who sponsors the research, might reasonably be expected to shape the answers given, suggesting that the epis-temological status of survey data is more complex than might at first appear (raising doubts about the transparency of face-value interpretations). The data that Eurobarometer and similar surveys report might, then, be interpreted to reflect variations in *public discourse* about food across Europe rather than actual levels and precise variations in consumer anxieties about food.

Similar issues are discussed by Judith Farquhar in her analysis of public atti-tudes to food and sex in post-socialist China where she suggests that social surveys do not merely *reflect* public attitudes but may also help *create* them

(2002: 220–21). Drawing on Steven Woolgar's (1988) work on the way science is involved in 'splitting and inverting' its object of study, Farquhar shows how modern sexual surveys bring into view a domain that is unproblematically identified as sexual while the object it creates (people's reported sexual behaviour) is probably both narrower and broader than anyone's personal experience. Through the very act of conducting survey research, the field becomes reorganized and delimited into a new (and largely hypothetical) object called 'Chinese sexual behaviour'. The survey that Farquhar refers to asked 'neutral' questions about people's sexual practices and attitudes. These questions are assumed to elicit true statements from informants about experiences and preferences which are assumed to have existed prior to the survey and which are assumed to continue more-or-less unchanged afterwards. There is little acknowledgement that surveys may shape their object of study rather than such objects simply existing 'out there', independent of the research having been conducted.[3]

This line of argument, when applied to the study of European attitudes to food, might help explain the paradox of relatively high levels of expressed anxiety among European consumers compared to the household-level data (gathered through ethnographic observation and reported in Chapters 7, 8 and 9) which reveal relatively low levels of anxiety in terms of people's everyday food practices and food-related talk. While research participants in the ethnographic research commonly expressed low-level worries about food hygiene and food safety issues (including concerns about the cleanliness of chopping boards or the importance of washing their hands before preparing food), they did not seem unduly troubled by food-safety concerns or by potentially risky food-related practices.[4]

There is, then, an apparent discrepancy between the high levels of food-related anxiety reported in survey data (from Eurobarometer and similar sources) and ethnographic evidence collected at the household level regarding everyday consumer practice and mundane 'food talk'. This can partly be explained by the taken-for-granted, routine character of domestic practice where people are unlikely to be self-consciously regulating their behaviour to meet current food safety guidance (even where they are aware of such advice). But it also suggests the need to attend to the epistemological status of different kinds of data, where reported behaviour in social surveys such as Eurobarometer may be more susceptible to 'social desirability' effects than other kinds of (qualitative, ethnographic) data where researchers aim to get 'beneath the skin' of such public discourses about food. This is not to suggest that one kind of data is inherently 'better' than another but that the epistemological status of different kinds of evidence should be duly acknowledged – as Lydia Martens (2012) argues in her discussion of 'talk about practice' (accessed via interview data) and 'talk as practice' (accessed through ethnographic observation).[5]

Returning to the mapping of Eurobarometer data, questions might then be asked about how differences in reported levels of food-related anxiety between countries should be interpreted. At one level, it could simply be accepted that consumer anxieties about food are higher in some countries than in others because the level of exposure to risk varies between countries. Citizens in Greece, for example, might be fully justified in being almost twice as concerned about pesticide residues in food as UK citizens, and those in Lithuania might be right to be almost four times as concerned about the risks of food poisoning as those in Sweden. But there are other ways of approaching these data as suggested by a previous European project on public trust in food.

A research team led by Unni Kjaernes used survey evidence to examine variations in consumer trust among citizens in Denmark, Germany, Britain, Italy, Norway and Portugal (Kjaernes et al. 2007). Taking theoretical inspiration from Beck (1992) and Luhmann (1979), they sought to challenge the notion that trust can be understood purely as an individual disposition (that some people are simply more trusting than others). Such an understanding, they suggest, leads to an overly technocratic response where it is assumed that trust in food can be restored simply by providing consumers with additional data or better information. This kind of 'knowledge-deficit' model assumes that trust is a cognitive issue that can be addressed at the individual level and that changes in knowledge will have a direct effect on consumer behaviour, influencing the decision-making process. This kind of approach has been highly influential in policy circles but is fundamentally flawed (as discussed further in the Conclusion). Critics point out, for example, that increased knowledge about some issues may lead to *increased* anxieties rather than allaying people's fears and increasing public trust. They also question the assumption of a direct link between knowledge, attitudes and behaviour (Shove 2010, Milne 2013).

Kjaernes et al. (2007) challenge the conceptualization of trust as an individual disposition by demonstrating systematic differences in levels of consumer trust across Europe. They show, for example, that there are high levels of public trust in food in Norway and Sweden and much lower levels in Italy and Portugal. Rather than seeking explanations in real or perceived levels of food risk, they pursue a different line of enquiry, exploring *institutional* differences in the way food markets are regulated, how consumers are organized and how food politics is conducted in these different countries. In subsequent reflections on this comparative institutional study, Kjaernes (2013) suggests that high levels of public trust among Scandinavian consumers are related to the relatively consensual nature of food politics in the Nordic countries and to the standardized and predictable nature of their food supply systems. By contrast, relatively high levels of consumer distrust in Italy and Portugal, Kjaernes suggests, can be understood in terms of their less transparent food institutions and higher levels of political contestation over food (ibid.: 420–21).

Kjaernes suggests that variations in consumer trust should be sought in terms of the character and performance of food markets and the nature of political systems rather than in terms of individual dispositions. Across their European sample, Kjaernes and her colleagues found relatively high levels of trust in food experts, mixed opinions on the trustworthiness of food safety authorities and the media, and widespread scepticism about commercial actors such as supermarkets (though, here too, there were variations between nation-states, as reflected in the Eurobarometer data reported earlier). As may also be true of the variations in consumer attitudes to food discussed above, variations in trust appear to be related to differences in regulatory structures, the relative concentration of the retail sector, the power of supermarkets to control their supply chains and the balance of power between public and private actors in the food system.

But this is a speculative line of argument and other differences in consumer attitudes are harder to explain. For example, Kjaernes et al. (2007) report high levels of consumer trust in Britain and Norway despite contrasting institutional arrangements: the former has an open market, has experienced wholesale reform of its centralized regulatory system, with globalized food provisioning while the latter is characterized by producer-dominated regulation, standardization and protectionism (Milne 2013: 215). Similarly, Britain and Germany both have high levels of political contestation over food issues but variable levels of public trust in food (with higher levels of consumer distrust in Germany than in Britain). A comparative institutional approach only goes some way in explaining these differences. For example, Kjaernes suggests that German consumers have a weaker position in national food politics than is the case in Britain and that they make more use of 'alternative' shops and familial networks than British consumers (Kjaernes 2013: 421). While more research would be needed to support or challenge these interpretative suggestions, the overall tenor of the argument is convincing and the emphasis on institutional and cultural factors is supported by the data where levels of trust in food vary more consistently *between* countries than among sociodemographic groups *within* countries.

A similar argument can be applied to variations in consumer anxieties about food where levels of reported anxiety may reflect differences in national food discourses rather than differences in actual food-related risks across Europe (however these differences might be measured in practice). But to be clear, the present analysis does not seek to arbitrate between 'real' (empirically justifi-able) concerns and 'perceived' (subjectively experienced) anxieties. Nor does it presume to judge whether some anxieties are more 'rationale' than others. Rather, as outlined in the Introduction, the analysis seeks to understand how food-related anxieties circulate within society whether or not they are justified by some external assessment of the actual risks.

Besides these epistemological considerations, the approach adopted here can also be justified empirically. Those who attempt to measure anxiety in an 'objective' way generally use an inventory of symptoms, with self-reported responses being converted to a standardized rating scale. Questions typically probe physiological responses such as the experience of sweating, numbness or tingling and emotional states such as 'fearing the worst', suicidal thoughts, restlessness or panic. Rating scales and similar approaches range in complex-ity from the Hospital Anxiety and Depression Scale (HADS-A), based on 7 questions, to the State-Trait Anxiety Inventory (STAI), based on 40 questions. Others measures such as the Hamilton Anxiety Scale (HAM-A) and the Beck Anxiety Inventory (BAI) have an intermediate degree of complexity, based on 14 and 21 questions respectively.[6] While there may be good reasons for using such inventories and scales in medical practice, social scientists have demon-strated that such scales are culture-bound and historically specific and that they are therefore unreliable as evidence of shifting patterns of public anxiety over time or between different geographical settings. In one particularly striking study of birth-cohort data, for example, Twenge (2000) found that the average American child in the 1990s reported higher levels of anxiety than child psychi-atric patients in the same country in the 1950s. While levels of anxieties may well have increased, the study calls into question the reliability of such measures when employed in this comparative way. Similar reservations might justifiably be held about cross-cultural or temporal measures of food-related anxieties such as those employed in the Eurobarometer data reported earlier.

Joanna Bourke (2003) raises a series of related questions in her historical research on fear and anxiety, asking whether archival records pertaining to fear of starvation in earlier centuries can be directly compared with modern-day fears about food allergies or intolerances (see also Bourke 2005). Rather than assum-ing that all such expressions of fear and anxiety are commensurate, Bourke suggests approaching the issue as a kind of 'language game' where research-ers should be sensitive to the terminology in which fears are expressed, paying due attention to the social, cultural and historical context of such reported concerns.[7] This book does not, therefore, seek to judge whether reported levels of consumer anxiety about food can be justified by 'objective' levels of risk. Its task is comparative and interpretative rather than normative or judgemental, seeking to understand how and why levels of anxiety within and between societies vary over time and place. The next chapter expands further on this goal, outlining a novel theory of anxiety as a social condition.

Conclusion

This chapter has reviewed some data from a respected European social survey regarding the extent of consumer anxieties about food. The data reveal high and persistent levels of anxiety about a range of food-related issues. While there are some geographical patterns and some identifiable changes over time, the interpretation of the data is far from straightforward. This is partly because the survey evidence is based on reported behaviour and publicly expressed attitudes rather than direct observation of actual behaviour. However, it has also been suggested that there are more fundamental epistemological and methodological issues with the data. Despite these difficulties, considered further in the Conclusion, the Eurobarometer data provide a valuable baseline for the discussion of different kinds of evidence in subsequent chapters concerning the extent and nature of contemporary consumer anxieties about food.

Notes

1. The maps in this chapter (Figures 2.1–2.11) were drawn by Jeremy Ely in the Department of Geography at the University of Sheffield using the GIS software package ARC-Info. The maps are based on the World Borders Dataset, which is available under a Creative Commons License (http://creativecommons.org/licenses/by-sa/3.0/). Thanks also to Steve Wise for an initial discussion about mapping these data.
2. Thanks to Mara Miele for posing the question in this way after a public talk I gave at the Cardiff School of Planning and Geography in November 2013.
3. Farquhar goes so far as to suggest that the questionnaire, in its explicit questions about different sexual practices, may itself have been an education for some respondents (2002: 226).
4. Pursuing this argument could have important implications for food safety authorities such as the UK FSA. For example, the FSA's 'Food and You' surveys report that most British consumers do not adhere to the Agency's guidelines in terms of the 'correct' temperature at which to store refrigerated food (below 5°C). But if most consumers fail to follow FSA advice and do not suffer from food poisoning, consumers may question the validity of the advice. An ethnographic study of Kitchen Life, commissioned by the FSA, raises similar questions about the gaps between expert

advice and lay understandings of public health and hygiene issues: http://food.gov.
uk/science/research/ssres/ foodsafetyss/fs244026/#.UrHwMrmYZYd (accessed
18 December 2013).

5. There is more discussion of these issues in the Conclusion.
6. For a useful review of three of these measures (the BAI, STAI and HADS-A scales),
see Julian (2011).
7. A comparable approach is taken to a range of contemporary 'food words' by Jackson
and the CONANX group (2013).

Chapter 3

Anxiety as a social condition

The distinction between individual and social anxieties is central to this book's argument. While individuals may have personal concerns about food, including food allergies or intolerances or a medical condition such as anorexia nervosa or bulimia, this book has a different focus, seeking to trace the rise and fall of social anxieties about food (historically and in the present day) and their patterning over space (mapping where they occur and how they spread). This is not to say that personal anxieties affecting individuals do not have a sociological dimension – they clearly do. But the book's focus is sociological and geographical rather than psychological or medical in orientation, seeking to understand *changing patterns of anxiety within society and space* rather than probing the causes of individual pathologies.[1]

Despite frequent claims about its centrality as a defining feature of modern life (e.g. May 1950, Wilkinson 2001), there is surprisingly little discussion of anxiety among the founding figures of social theory. Marx wrote about alienation, Durkheim about anomie, and Weber about disenchantment but none of them wrote at any length about anxiety. Even though Simmel's discussion of 'The metropolis and mental life' (1903) could be read as an account of urban anxiety, it was not named as such. It was only with the rise of Freudian psychoanalysis that there is any sustained treatment of anxiety as a psycho-social phenomenon and it is in the work of existential philosophers such as Kierkegaard that the concept is most fully developed. For Freud, anxiety was a normal fact of everyday life rather than an acute personal affliction. Freud saw the increase of anxiety as an inevitable response to the evolution of civilization which, he argued, had been achieved through the 'sublimation of instinct' (1930: 63). In his later works, such as *The Problem of Anxiety* (1936), Freud debated whether anxiety was a result of repression or whether anxiety was its cause.

The neglect of anxiety among social theorists is all the more surprising, given the centrality that the concept occupies within theories of modernity. Indeed, as noted in Chapter 1, the modern era has often been described as an 'age of anxiety' from the poetry of W. H. Auden (1947) at the end of the Second World War to more recent analyses of our current economic, social, political and environmental insecurities (e.g. Dunant & Porter 1996). For many commentators, it is its pervasiveness as an everyday social condition that distinguishes anxiety as a distinctively modern phenomenon. According to Bauman (2006), for example (quoted at more length in the Introduction), anxiety has become a normal, everyday condition of modern life, with more and more people living in a state of constant anxiety. Relatively few voices have questioned the presumption that we are living in a qualitatively new or distinctive 'age of anxiety', asking, as does Wilkinson (1999), whether our present-day anxieties (about the environment and climate change, the resurgence of nationalism or the demise of communism, for example) differ in a qualitative way from the anxieties of earlier historical periods. Rather than seeking a direct answer to Wilkinson's question, his caution should be held in mind as this chapter seeks to clarify the nature of anxiety as a social condition.

Defining anxiety

The word 'anxiety' has Anglo-Germanic roots and refers literally to feelings of constriction or throttling. Its etymology establishes that the concept refers to an embodied as well as an emotional state. In contemporary English usage, 'anxiety' has at least four separate meanings referring to a state of agitation, being troubled in mind, a solicitous desire to effect some purpose, and a sense of uneasiness about a coming event (Tyrer 1999: 3–4).[2] According to this definition, anxiety is a physically embodied state involving mental and emotional distress, combined with a more diffuse sense of uneasiness about impending events. Its future orientation is fundamental though it may refer to a sense of dread about the consequences of current events as well as to more general fears about the future. Anxiety may also affect social entities such as organizations and governments, whether or not particular individuals are troubled in mind.

As mentioned in the previous chapter, social historian Joanna Bourke (2003) suggests that anxiety (and other emotions) can be approached as a kind of 'language-game', tracing the circumstances and terms in which anxieties are expressed and how they are articulated within wider social relations of power. While we might be uneasy about identifying the concerns of premodern societies as a form of 'anxiety', we can nonetheless begin to trace how anxieties have shifted between different domains over time and what sources of authority might be invoked to quell such feelings. So, for example, where science and technology may once have been looked to for the solution to contemporary anxieties, science itself is often now regarded with suspicion. Rather than the Enlightenment replacing fear and superstition with rationality and scientific knowledge, Bourke suggests, such fears have been displaced to new sites of anxiety which can be equally as troubling as the role of magic or witchcraft in the Middle Ages. Bourke concludes that harmful microbes and bacteria are as capable of evoking fear as the evil spirits they replaced: scientists, she suggests, are potentially as worrisome as sorcerers (Bourke 2003: 112).

The relationship between fear and anxiety has been the subject of lengthy debate. Many authors seek to distinguish between fear in terms of its orientation towards a specific object and its rational nature, compared with anxiety's apparently irrational nature and lack of a definable object. But this distinction is scarcely tenable as ostensibly rational fears (about crime, for example) are often associated with irrational anxieties (about racialized Others, for example). While psychoanalysis may seek to identify the rational object of fear that lies behind a subject's irrational anxieties, the analysis of social anxieties requires no such formal distinction and both terms (fear and anxiety), together with other terms such as concern or worry, will be used interchangeably as circumstances demand.

Specific anxieties such as those that revolve around 'food scares' (discussed in more detail in Chapters 5 and 6) might invoke parallels with the concept of 'moral panics' where self-appointed moral guardians (such as local newspapers or community groups) identify a convenient 'folk devil' to blame for current social ills. According to Cohen (1972), the process leads to an amplification of anxiety beyond that which might be considered proportionate to the perceived threat, with those held responsible for undermining the social order being vilified in moral terms. Teenage mothers have been subject to such a process (McRobbie 1994), for example, as well as subcultural groups such as the Mods and Rockers in 1950s Britain who formed the object of Cohen's original analysis. The extent to which recent 'food scares' can be analysed in this way is a moot point, particularly in terms of the difficulty of identifying a specific folk devil – which might variously include foreign competitors driving down prices paid to local farmers, lapses in governmental regulation, the excessive concentration of retail power or consumers who are alleged to lack appropriate culinary skills or who pay insufficient attention to expert advice. The case of the 'sinner ladies' at Rawmarsh school in Rotherham, South Yorkshire, who were alleged to have defied the authorities by passing 'junk food' to their children through the school railings probably comes closest to a classic moral panic from the range of examples covered here (discussed in more detail in Chapter 7).

In his account of *Anxiety in a Risk Society,* Iain Wilkinson (2001: 15) defines anxiety as a complex combination of affective experiences, bodily reactions and behavioural responses. This definition suggests that anxiety has various dimensions: emotional, embodied and behavioural. Wilkinson maintains that while anxiety may be experienced at a personal level, its incidence can be exacerbated by what he calls 'social predicaments and cultural contradictions'. To quote him in full: 'anxiety is conceived not so much as a personality defect but, rather, as a function or consequence of the social predicaments and cultural contradictions in which individuals are made to live out their everyday lives' (2001: 17). It is this relationship between individual anxieties and changing socio-cultural circumstances that we refer to here in terms of the social condition of anxiety.

Another useful way of thinking about the social dimensions of anxiety is suggested by Sheldon Ungar's attempt to identify the shifting sites of anxiety associated with environmental, nuclear, chemical and medical threats. As mentioned in the Introduction, Ungar (2001) sees anxiety as a response to uncertainty and ambivalence where concerns about public safety lead to an exaggerated response, similar to the process that Cohen described as a 'moral panic'. Commenting on Ungar's argument, Sean Hier (2003) identifies a growing gap between the 'techno-scientific rationalities' of expert systems and the 'social rationalities' of everyday living – a gap that provides fertile ground for the development of social anxieties (as described in more detail below).

The distinction between anxiety as an individual pathology and anxiety as a social condition can be illustrated via a number of examples. Consumer anxieties about food in the Global North were heightened by a series of 'food scares' (such as BSE in cattle and Salmonella in eggs) where public anxieties rapidly extended from specific health concerns about eating beef or eggs to wider debates about environment and society (cf. Stassart & Whatmore 2003). The same could be said about contemporary anxieties about global food insecurity, the explanation for which can be sought in climate change, population growth, fluctuations in agricultural commodity prices, political instability, rising demand from middle-class consumers in the 'emergent economies' of India, China and Brazil, the conversion of land to biofuel production and a host of other factors. All these factors contribute to contemporary anxieties about food, affecting individuals differently and having very different personal consequences depending on people's circumstances. They are also rooted in wider social, political and environmental changes. Taken together, they contribute to a social condition of anxiety while different groups and individuals will experience that condition in very different ways.

A similar argument is developed by Rachel Pain and Susan Smith (2008) in their work on the geopolitics of fear and its impact on everyday life. Fear, they stress, 'is a social or collective experience rather than an individual state', embedded in a wider network of moral and political geographies. Such fears, they insist, should be understood as an 'increasingly ingrained material practice' (ibid.: 12). These insights helped inform a specific research agenda:

> Recognising the materiality of fear means that there are tracks and traces between the different lives of those who seek to control fear and those whose lives are pervaded by it. It is possible to follow the materialisation of certain fears into local landscapes; and it is important to show how everyday practices might be inspired by this, might tolerate it, could ignore it, will certainly pose alternatives, and may well have other, more pressing, 'things' to contend with. (ibid.: 13)

It is this agenda that we seek to develop here, following the 'tracks and traces' of contemporary food anxieties. Before outlining that agenda in more detail, it is useful to outline some relevant ideas about the existential nature of anxiety.

Existential anxiety

Modern theories of anxiety are rooted in the existential philosophy of Kierkegaard, Nietzsche and Heidegger.[3] In his seminal work on *The Concept of Anxiety*, Soren Kierkegaard (1980) describes anxiety as an internal condition of human beings rather than as something that intrudes on the individual from outside. Anxiety is simultaneously terrifying and humans seek redemption from it at the same time as they are irresistibly drawn into it. In a state of anxiety, humans come to realize their position in the world and to distinguish themselves from their surrounding environment. Experiencing a state of existential anxiety, individuals pass through different stages, from ignorance and purposelessness, seizing on this or that opportunity, through becoming a thoughtful and responsible individual, to the realization that everything is grounded in nothingness, opening up the possibility of true faith, grounding the human being in the eternal and recognizing that 'anxiety is freedom's actuality' (1980: 42). While anxiety can lead to inaction and paralysis, Kierkegaard also saw anxiety as a spur to creativity and freedom, for 'whoever is educated by anxiety is educated by possibility' (ibid.: 156).

In a similar vein, Nietzsche (1961) identified three stages of spiritual development the first of which involves a belief in ideals, then those beliefs are destroyed before finally nothingness is accepted, giving way to a new, child-like affirmation of life. Between the realization that all meaning is relative and the acceptance of nothingness lies the transition that Nietzsche famously called nihilism: the realization that humans have no purpose in the world apart from those they craft themselves, that the world is indifferent towards human life, and that death is inevitable. For Nietzsche, however, this is not a cause for desperation. It is the beginning of a glorious new age where humans live their lives free from prejudice and traditional biases.

A parallel trajectory can be traced in the work of Martin Heidegger. In *Being and Time* (1978), for example, Heidegger analyses Angst as a phenomenon which is at the heart of the human condition. For Heidegger, Angst is directed towards the condition of being itself where anxiety is experienced as a sudden awareness of the nothingness that is 'nowhere' but everywhere. Anxiety reveals the relativity of all meanings to the individual. In more sociological terms, this refers to the insight that the world as it is experienced by human beings is always-already interpreted and filled with meanings. But in the face of anxiety, an individual realizes that these meanings are not stable or absolute and that people are themselves the creators of these meanings. Anxiety also reveals the inevitability of one's own death which is the annihilation of being. Death therefore is the end of all meaning. These two, separate but interrelated, aspects characterize the state of anxiety. The anxious person realizes the relativity of meaning and recognizes his or her own mortality. Following Kierkegaard and Nietzsche, Heidegger encouraged people to face their anxieties in order to lead more authentic lives, accepting the truth of nothingness.

This philosophical sketch of the nature of existential anxiety can now be applied to a range of food-related issues. One of the reasons why 'food scares' give rise to heightened anxieties is because of the way they threaten the very taken-for-granted nature of our everyday lives and the consumption practices that punctuate them. As Heidegger argued, social life is characterized by daily routines which ensure that life goes on in a routine manner without the need for conscious thought. The experience of Angst disrupts the flow of everyday life, calling into question received ideas and social conventions. Heidegger believed that most people flee from this conclusion and try to maintain their everyday routines in spite of the revelations that Angst provides. By facing our anxieties, Heidegger asserts, life's authentic possibilities can be grasped. Kierkegaard reaches a similar conclusion, arguing that anxiety helps people to reflect on the full range of life's opportunities, to assess their consequences and to make considered choices.

These ideas are of direct relevance to the theory of social anxiety outlined here where events such as 'food scares' rupture the fabric of everyday life, threatening consumers' very existence (in the rare instances when food safety risks become a matter of life and death) or disrupting common understandings of the world and established ways of 'making sense' of our place within it. These ideas are also relevant to what Milne et al. (2011) describe as the 'modulation of anxiety' where authorities seek to raise public anxiety to levels that encourage people to act without causing such high levels of anxiety that they are rendered incapable of action.

As Tyrer writes about the anxieties of everyday life, a world without anxiety would be a grey and boring place, leading to frustration and torpor (1999: 1), an argument with which Salecl would appear to agree:

> While anxiety is today perceived as something one needs to be able to control and hopefully in the long run get rid of . . . it is almost forgotten that philosophy and psychoanalysis discussed anxiety as an essentially human condition that may not only have paralysing effects, but also be the very condition through which people relate to the world. (2004: 15)

As already noted, Heidegger argued that Angst reveals the relativity of meaning and the recognition of one's own mortality. Everyday life is ruptured by events such as 'food scares', the social significance of which depends on how they are framed.[4] Typically, such events precipitate a disruption of one's being-in-the-world, leading to the recognition of subjects and objects of anxiety and to attempts to annihilate one or other (or both) in order to annihilate anxiety itself. An example may help to explain how this theory of anxiety can be applied in practice.

The death of several dozen people in 2005–6 led to widespread social anxieties about avian influenza ('bird flu') with heightened fears about the potential for a global epidemic (Davis 2005). Official anxieties centred on the prospect of the highly pathogenic H5N1 virus spreading from birds to humans, with the potential to infect many thousands of people.[5] In this case, the objects of anxiety (the virus and the birds) were relatively easily identified and could be closely monitored through conventional biosecurity methods (cf. Hinchliffe & Bingham 2008). In practice, thousands of infected and vulnerable birds were destroyed as a preventative measure to ensure that the virus did not spread from birds to humans. So, too, according to Haraway (2008: 268), did the fear of a global pandemic lead to the prophylactic slaughter of 20 million chickens in Thailand. In other cases, such as the perceived threat of international terrorism, it may not be possible to eliminate the threat by annihilating the object of anxiety but people have come to tolerate a range of precautionary measures that have been introduced to allay public anxieties including ever-more intrusive airport security checks and increasingly stringent passport controls, while the perceived object of anxiety persists.[6] Indeed, the constant presence of such measures and their periodic elevation may serve to perpetuate or exacerbate anxieties rather than relieving them.

As noted above, existential anxieties centre on the threat of death and/or meaninglessness. 'Food scares' may involve either or both, in extreme cases becoming a matter of life or death or, more usually, undermining consumers' confidence in the safety of the very things that can usually be relied upon to sustain their lives. As well as affecting individuals and groups, social anxieties also pose a potential threat to organizations and institutions, such as food businesses and national governments. Moreover, as argued in the next section, the institutionalization of anxieties can evolve independently from individualized fears as when a 'food scare' leads to products being removed from sale, implicating consumers in a social condition of anxiety, regardless of whether they are themselves fearful of consuming the product in question.

Social anxieties

The previous discussion has brought the argument to a point where it is possible to articulate a theory of anxiety which emphasizes its social nature as much as, if not more than, the way anxiety is experienced by particular individuals. As suggested elsewhere (Jackson et al. 2013), arguing that anxiety is not reducible to individual subjective experience is not to say that it can float entirely free from the embodied human subjects who are experiencing the distinctive psychological and physiological symptoms of anxiety. But, it can be argued, the moment of individual subjective experience has a before and an after, both of which stretch beyond the personal biography of the individuals concerned (and beyond the immediate time and place of their subjective experience). So anxiety's social presence is apparent through the relations which constitute moments of individual subjective anxiety. It can also be noted that anxiety as subjectively experienced is constituted relationally from direct personal interactions with other people and/or with material things (such as packaged foods with health warnings and date labels) and/or with particular spaces and places (such as supermarkets or domestic kitchens) and/or with specific institutions (including regulatory authorities such as EFSA) and/or with discourses and representations circulating through the media (such as stories about 'food scares' or the obesity 'epidemic').[7] Social anxieties are a relational effect of all of the forces and entities involved in their articulation.

Anxiety also has a presence in the social through the consequences which flow from those moments of subjective experience. This is true across scales, from consequences at the level of individual action in response to personal anxieties, to legislative and regulatory action at the level of national or supra-national governments in response to collective anxieties (as exemplified by recent debates in the UK and elsewhere about the quality of school meals). While not free-floating, these intersubjective and institutional forms of anxiety extend well beyond the level of individual experience and are the principal focus of this book.

A useful parallel can be drawn with the way individual memories cohere into a more collective consciousness of past events which come to be shared even among those who have no direct memory of the events in question. This idea is developed in Maurice Halbwachs's (1950) work on collective memory which raised the spectre of a reified *conscience collective*. It is exemplified and debated by Samuel and Thompson (1990) in their work on national memory and 'the myths we live by', which asks to what extent nations share a 'collective memory' of the past, beyond the individual memories of their citizens, including the role such shared memories play in the 'imagined community' of the nation (cf. Anderson 1991).

Theodore Schatzki (2002) takes these ideas further in his work on 'practice memory' where he argues that it is possible to attribute memory to social enti-ties without ascribing to society some sort of reified or quasi-reified mind or consciousness. For example, it is possible to think of a community of people who are held together by collective memories that are shared and communicated via common narratives and public memorials. Schatzki argues that this 'presence in public' demonstrates the existence of social memory without hypostatizing the existence of any kind of collective mind. Paul Connerton (1989) makes a similar argument about 'how societies remember' drawing attention to bodily practices and social rituals that show how memory is a cultural rather than a purely indi-vidual phenomenon.

Extending this notion of practice memory to the context of food anxieties might involve examining the way war-time rationing (in force in the UK until 1954) led to deeply embedded social attitudes towards thrift and waste, insti-tutionalized through agencies such as the Ministry of Food whose cultural resonance continues to be felt by British consumers today (as explored in Chapter 7). Prompted by war-time memories, anxieties about food waste are now being experienced among younger generations of consumers who themselves have no direct experience or personal memory of the Second World War. Its traces, however, remain tangible in public consciousness, media commentary and political debate, circulating widely and having continued cultural resonance.

To pull these arguments together, the theory of social anxiety suggests that consumer anxieties about food are intensified by specific *events* (such as 'food scares') where they form part of an underlying *condition*, perpetuating food-related anxieties even at times when there are no specific events to trigger particularly intense moments of anxiety. The theory suggest that 'food scares' and similar events are effective in rupturing the fabric of everyday life, disrupting established routines and rhythms, and persisting until a new order of understanding is put in place and a new consensus is firmly established. Such events can be analysed in terms of the identification of specific objects and subjects of anxiety, with the condition persisting until either object or subject is eliminated. Food-related anxieties derive their intensity and disruptive power because of food's intimate connections with our embodied experience and because of the everyday nature of food consumption. When food's taken-for-granted and life-sustaining properties are thrown into question, anxieties are inevitable and spread rapidly among the population deemed to be at risk.

The theory also suggests that anxieties are framed by different 'communities of practice', including news media, government bodies, regulatory authorities, scientists and other kinds of 'expert'. In their original formulation of the concept, Lave and Wenger (1991) defined communities of practice as formed by groups of people who engage in a process of collective learning in a shared domain of human endeavour, who share a common concern or a passion for something they do, and who learn how to do it better as they interact regularly. In a later commentary, Wenger (1998) added that communities of practice are brought together by their participation in common activities, having a shared domain of interest, engaging in joint activities and developing a shared repertoire of resources. All these ideas can usefully be applied to the study of 'food scares' and other food-related anxieties such as those discussed in Chapters 5 and 6.

The framing of anxiety events crucially affects their social and geographical reach. Some social anxieties may generate a demand for long-term change such as new modes of production and consumption, investment in new infrastructure or novel vaccination programmes, for example. Others may, after the successful destruction of the object of anxiety and with the benefit of hindsight, only appear as a scratch on the surface of history. Some may spur technological innovations or institutional reform, while others encourage a retreat into more 'traditional' ways of life. Some events will be regarded as exceptional, requiring radical change, while others are 'handled' in the flow of everyday practice, as when people routinely buy or avoid particular kinds of food.

As subsequent chapters demonstrate, food-related anxieties commonly move between social fields, spreading across time and space until they are eliminated or contained. What may begin as a 'health scare', for example, might raise questions about the effects of agricultural intensification or the relationship between rural and urban environments (as in the case of the melamine scandal in China, discussed in Chapter 6), while other 'scares' (such as the 2013 horsemeat 'incident', discussed in Chapter 5) may raise concerns about the governance and regulation of food supply chains even when there is no direct threat to public health. Other events, such as Foot and Mouth Disease, have become entangled in public memory with 'food scares' such as BSE, even though the former was more strictly a farming crisis than a food safety issue (cf. Ward et al. 2004).

The emphasis here is on tracing how and why some anxieties intensify and spread while others are contained and remain purely 'local' concerns. Why, for example, did swine flu become recognized as a global pandemic (proclaimed by the World Health Organisation in June 2009) while other diseases, such as malaria and TB, which pose much greater threats to human health worldwide, have been much less conspicuous as social anxieties at least in Europe? Only when these persistent diseases, mostly confined to populations in the Global South, begin to show resistance to current medicines, when more deadly mutations occur, or when they threaten to spread to new areas outside the Global South does the potential for social anxiety in the more 'developed' parts of the world increase.

Social anxieties can therefore be analysed in terms of their life-cycle, social context and political geographies. In the case of swine flu, for example, responses to the object of anxiety clearly varied geographically as the impact of disease was monitored and reworked by different institutions. In one case, the Egyptian government ordered the destruction of all swine stocks to prevent further infection (inflaming religious tensions among the Koptic minority who kept most of the pigs), while several Asian countries stopped importing pork from the United States and Mexico, fearing that the consumption of pork products posed a threat to human health (Johnson 2009). Meanwhile, in the United States, the farming lobby stressed that there was no evidence to associate swine flu with pork consumption, blaming the media for creating 'false' anxieties. While swine flu is still framed as an emerging pandemic with potentially fatal effects for humans, it has already had real consequences not only for

infected individuals and animal populations but also on societies and economies more widely.

These examples suggest that social anxieties proliferate in conditions of
ambivalence and contradiction, particularly where there are gaps between
expert knowledge and lay understandings. This is exacerbated in cases where
scientists are unable to reach a consensus on which to base their advice to the
public or when new evidence appears which challenges the previous consensus.
This raises particular issues for public policies that claim to be evidence-based,
when the nature of that evidence is contested or appears to be inconsistent.
It also poses challenges for the public communication of science where the
evidence is probabilistic rather than definitive and where consumers may have
an imperfect understanding of risk-based assessments, expressed in statistical
terms.[8] Similar issues arise when government authorities change their advice
on common domestic practices, such as whether or not to wash raw poultry
prior to cooking it. Such circumstances may lead to confusion and increase
consumer anxieties about food safety even when the advice is intended to allay
such fears by encouraging appropriate preventative behaviour. Likewise, when
official advice does not coincide with people's everyday experience or when
advice takes multiple forms, as has occurred over the interpretation of food
expiry dates in the UK (with a proliferation of different labels indicating 'best
before', 'use by' or 'display until', for example), it should not be surprising if
some consumers fall back on common-sense understandings or rely on their
own senses of sight, taste and smell to judge when food is no longer considered safe to eat.

Food safety authorities are aware of these issues and are using a variety
of different channels, including social media, to target their advice to specific
groups, including those who are considered to be most 'vulnerable' or most 'at
risk'. Helene Brembeck's (2013) study of the Swedish National Food Authority's
(NFA) use of Facebook to communicate with pregnant women is a case in point
where the authority sought to communicate information in ways that would be
of most use to consumers, in language they could understand and at times
when they were likely to be most receptive to it. The NFA was a trusted source
of advice for these consumers and the messages were cast in a tone that was
intended to be both authoritative and personable. The NFA's biggest challenge,
however, was to provide sound advice in cases of scientific uncertainty, about
pesticide residues, for example, generally erring on the side of caution. Official
advice from food safety authorities also needs to be understood in terms of the
wider 'ecology' of information sources that consumers rely on in making sense
of sometimes conflicting advice, starting from where consumers currently are in

terms of their understanding of food safety issues rather than where the authorities might wish them to be.

The moralization of food anxieties

The approach to consumer anxieties about food being adopted here also seeks to grasp the many ways such anxieties are moralized. Without such understanding it is all too easy for those in authority to 'blame the victim' for social practices that may appear ignorant or morally reprehensible from an official perspective but which might be perfectly logical (and ethical) when viewed from the consumer's perspective (cf. Evans 2011, Meah 2014). A good example is Felicity Lawrence's report on Tim Lobstein's research on family food expenditure (reported in *The Guardian*, 1 October 2008), which occurred during a discussion of the relationship between food and class, provoked by Jamie Oliver's *Ministry of Food* television series (examined more closely in Chapter 7). Lobstein calculated the cost of consuming 100 calories of food energy, showing that frozen chips (at 2 pence per 100 calories) were a much cheaper source of calories than broccoli (at 51 pence) and that orange squash (at 5 pence per 100 calories) was much cheaper than fresh orange juice (at 38 pence). Rather than condemning poorer families for favouring 'unhealthy' food, as can happen if emphasis is placed on the deleterious consequences of apparently ill-informed 'consumer choice', Lawrence argued that the cheaper options were quite rational in the circumstances (and might lead to less food being wasted). When you are on a low income, Lawrence argued, 'you buy the food that fills you up most cheaply. What may seem ignorant choices to others are in fact quite rational'. Rather than framing the argument about working-class diets in terms of an absence of parental care or a lack of culinary skill, Lawrence emphasized the rationality of such (financially constrained) food 'choices'. Her argument resonates with an earlier discussion of well-intentioned food advice in George Orwell's *The Road to Wigan Pier* (1937: 92) where he criticized middle-class do-gooders 'who first condemn a family to live on thirty shillings a week and then have the damned impertinence to tell them how they are to spend their money'.[9]

Finally, the social nature of food-related anxieties suggests that they might be better understood as a necessary or normal part of the human condition rather than as some exceptional state associated with individual phobia or personal pathologies. Moreover, food-related anxieties should be understood in dialectical relation to the pleasures of food and eating. Rather than seeing anxiety as a condition to be avoided at all costs, it might be understood as a normal part of everyday life, albeit one that can escalate to a point that is temporarily out of control, threatening people's sense of health and well-being. While extreme anxiety can be disabling, a life without any degree of anxiety would be extremely dull. At a trivial level, for example, one might be anxious about consuming particular foods in terms of their spiciness or flavour, or one might be worried about the social acceptability of certain kinds of food, or concerned about one's ability to cook them to an appropriate standard. But these kinds of anxieties are unlikely to deter us from cooking or eating them, serving as a marker of anticipated pleasure or what is socially at stake, where the benefits are expected to outweigh the risks. Consumer anxieties about food are therefore subject to constant modulation (Milne et al. 2011), with a variety of (public and private) institutions vying to control our level of anxiety.[10] Understanding the nature and causes of contemporary food anxieties may help consumers gain more control over that process but it will never – and probably should not seek to – eradicate them altogether.

Conclusion

This chapter has presented a theory of anxiety which emphasizes its social rather than its purely personal dimensions. It has argued that anxiety events such as 'food scares' rupture the fabric of everyday life, threatening consumers' mortality and/or their established systems of meaning and ways of 'making sense' of the world. The chapter has argued that anxieties can be creative or disabling (in the sense of Kierkegaard's claim about the possibility of being 'educated by anxiety'). As well as taking an episodic form (as is the case with periodic 'food scares'), anxiety can also be understood as a pervasive feature of modern life (both in terms of specific *events* and as an underlying social *condition*). The analytical separation of individual and social anxieties also enables an understanding of how consumers can be drawn into a social condition of anxiety whether or not they are themselves anxious.

Having reviewed the existential and social nature of contemporary food-related anxieties, this chapter has outlined a theory of anxiety as a social condition whereby events (such as 'food scares') were seen to disrupt established routines, disturbing the rhythms of everyday life, creating objects and subjects of anxiety which persist until either or both are destroyed and a new consensus is put firmly in place. The chapter argued that anxieties are framed by different 'communities of practice', moving between different sites or social fields, and varying across time and space. Anxieties spread and/or are contained.

They proliferate in conditions of ambivalence and uncertainty and are moralized to varying degrees. The remainder of the book seeks to 'apply' this theory to a range of food-related anxieties, exploring their sociological, historical and geographical dimensions rather than treating anxiety as a purely individual experience or personal pathology.

Notes

1. The roots of this distinction can be traced back to the work of Emile Durkheim. In his classic study of suicide, Durkheim (1897) showed that there were different *rates* of suicide among different social groups (higher among Protestants than among Catholics, for example, and higher among men than women), irrespective of the causes of any individual suicide, which might be intensely personal.

2. The German word *Angst* has rather different connotations from the English word 'anxiety'. In his pioneering study of *The Meaning of Anxiety* (1950), Rollo May comments on Walter Lowrie's translation of Kierkegaard's classic study of anxiety as 'The concept of dread': 'It is certainly to be agreed that the term "anxiety" in English often means "eagerness" ("I am anxious to do something") or a mild form of worry or has other connotations which do not at all do justice to the term *Angst*. But [May continues] the German *Angst* is the word which Freud, Goldstein, and others use for "anxiety"; and it is the common denominator for the term "anxiety" as used in this study' (1950: 32).

3. This section draws on ideas that were first elaborated in Jackson and Everts (2010).

4. In her work on obesity, for example, Lauren Berlant (2007) challenges the tendency to frame events in the language of 'crisis' or 'epidemic'. Such terminology, she argues, should be limited to relatively rare or extreme experiences, calling for heroic agency and diverting attention from the everyday 'zone of ordinariness' through which events are routinely reproduced. Berlant distinguishes between event and environment, focusing on the way that events become occasions for justified moralizing within a wider social environment, with the potential to misrepresent the duration or distort the scale of contemporary anxieties.

5. 'How many people could bird flu kill?' (ABC News, 30 September 2005), available at http://abcnews.go.com/Health/Flu/story?id=1173856 (accessed 9 April 2015).

6. Many other drastic measures have been justified by invoking the precautionary principle as Anderson (2010) explores in his work on anticipatory action.

7. The World Health Organisation declared that Western society was facing an obesity 'epidemic' over a decade ago (WHO 1998) but its nature, extent and underlying causes are strongly contested (see, e.g. Colls & Evans [2009] and Guthman [2011] for a range of alternative perspectives). On the mediation of 'food scares', see Miller and Reilly (1994).

8. See, for example, Gene Rowe's (2010) report to the UK FSA's Committee on Toxicity on the challenges of communicating uncertainty in scientific risk assessments: http://multimedia.food.gov.uk/multimedia/pdfs/evaluncertframework.pdf and the additional commentary provided by members of the Agency's Social Science Research Committee: http://multimedia.food.gov.uk/multimedia/pdfs/riskuncert (both accessed 11 July 2014).

9. Leading up to this expostulation, Orwell wrote that: 'The ordinary human being would sooner starve than live on brown bread and raw carrots . . . A millionaire may enjoy breakfasting off orange juice and Ryvita biscuits; an unemployed man doesn't . . . When you are unemployed, which is to say when you are underfed, harassed, bored and miserable, you don't *want* to eat dull wholesome food. You want something a little bit "tasty" . . . Let's have three pennorth of chips! Run out and buy us a twopenny ice-cream! Put the kettle on and we'll all have a nice cup of tea!' (1937: 88).

10. Consider government campaigns about 'healthy eating', for example, or the commercial promotion of dieting products and lifestyle advice.

Chapter 4

Technological change and consumer anxieties about food

This chapter examines the consumer anxieties about food that have arisen from the intensification of agriculture and the way these anxieties are shaping the development of the contemporary food industry, using the broiler chicken industry as a case study. It argues that the development of 'cold chain' technologies and related innovations enabled the widespread consumption of fresh chicken, previously regarded as a luxury item, consumed by the few and restricted to special occasions. But these developments also had a number of unintended consequences, leading to lengthening and more complex supply chains, negative impacts on animal welfare and increased risk of food-borne diseases such as Campylobacter.[1] Consumer anxieties about these issues have had direct commercial implications for the development of the poultry industry, impacting on new product development, branding and food marketing.

Despite the benefits of agricultural and technological innovation in making fresh chicken and other products more widely available, consumers often complain about the lack of taste of intensively reared chicken, comparing it nostalgically with their perception of how chicken used to taste in a real or imagined past. This chapter examines the impact of these changing consumer attitudes which have played a key role in shaping the poultry sector. The chapter also explores the context in which these attitudes have been shaped, including the growing disconnection between food producers and consumers, often identified as a major cause of declining consumer trust in food (see, e.g. the Policy Commission on the Future of Farming and Food 2002).

The growing separation of producers and consumers has also given rise to significant challenges for the retail industry which seeks to promote the 'naturalness' of animal products such as chicken without making consumers feel uncomfortable about having close contact with raw flesh and other uncooked ingredients.[2] Food retailers have had to confront the increasing squeamishness of their customers, as reported in previous research (Jackson et al. 2010) where one interviewee claimed that 'the meat that you worry about most is chicken isn't it? Cause it's like you can get so many different things from it'. Previous research also suggests that many consumers are concerned about animal welfare, worried about the rearing of chickens in battery cages (for egg production) or in broiler sheds (for meat), anxious about them being 'squashed together in . . . some sort of big monstrosity like the Bernard Matthew's thing'.[3] Whether or not one accepts the premise on which these anxieties are based, chicken remains a major source of food-borne illness and is a key area of current attention from food regulators such as the UK FSA. It is this confluence of interests among regulators, retailers and consumers that is at the heart of the present chapter.

The chapter begins by outlining the history of chicken production. It provides an account of the socio-technical innovations that enabled the intensification of poultry production, first in the United States and then in the UK. It goes on to outline the development of the 'cold chain', which enabled the widespread consumption of fresh as opposed to frozen chicken, drawing on a unique collection of life history interviews with some of the key actors in this process. The chapter then reviews one recent episode in this longer history (the development of 'Oakham' chicken by British retailer Marks & Spencer), including some focus group and interview material from British consumers concerning the anxieties that have been prompted by these socio-technical changes. The chapter concludes with some thoughts on the commodification of nature, its limits and implications.

The historical development of chicken production

The rearing of chicken for human consumption can be traced back at least 5,000 years (Potts 2012). Specialization and technological innovation were at the heart of chicken rearing from the earliest times. In their history of chicken, for example, Smith and Daniel describe how the invention of chicken incubators in Ancient Egypt was 'the accomplishment of a social and political order in which the mass production of food was already highly organized' (1982: 15). What followed, depending on your point of view, is a story of incredible human ingenuity and the forward march of technology, subordinating this humble creature to meet the seemingly insatiable appetite of an increasingly urbanized population, or a sorry tale of moral decline as the 'industrialization of the chicken' was quickly followed, in Smith and Daniel's terms, by 'the fall of the chicken (and almost everything else)'. From being an object of veneration and pleasure, curiosity and delight, *Gallus domesticus* became a commodity or a product 'not much different from a galosh or a bar of soap' (ibid.: 272). Those involved in the intensification of chicken production, Smith and Daniel conclude, demonstrated callous disregard for a living creature and a reckless confidence in the irresistible logic of technology (ibid.: 298–99).[4]

Donna Haraway adopts a similar line of argument in her provocative book, *When Species Meet*, inviting readers to 'Follow the chicken and find the world' (2008: 274). Her analysis of the contemporary 'animal-industrial complex' describes the postwar intensification of poultry production based on genetic manipulation, the widespread use of antibiotics and forced maturation to the point where chickens are 'unable to walk, flap their wings, or even stand up': 'Muscles linked in evolutionary history and religious symbolism to flight, sexual display, and transcendence instead pump iron for transnational growth industries. Not satisfied, some agribusiness scientists look to post genomics research for even more buffed white meat' (ibid.: 267).

Equally unrelenting in tone, Annie Potts talks of the transformation of chicken 'from reverence to ruination' as birds that were once admired and respected have been subordinated to the dictates of industrial production. Along the way, she argues:

> They have lost their natural births and relationships with mother hens and siblings to incubators and brooders; their immune systems to compulsory antibiotics; their connections to the earth and sky to confinement in overcrowded barns; their enjoyment of nesting and dust-bathing to barren cages; their sociability to the constant stress of immersion in a crowd of strangers; their love of sunlight and the changing seasons to Vitamin D regimes and artificial lighting; their capacity to fly, run or just stand to enforced obesity. (2012: 172)

Once revered for their bravery, fortitude and devotion to parenthood, Potts argues, chickens have become 'the least respected and most manipulated beings on the planet' (ibid.: 139).

Harold McGee is similarly scathing about the rise of the modern broiler chicken. As he writes in his encyclopaedia of kitchen science, history and culture:

> The modern chicken is a product of the drive to breed fast-growing animals and raise them as rapidly and on as little feed as possible. It's an impressive feat of agricultural engineering to produce a 4-pound bird on 8 pounds of feed in six weeks! Because such a bird grows very fast and lives very little, its meat is fairly bland, and that of the young 'game hen' or 'poussin' even more so. (2004: 139)

The scale of the modern poultry industry is, indeed, truly remarkable, with some ten billion chickens slaughtered annually for meat in the United States and a global population of around five billion laying hens (Haraway 2008: 266). Worldwide, chicken meat production has risen from just over 35 million tonnes in 1990 to over 85 million tonnes in 2010. In Roger Horowitz's (2004) words, chickens have been reworked 'as commodities and creatures' to the point where their lifespan is measured in days rather than weeks. Consumer anxieties about chicken focus, in particular, on the postwar intensification of poultry production.

The intensification of poultry production

Chicken is arguably the defining example of the industrialization of food production, the paradigmatic case of agricultural intensification. There can be few other examples where technological change and corporate power have reshaped food supply chains and production systems so dramatically as in the case of the intensively reared broiler chicken. Prior to the 1960s, eating chicken was generally regarded as something of a luxury, a rare treat, confined to 'high days and holidays' (Burnett 1966, Visser 1999). Chicken consumption was mostly a by-product of egg production, with spent laying hens destined for the cooking pot. War-time rationing led to the expansion of domestic egg production in the UK, based on a proliferation of small-scale producers, with over one million poultry keepers accounting for 30 per cent of the national laying stock in 1945 (Holroyd 1986: 155). But chicken meat was not included on the ration list as so little was consumed at that time.

In the United States, the transformation of chicken from a luxury food to a staple part of people's everyday diet was signalled by Herbert Hoover's electioneering slogan 'A chicken in every pot' in 1928 and it was the American preference for dry frying or broiling that gave the intensive broiler chicken industry its name. The emergence of the integrated broiler industry has been described as the first modern 'agribusiness' (Sykes 1963, quoted in Godley & Williams 2007: 4). It led to 'a watershed in the history of American dietary culture' (Boyd & Watts 1997: 192), when, in 1990, US consumption of chicken first outstripped beef consumption, with world consumption of broiler chicken overtaking beef and veal in 2001.

Learning from the American experience, the first broiler shed was built in Britain in 1953, marking the beginnings of the UK intensive broiler industry. As the number of broiler farms expanded, the price of poultry fell and consumption increased. Between 1960 and 1980 the average British person's weekly consumption of poultry increased threefold (MAFF 1991: 37). In the space of about 50 years, chicken production in the UK metamorphosed from being a localized cottage industry to a 'highly concentrated and industrialised sector with production and distribution dominated by a relatively small number of economic actors' (Yakovleva & Flynn 2004a: 229). Godley and Williams (2007: 2) refer to 'a revolution in modern British agriculture' as UK chicken production increased from around one million birds in 1950 to over 150 million in 1965, exceeding 200 million by 1967. Broiler companies such as Buxted Chicken, founded by Antony Fisher in the 1950s, experienced phenomenal growth, commanding annual sales of £5 million within five years of its establishment, employing 200 people and handling 17,500 chickens a day. Fisher sold the business in 1968 for £21 million, having, in the words of one observer, 'transformed the eating patterns of the British public' (Cockett 1995: 125).

The expansion of poultry production was enabled by a steady reduction in the time broiler chicks take to grow to maturity. Through a careful process of genetic selection, chicks can now be reared to their slaughter weight of 2 kg within about 40 days of being hatched. This time has halved in the last 30 years, with a reduction of roughly one day every year since the mid-1970s. Similarly, the amount of feed needed to achieve this weight gain has been reduced by almost 40 per cent since 1976 (Compassion in World Farming 2003: 7), with chicken now being reared on a truly industrial scale (see Figure 4.1). While the development of modern poultry farming in the United States was strongly guided by the Department of Agriculture, in Britain the 'revolution' was led by food retailers such as J Sainsbury and Marks & Spencer. The British industry also grew in a more integrated fashion than its American counterpart, with Sainsbury's having around 15 per cent of the total trade in the 1960s. Taking control of the supply chain, Sainsbury's was active in breed selection and in organizing chicken production on a regional basis. They also introduced new self-service store formats with greater shelf space and refrigerator capacity.

Sainsbury's led the development of 'ready-to-cook' frozen chicken, the preparation for which took place at dedicated packing stations rather than within each store, a process that required significant improvements in refrigeration and transportation as chicken meat deteriorates rapidly after evisceration.[5] Leading firms such as Buxted developed automated conveyor-belt processing systems and quick-freezing methods that were capable of handling 1,800 birds per hour (Godley & Williams 2007: 13).

Besides these innovations in factory processing and refrigeration, rearing methods also underwent rapid change, with a reduction in the average size of chickens enabling a shortening in the length of the growing cycle from

Figure 4.1 A modern broiler shed.
Source: People for the Ethical Treatment of Animals.

12 to 10 weeks, allowing growers to harvest birds three or four times a year. Improvements in feedstuffs led to a further reduction in the growing cycle to around 9 weeks (ibid.: 15). Flock sizes expanded from hundreds to thousands of birds in order to exploit economies of scale, as retailers began to exercise greater control over their suppliers. Processors such as Buxted also integrated other parts of the supply chain, moving backwards from rearing into commercial hatcheries and developing closer ties with feed manufacturers with the object of producing a more thoroughly integrated business.[6] Innovations in the use of pharmaceuticals (such as growth hormones and chemical supplements) enabled growers to produce more meat using less feed, with antibiotics reducing the mortality rate of chickens, enhancing their speed of growth and increasing their shelf-life.

There are four stages in the modern chicken supply chain: breeder farms, hatcheries, growers and processors, with different degrees of concentration at different stages in the chain. Breeder farms provide the genetic stock for poultry flocks and three breeder companies (Aviagen, Cobb-Vantress and Merial) supply the entire UK's poultry genotypes. The parent stock (mainly Ross and Cobb) produce eggs which are hatched at one of the UK's 12 hatcheries (see Figure 4.2) before being sent to a much larger number of growers. Although the UK broiler population is spread across a large number of holdings, the vast

Figure 4.2 Newly hatched chicks – industrial scale.
Source: © Polly Russell.

majority of chickens are held in flocks with more than 20,000 birds (Sheppard 2004). Once the chickens have reached the desired culling weight they are sent to a processing plant of which there are around 100 nationwide, each grossing several million pounds a year (Yakovleva and Flynn 2004b: 16). The retailing of chicken is also highly concentrated in the UK, with over 70 per cent of fresh chicken sold through the four main supermarket chains (Randall 1999, Blythman 2004).

Despite a rapid increase in consumption during this period, consumer confidence was not assured. Godley and Williams (2009: 268) refer to a crisis of confidence among British consumers in the early 1960s as the public questioned the probity of recent socio-technical innovations in chicken production, including the increasing pharmaceutical content of the diet on which intensively reared chicken were fed. Consumer concerns about the long-term consequences to human health of chemical residues in broiler chickens proliferated, the intensification of poultry production having required 'the forced ingestion of large quantities of hormones, antioxidants, coccidiostats, and antibiotics', in addition to vitamins and mineral supplements (Godley & Williams 2009: 284).[7] In what has become a frequent refrain among critics of agricultural intensification, a scientist at the Houghton Poultry Research Station asked in October 1955: 'Are we going too fast in our efforts to apply industrial methods to stock farming?' (Robert Gordon, quoted in Godley & Williamson 2009: 284). Fears about pesticide residues, growing antibiotic resistance and Salmonella in eggs all rang warning bells with the public until, in 1970, the British government prohibited the indiscriminate use of antibiotic growth promoters in animal feed.

Concluding their analysis of the invention of the 'technological chicken', Godley and Williamson (2009) argue that the retail industry played a key role in managing the risks associated with the intensification of chicken production. The risk was shared between the supermarkets and their suppliers, each knowing that a loss of consumer trust would damage them commercially. But it was the supermarkets that stood to lose most and who were the driving force of changes in safety standards and quality control, requiring their suppliers to meet quality standards that were well above the legal minimum. It is from this period that current retail-led systems of quality assurance derive, posing persistent questions about the governance and regulation of food supply chains (cf. Marsden et al. 2000).

Developing the 'cold chain'

While Sainsbury's led the retail revolution in terms of the widespread consumption of frozen chicken, it was the development of the 'cold chain' by one of Sainsbury's high-street rivals, Marks & Spencer, which enabled the mass consumption of fresh chicken.[8] Recalling this period, retired food technologist Norman Robson relates how senior management at Marks & Spencer felt that frozen food was 'slightly infra-dig' and how they sought to differentiate themselves from competing stores such as Sainsbury's and MacFisheries, who were 'completely sold on frozen chicken'.[9] Robson's objective was to develop 'fresh not frozen' chicken, a phrase that became the company's publicity slogan. The problem was, of course, that fresh chicken had a much shorter shelf-life than frozen chicken. The answer to prolonged shelf-life lay in improved refrigeration (see Figure 4.3).

According to Norman Robson, refrigeration was at the heart of the company's move into fresh food:

We accepted from the moment that we went into what in those days we called 'provisions' . . . which consisted of ham, bacon, chickens, cheese [and] dairy products in general, that these products would have to be not only displayed in refrigerated counters but also distributed in refrigerated vehicles.

Figure 4.3 Refrigerated chicken display, Marks & Spencer, 1960s.
Source: The Marks & Spencer Company Archive.

Maintaining food at a constant temperature was critical to food quality and safety, yet refrigerated vehicles scarcely existed at that time. Robson recalls how Marks & Spencer used solid carbon dioxide to cool ordinary delivery vehicles in the hope that cold dry ice would reduce the atmospheric temperature sufficiently to transport goods safely to the store. The first refrigerated display units were introduced in 1961 when the UK broiler industry was still in its infancy and Robson recounts how the firm was gradually able to build in a sufficient safety margin to enable fresh chicken to remain in store overnight rather than having to be restocked each day:

> Better equipment flowed through, the temperature control got better and better, my technologists started doing shelf life tests which proved that you could keep a chicken quite happily over one night and the consumer could cook it on the third day and it would be quite safe . . . and that's what cracked it.[10]

Customers preferred fresh chicken, Robson maintains, because the texture of frozen chicken was coarse and chewy, whereas the texture of a chilled bird was tender, with much better flavour. Around this time, too, David Gregory, former head of technology at Marks & Spencer, recalls the firm's partnership with the British Oxygen Company (BOC) with whom they developed polar stream nitrogen-chilled vehicles (for retail distribution) and piped refrigeration (to ensure consistent chilling capacity in-store).[11]

Fresh chicken was an ideal product for Marks & Spencer in terms of 'value, consistency, acceptability [and] versatility'.[12] It was acceptable to all cultural and religious tastes and reliable in terms of tenderness and consistency. Agriculturally, too, chicken was more economical in terms of carcass balance than beef, lamb or pork, with fewer off-cut problems. Besides selling fresh whole birds, Marks & Spencer pioneered the introduction of added-value products such as Chicken Kiev, introduced in 1979 and designed to mirror the quality of food that customers were becoming accustomed to in restaurants as the experience of 'eating out' became more popular. Prepared dishes such as Chicken Kiev and Chicken Cordon Bleu were the precursor of the modern 'ready-meal', including Chinese and Indian ranges, introduced in the 1980s (discussed further in Chapter 9). Through these innovations, Marks & Spencer claim to have made chicken 'convenient', justifying their reputation for quality and innovation.[13]

Marks & Spencer's suppliers share the company's pride in product innovation. Former Marks & Spencer chicken supplier Fred Duncan suggests that the work he did at Grampian Foods 'set a new standard for animal welfare and performance in chicken growing'.[14] He also draws attention to the company's record in taking artificial growth promoters out of chicken feed before the government required it and introducing better animal husbandry methods, anticipating a trend that the company would return to in later years.

Rebranding intensively reared chicken

Although the intensification of poultry production led to a massive increase in chicken consumption, making fresh chicken available to the mass market, it also had a series of unintended consequences in terms of lengthening supply chains and increasing consumer anxieties about provenance and animal welfare. In Britain, chicken became available year-round and was sourced from throughout the UK (and later from abroad) rather than only being available from local butchers. But the quality of the finished product tended to be rather bland compared to free-range or organic chicken, lacking in taste and texture. Marks & Spencer's category manager Andrew Mackenzie describes intensive chicken as: 'a canvas upon which people paint, because actually in itself, it doesn't offer much. It's a source of protein but in textural terms, unless it is free range or organic, in flavour terms . . . it doesn't really deliver.'[15] Currently, around 94 per cent of UK chickens are reared intensively and 6 per cent are free-range, half of which (3%) are certified organic. The official definition of 'free range' specifies a maximum indoor stocking density of 12 birds per square metre, with continuous daytime access to open-air runs for at least half the bird's life at a maximum outdoor density of 1 bird per square metre (Miele 2011: Table 1).

In the late 1990s, Marks & Spencer found themselves competing with Britain's other major retailers most of whom offered broiler chickens on an 'everyday low price' basis or even as a loss-leader. Unable or unwilling to compete on this basis, Marks & Spencer set about rethinking their poultry offer to re-establish their distinctiveness from their high-street rivals. Their proposed solution also responded to growing consumer anxieties about animal welfare and concerns about the perceived quality of the product. Andrew Mackenzie recalls how Marks & Spencer challenged their suppliers to help them establish a 'point of difference' from their competitors:

> I felt that our chicken business could be more . . . I didn't feel we were different enough, I didn't feel we were special enough . . . so we wrote a blueprint which was about a three page document, which was, what brand values do we want, what visual appearances do we want and what are the main things that we want to achieve? And it was about visual appearance to the customer, it was about leading standards in terms of growing the bird, it was about great standards in terms of slaughter.[16]

Andrew Mackenzie admits that the points of difference with intensively reared chicken are 'relatively slim'. The changes they proposed to introduce were 'incremental rather than step changing'. 'If you want to go step changing,' he concedes, 'then you're into your free range and if you want to go step changing again, you're into organic, so that's how you actually achieve [major differences] in this area.'

Articulating this vision and putting it into practice resulted in the development of the 'Oakham' brand. It coincided with a time when Marks & Spencer's food business was ailing and when relaunching several popular lines including chicken was a company priority (Mellahi et al. 2002). The company was judged to be over-reliant on its own brand ('St Michael'). It had been later than other retailers in accepting credit and debit cards, and the company had a low profile in rapidly developing 'out-of-town' retail parks. Marks & Spencer had a low advertising spend and faced increasing competition from other supermarkets' premium brands (such as *Tesco's Finest* and Sainsbury's *Taste the Difference* ranges). The company had engaged in some ill-fated overseas acquisitions where many of their traditional ways of doing business, including their 'buy British' policy, were hard to adapt to a different retail environment (Burt et al. 2002). By 2004, the company was in the throes of an attempted takeover by the Arcadia Group, led by the owner of British Home Stores, Philip Green. A new wave of innovation in its food business was identified as a key part of the company's strategy for commercial revival.

Aware of its history of innovation and its reputation for quality produce, the company began a major review of their poultry lines, leading to a change of suppliers and the launch of the Oakham chicken brand in 2003. According to Marks & Spencer's agricultural technologist Mark Ranson (interviewed January 2004), the development of the Oakham brand took 18 months and was 'a joint team effort' involving the company's chicken buyer, product technologist and himself, working with the breeder company Aviagen, a nutritionist from Buxted and their suppliers. Several suppliers were invited to tender for the company's chicken business, proposing long-term strategies for improving poultry sales, profitability and quality. The successful strategy proposed by Two Sisters Food Group included a plan to differentiate Marks & Spencer's chicken products from their rivals, striving to produce 'chicken the way it used to be'.[17]

Oakham chicken are a standard breed (the Ross 508), owned by the international poultry breeding company Aviagen from whom Marks & Spencer obtained exclusive rights to the breed. The Ross 508 is a slower-growing bird, known for its high meat-yield and good feed-conversion ratio.[18] As agricultural technologist Mark Ranson explained, it would have been prohibitively expensive to develop a new breed from scratch, so Marks & Spencer worked with Aviagen to select the ideal bird for their needs:

> [Aviagen] had this bird available and it was . . . it wasn't being used anywhere else because it had been originally developed for the fast food industry. What they wanted was a bird with lots of breast meat with very little leg so they could use the breast meat for cutting up into portions and nuggets and God knows what else. So it was a slower growing bird overall, but you got this bigger, larger breast meat from it.[19]

What distinguishes Oakham chicken from standard broilers was, however, less to do with the breed and more about how the birds are reared. A press release promoting the Oakham brand explained that the chickens are fed on 'a nutritious feed ration which is non-GM, cereal-based and free from antibiotic growth promoters and encourages health and welfare too'. Besides the specifications for the feed regime, Oakham chickens are housed at lower stocking densities (34 kgm^2 compared to the industry standard of 38 kgm^2) and have a slower growing cycle (living on average 4–5 days longer than the typical 39–40 days

of conventionally produced broiler chickens). Although lower than the industry standard, a density of 34 kgm^2 is still 4 kgm^2 above the Royal Society for
the Prevention of Cruelty to Animals' recommended maximum stocking density
(RSPCA 2005). High stocking densities can lead to hock burn, where the ammo-
nia from the waste of other birds causes a burning of the skin on a chicken's leg
and other joints. A study by Broom and Reefman (2005) identified the presence
of hock burn in 82 per cent of supermarket chickens. Campaign reports from
animal welfare charities also focus on the adverse effects of genetic selection
and inappropriate lighting arrangements as well as excessive stocking densities (Sustain 1999, RSPCA 2001, 2005). Oakham chickens also have access to
'natural behaviour enablers' (such as bales of straw that the chickens can claw
and peck at). Thus, Oakham chickens can be marketed as slower-growing birds,
reared under more welfare-friendly conditions (though still not to free-range or
organic standards).[20]

The development of the Oakham brand can be seen as a direct response
to consumer anxieties about the acceleration and intensification of chicken
production, designed precisely to allay consumer fears about the pace and
direction of change in chicken production and to address changing customer
tastes and perceptions. Compared to the cheaper year-round prices offered by
Tesco or Sainsbury's, for example, Marks & Spencer sought to offer a higher
quality product, representing what the company's poultry buyer, Catherine Lee,
described as 'a unique proposition on the high street'.[21] Unlike their commercial rivals, she explained, Marks & Spencer was not about economy fillets or
buy-one-get-one-free special offers, as such strategies 'don't fit with anything
else in our proposition', not 'what an M&S customer expects'. Marks & Spencer
were also able to claim 100 per cent traceability, putting the name of the farmer
on the pack.[22] Marketing references to how chicken 'used to taste' suggest a
sense of nostalgia for a previous, real or imagined, world in which food was
more authentic and tasted better. An interview with hatchery manager Ray Moore
provides several examples of this sentiment. Describing himself as 'oldy-fash'
[old fashioned] and 'traditional', he talks about growing up in the 1960s when
you 'used to just have chicken', 'you never had all these breast fillets and drum-
sticks and all that jazz'.[23] Chicken grower Audrey Kley also argued that 'chicken
used to be special but now it's everyday', while agricultural technologist Mark
Ranson talked about how 'chickens today are very different to how they were
twenty, thirty [years ago] . . . In terms of flavour, texture and everything else [it]
was very . . very different'.[24]

The Oakham brand was introduced as part of the company's commitment to bringing customers 'the best tasting, freshest products' (press

release, 4 November 2003). In the same statement, Mark Ranson is quoted as saying that:

> The introduction of the Oakham chicken is based around listening to our customers and their concerns about issues such as the welfare of animals and what they are fed . . . Our customers told us they wanted chicken to 'taste like it used to taste'. So, responding to this, we've introduced birds that are grown in enriched environments, with the Oakham White grown in barns with straw bales enabling the birds to perch and rest, and as a result, the Oakham is a slower-growing bird.[25]

Mark Ranson's description suggests a shift from a producer- to a market-driven supply chain.[26] Understanding customer concerns, applying new agricultural standards and putting these practices on display via packaging and marketing were integral to the product development process. According to Catherine Lee, however, the difference between Oakham and rival brands was 'essentially a marketing message' for what Marks & Spencer specified agriculturally and in terms of processing and packaging.

The Oakham brand attempted to respond to a range of consumer anxieties associated with intensive poultry production. For example, Mark Ranson emphasized the importance of a longer growing cycle to determining taste and texture, compared to the 40-day industry standard, while agricultural technologist Paul Willgoss referred to the animal welfare problems (such as hock burn) associated with intensive poultry production to which the development of the Oakham brand was a direct response.

The naming of the Oakham brand was also driven by consumer concerns and the need for what Catherine Lee called 'some provenance-type imagery'. Oakham is, in fact, a small market town in Rutland in the east of England but Oakham chickens have no direct connection with the town. The name was chosen because of its positive association with 'countryside imagery and nice places'.[27] As Catherine Lee explained:

> It's more about an image than it is a place and provenance. I suppose it does sound British, there's a Britishness to it . . . and there's a provenance feel, a bit like Aberdeen Angus. Because that's effectively what we were looking for . . . the Aberdeen Angus of the poultry world.

There is, however, a key difference between the two products as Aberdeen Angus is a specific breed linked to a particular place, while Oakham chicken are a generic breed (originally produced for the fast-food industry), with no specific connection to the town of Oakham.

Rather than switching over entirely to free-range or organic production, the development of the Oakham brand enabled Marks & Spencer to implement some improved environmental and welfare practices which justified a premium price without unduly sacrificing intensive production methods, relatively high volumes and low costs. The brand's success contributed directly to the firm's commercial revival following its launch in 2003, generating 30 per cent sales growth, well ahead of the rest of the market.[28] The company's share price almost doubled, reaching a high of £7.66 in May 2007. Marks & Spencer won an award for the development of the Oakham brand from the animal welfare group Compassion in World Farming and a commendation from the RSPCA for the company's commitment to improving farm animal welfare. Competitors quickly sought to copy the success of the Oakham brand with similar rebranding exercises involving Tesco's Willow chicken and Sainsbury's Devonshire Red. Unlike Marks & Spencer, however, these other companies did not extend the changes across their entire chicken range, restricting them to specific 'hero brands'. Marks & Spencer have since attempted to 'Oakhamize' other protein species (including duck, turkey, salmon, pork and lamb).

Chickens as creatures or commodities?

The intensification of chicken production raises critical questions about the commodification of nature or, more pointedly, what happens to chickens when they are transformed from a live creature into an object to be bought and sold for human consumption.[29] Chicken hatchery manager Ray Moore provides a good point of entry into this discussion. He clearly sees chickens as a tradable commodity, where his job is to anticipate future demand and to acquire and hatch sufficient chicks to meet that demand. As he puts it: 'It's all to do with money, with chickens really, you shuffle chickens like you shuffle money'. Yet he also identifies closely with the product and describes himself as 'a Ross man' whose 'life was made with chicken'. He continues:

> Chicken talk to you, they do. You know if they're cold, hungry, too hot. You know by your atmosphere anyway . . . You got to keep walking these chickens . . . You've got to look after them just like I look after my wife. They need tender loving care and that's all that matters to them really and if you look after them they'll be alright.[30]

Ray Moore spoke about his concerns over the acceleration of production and its possible implications in terms of increased consumer anxiety. He talked of the need to slow the production cycle down 'to give the bird a bit more chance'. Asked why the increasing speed of modern broiler production makes him uncomfortable, he replied: 'Well they just grow them on so damn fast . . . I mean you're killing the bird now in less than six weeks for a four pound bird, so you've got to do something somewhere.'

Contrasting the current state of the poultry industry with the time when he entered the business, Ray Moore reflects nostalgically: 'We had proper free-range chickens [then], proper free-range, not like they tell you now.' He is also critical of contemporary consumers' lack of knowledge about how chickens are produced and where they come from: 'To be quite honest, I don't think town kids know where eggs and chicken come from . . . Some people might just think milk comes from a bottle [and] eggs come from a cardboard box, but there's a chicken at the end . . . a live thing at the end.'

Compared to Ray Moore, chicken grower Audrey Kley has a less ambivalent attitude towards the birds that provide her livelihood:

> You've got to be hardened to it. It's not like your own pet dog when it dies and you get very upset . . . with the chickens there is no sort of affection towards them because they all look alike and it's part of your work and you don't think about it. When they come in [from the hatchery], you know they're going to be killed and you worry about them having enough food and that they'll pay but you don't worry about the rest of it.

Agricultural technologist Mark Ranson provides another perspective on this issue, contrasting the 'lethargic' nature of intensively reared birds with the 'sparky and flighty' nature of free-range chickens:

> If you go and see, just go into a broiler shed, even the Oakham White ones where they're a little bit more . . . the birds are a little bit more attentive and so on, and then go and see a flock of free-range birds, and they're sparky and flighty, they're excited, they're running in and out, they're having a great time. They still die, but . . . And you go into a broiler shed and they are lethargic and whilst I think ours are probably less lethargic and particularly the Oakhams would be, I still think that at the end of the day maybe it's something that goes right back to my childhood of walking round farms with friends and whatever, who had free-range, you know, chickens just scrabbling around for eggs . . . And chickens roam around and they roost . . . you know, that's how chickens are.[31]

Ray Moore's acknowledgement that there is 'a live thing' at the end of the supply chain is taken up by poultry buyer Catherine Lee when she tries to explain the 'agricultural proposition' of improved welfare standards that is used to justify the premium prices that Marks & Spencer seek to charge. She suggests that customers 'don't want to know that that's a dead body sitting in front of them', an attitude which she disparages as squeamish and which she seeks to explain in terms of the increasing distance between modern consumers and the sites of agricultural production:

> We've moved so far away from a rural lifestyle that they don't want to know what's happened on a farm. They don't see chickens any more. They've become squeamish with the consequences of that . . . We've moved so away from a rural environment . . . that the majority of the population live in a town, you know, they don't really see a live chicken on a day to day basis anymore and therefore they've become squeamish about dealing with the conse- quences of that. They've become disassociated with it you know.[32]

Consumer interviews and focus groups provide further support for Catherine Lee's argument. As one interviewee remarked: 'I think we're probably, in this kind of Western culture, far too removed from what we're actually eating . . . It's not because I'm squeamish about what I'm eating . . . I think there's this whole kind of silly thing, that's almost making what we're eating as less like an animal as possible which is daft because at the end of the day, it *is* an animal' (consumer interview, December 2006). The 'squeamishness' to which this interviewee alludes was a common feature of other interviews. As one female consumer reported: 'I don't like whole chickens. I don't like cutting them up – the gunge and the fat and everything . . . all the fat and mess . . . it's just a mess really [and] you're left [with] your bread board and your kitchen bench and everything all covered in this slimy horrible gunge.' Other interviewees spoke about their dislike of the 'bone and gristle' associated with chicken and all the 'veins and things', while others took extreme measures to avoid touching raw meat:

> I hate handling raw chicken. I tend to do it with rubber gloves because I keep thinking Salmonella urgh or whatever . . . and I'm quite careful about how I handle it because I think probably all chicken's got Salmonella . . . I don't like touching it either, so I do it with rubber gloves and then wash my hands really well.

Or, again:

> I bleach all my knives and boards and wash them down after cooking to make sure it's free of any bugs and then make sure that it's obviously cooked really well . . . so I don't poison me and my housemates!

These anxieties pose problems for people further up the supply chain, who tend to be critical of what they regard as a lack of consumer knowledge. For example, Audrey Kley can barely hide her contempt for the supposed ignorance of contemporary housewives:

> I'm very worried about the housewife because she'll go and buy the cheapest that she can but she won't look or know where they're produced or where they come from . . . They don't bother to cook it properly, do they. They just sling it in the microwave . . . or they fling it in the oven half frozen and they don't wash it or anything . . . Part of the problem with the housewife is that she isn't taught to cook good simple food . . . besides they don't want to bother with that do they . . . and then they wonder why they've got all these nasty bugs and it's nothing to do with the growers, it's the housewife.[33]

Consumers' squeamishness about touching raw poultry poses particular problems for those at the higher end of the retail market (like Marks & Spencer) who wish to differentiate their product in terms of quality.[34] As Catherine Lee argues, it is hard to change the texture and flavour of chicken, unlike red meat, where hanging improves the quality. While customers will debate the texture of a steak, she argues, 'they don't want to reflect on what the chicken ate because then it's a live thing'. This is particularly problematic for firms such as Marks & Spencer, she argues, who cannot compete simply on price:

> If I was at Asda [a lower-cost supermarket chain] this would make life much easier but when you're at the other end of the market, when you're trying to get customers to understand quality and a whole proposition of agriculture when they don't really want to know, well it's really hard. You want a customer to understand why it costs 10p more but it's hard when it will make them squeamish. When I was at Safeway [her previous employer], it wasn't about that, it was about [the financial] margin.

Mark Ranson also found it 'amazing that customers don't want to touch raw meat'. But he revealed how Marks & Spencer have responded to consumer requests by developing oven-able trays which can go straight into the oven without customers having to lift the product out of the tray: 'That's a direct request from customers', he confirms, 'saying they don't like to touch [raw] meat'.

Our research also suggests that attitudes to chicken vary significantly when compared to other animal species and, even within the same species, comparing whole birds or chicken portions with processed foods such as ready-meals or chicken nuggets. This distinction is nicely captured by Mark Ranson, commenting on the amount of meat that is wasted in routine consumer testing and new product development. Describing chicken as 'much more of a commodity than other protein species', he deplores the amount of wasted meat, particularly where whole chickens are disposed of after a couple of slices of meat have been tasted:

> When it's the whole bird and you think it was a living animal . . . All right, it's been bred for food and there's a reason we do it, but from a moral perspective, if there was a way to do the tasting without killing the animals . . . I've got nothing against eating animals for food as long as its welfare is being cared for but that is just such a waste. I find it a bit objectionable actually.[35]

He adds: 'I wouldn't feel so bad if it was just portions, because the rest would've gone to the use it was meant for . . . it's the waste, it's a reminder of it as a whole animal.' This distinction is also commonly made by consumers:

> From a customer's perspective, once an animal has been cut up, it's lost . . . in the customer's mind, it's lost what it was . . . Once an animal has been cut up, it's lost . . . In the customer's mind, it's lost what it was and customers' questions about chicken, in their mind as it's a whole bird or a portion . . . but once it's in a recipe dish the same concerns don't exist [as] for a whole piece of meat.[36]

A similar argument applies to the supply side, where Marks & Spencer source all of their raw chicken (whole birds, fresh or frozen portions) from Europe but import chicken for ready-meals and other processed food from Thailand. Mark Ranson pointed out the irony in this process, arguing that a lot of people buy purely on price rather than quality or flavour, confirming that these attitudes apply more to whole birds than to processed chicken or ready meals:

> If their retailer started selling whole chickens from Thailand or Brazil, [British customers] wouldn't buy them. But they're quite happy buying a ready-meal which is being made with ingredients from Thailand or Brazil and standards-wise there may be no difference and in some areas the standards may be as good if not better.

He also suggests that consumers are less interested in the provenance of frozen as opposed to fresh chicken:

> When something is cut up and is not visibly a piece of raw meat, people lose their interest in where it's come from . . . but I think certainly where there are issues about where things have come from, that's because customers think that standards are bad or because they are reported that way by the media

or you get things like meat from Denmark or Belgium injected with water . . .
so that is really about making a generalisation, like if it's come from one country it's bad. But from a retail perspective, retailers will put their standards in
place and it might not be exactly the same as with fresh but they do have
standards.

As Mark Ranson suggests, an ethical inference can be drawn from these issues
about the agricultural origins of food: 'Ethically, people should know where it's
come from and been produced because I think . . . if there was an understanding
of the lengths that had gone into producing that animal, I think there'd be greater
appreciation for it.'

The most revealing commentary on these issues comes from category
manager Andrew Mackenzie, describing chickens as 'strange things', produced
in such large quantities, via a production line which 'works on volume' but where
ultimately, he acknowledges, 'something dies'. His reflections are worth quoting
at length:

> The thing which I feel is because chicken is so cheap and so available now,
> I think people's aspirations and expectations of chicken have lowered in the
> course of the last number of years . . . And I think that because it's eaten so
> regularly and we eat such vast quantities of it – and you talked about it down to
> a unit or a commodity, I think that's a really good analogy because, the other
> thing is, you know, chickens aren't the most appealing of things, because I
> mean you know, you don't think of them as you do a robin or a swan or some-
> thing which is quite appealing – or a duck. People think of them mostly in
> connection with either when they think of them, either in a cage as a caged
> battery egg or as something they see scratching around in a farmyard but they
> would have very little perception of the way that chickens are actually grown
> in the modern broiler world. And I think that they don't want to think about it
> because you know, they're not particularly easy to empathise with, whereas
> people see a lamb outside become a sheep and they see a calf become a
> heifer or a steer and they are much more visually appealing.

Andrew Mackenzie relates these differences in consumer perception to the relative invisibility of chicken production compared to the farming of other species:

> The other big difference is that you can see cows and sheep out in fields if
> you go to the countryside – you'll never see any chickens grown commercially
> unless you happen to see free range or organic but often they're hidden away
> so you don't see them. But you'll see cows and you'll see sheep all the time.
> And therefore, there's a kind of connection that they've been outside, and so

they've had quite a decent life really haven't they? So I think that people can make that connection a bit more with four-legged things than they can with chicken.

At this point, Polly Russell (the interviewer) interrupts the speaker to ask:

And just coming back to your comment, just to sort of push you a bit further, you said you don't think about it that much, is that because if you think about it, you don't fundamentally believe on some level that it's right?

After a long pause, Andrew Mackenzie continues:

It's a very interesting question, and if you do push me on it I would say the following – I think that it is right that we eat flesh, animals, 'cause I think if you think back through tens of thousands of years, that's what we've done. The thing I struggle with – no, struggle's the wrong word – the thing if I were to think about it too much that I might struggle with is the way that we have exploited it and moved it to such a clinical and efficient way of doing things . . . That kind of, I don't know, that kind of, I mean I'm obviously not that sentimental about it because I still eat chicken and I still do my job – but if you are pushing me – that kind of thing just doesn't quite feel right and natural.[37]

To paraphrase his argument, Andrew Mackenzie feels that the intensification of the broiler industry, which has made chicken 'so cheap and so available now' – reared in 'such vast quantities' – has affected the way consumers (himself included) think about chicken (as 'less appealing' than other species such as robins, swans or ducks). These attitudes derive, he suggests, from the fact that consumers rarely see chickens being grown 'in the modern broiler world', making it harder for people to 'make that connection' with them (compared to sheep or cows for example). As a result of the 'clinical and efficient' way in which they are grown, chickens come to be thought of 'as a unit or a commodity', as part of a system that 'just doesn't feel quite right and natural'. This is a very telling commentary in terms of consumer anxieties about food, demonstrating the power of life history interviewing to reveal the subtle interweaving of personal and corporate narratives, as well as providing specific insights into the world of modern chicken production and its associated anxieties.

Conclusion

This chapter has argued that the history of the chicken industry can be regarded as a paradigmatic example of agricultural intensification. While it has provided a cheap source of protein for a large section of society, no longer a rare luxury for the privileged few, the intensification of production has come at a price. Consumer anxieties about chicken have arisen as a direct consequence of the process of intensification (where chickens are treated as commodities rather than as living creatures) – a predictable response to the commodification of nature and the growing separation between food producers and consumers.[38] While the intensification of chicken production can be interpreted as a technological triumph, providing cheap year-round food for mass consumption, there are limitations to the human subordination of other animal species which are manifest in various ways. Chicken's organic properties – including its susceptibility to damp, cold and disease – constantly threaten to undermine the imposition of technocratic control and limit their commercial exploitation. When kept at high densities, without access to fresh air and open space, chicken develop visible imperfections such as hock burn or diseases such as coccidiosis.[39] When subject to genetic selection to increase the volume of breast meat relative to their leg strength, chickens have a tendency to collapse and 'come off their legs'. Modern chicken rearing and industrialized processing has also increased the incidence of food-borne pathogens such as Campylobacter that pose a significant risk to human health.[40]

For these reasons, among others, consumers have come to express a nostalgic yearning for chicken 'the way it used to be'. Some who can afford the price have turned to free-range or organic chicken, bought from butchers or farmers' markets or from high-street supermarkets. Meanwhile, food retailers such as Marks & Spencer have developed products such as Oakham chicken which combine the reliability and volume of intensive broiler production with some of the qualities that consumers look for in a slower-growing bird with higher welfare standards, improved diet and enhanced animal welfare.

The evidence presented here suggests that many British consumers are squeamish about coming into contact with raw meat, especially poultry, encouraging producers to experiment with technical innovations that reduce the contact between human and other animal species until the product is transformed into a more palatable (cooked) form. Here, it seems, consumer anxieties about food result from undue *proximity* to other species, while in other circumstances it is consumers' growing *distance* (or disconnection) from agriculture that is thought to be at the heart of consumers' troubled relationship with food. Elspeth Probyn makes this argument in her essay on 'anxious proximities' where she argues that changing relations of proximity have become a major site of contemporary anxieties (2001: 173).

A government report highlighted the 'dysfunctional' nature of contemporary agri-business and called for a 're-connection' between UK food producers and consumers. The Curry Commission reached this conclusion in its investigation into the future of UK farming, arguing that:

> Our central theme is *reconnection*. We believe the real reason why the present situation is so dysfunctional is that farming has become detached from the rest of the economy and the environment. The key objective of public policy should be to reconnect our food and farming industry: to reconnect farming with its market and the rest of the food chain; to reconnect the food chain and the countryside; and to reconnect consumers with what they eat and how it is produced. (Royal Commission on the Future of Farming and Food 2002: 6)

In this analysis, it is the growing disconnection between food producers and consumers that is at the heart of contemporary anxieties about food. Meanwhile, Joanna Blythman has pointed out the irony in present-day agri-food systems where 'the white-coated, hair-netted and thoroughly scrubbed-up and hosed-down food safety establishment talks the language of "bio-security", "hazard analysis" and "critical control points"' but where, she suggests, true food safety can only be delivered by pursuing a radically different model of food and agriculture, based on smaller scale production, where control is no longer concentrated in the hands of a few global corporations and vested interests.[41] Rather than seeing its goal as the elimination of risk in order to guarantee the health and safety of consumers, Blythman suggests, the food industry defines its responsibility in terms of the management of risk, achieved through a variety of socio-technical strategies.[42] Joanna Blythman's own vision of Britain's agricultural future is very different from the conventional emphasis on agricultural intensification, putting 'diversity at its heart and respect[ing] the limits of the natural world'. This debate between competing agri-food visions, illustrated here through the intensification of chicken production, goes to the very heart of contemporary consumer anxieties about food.

Notes

1. Campylobacter is the most common food-borne pathogen in the UK, causing around 280,000 cases of food poisoning per year (FSA 2013b).
2. Noëlie Vialles (1994) explores these ideas in her study of the abattoirs of South-West France which focuses on the transformation of 'animal to edible' and the complex system of avoidances (including the distancing of animal slaughter from butchering)

that has resulted in urban consumers rarely if ever being brought face to face with the animal origins of their food.

3. Bernard Matthews is one of the largest poultry processors in Europe with an annual turnover of £400 million. He was at the centre of a public health crisis in February 2007 when the H5N1 strain of avian influenza was detected at one of his farms in Suffolk. He was subsequently accused of importing poultry from an avian flu exclusion zone in Hungary (*Times OnLine*, 9 February 2007).

4. For other accounts of the industrialization of chicken production, see Dixon (2002), Stull and Broadway (2004), Striffler (2005) and Ellis (2007).

5. Godley and Williams (2009: 279) report that, after evisceration, poultry meat becomes inedible within 24 hours at 20°C. Contamination with Campylobacter, one of the most common causes of food poisoning, occurs most readily at the de-feathering and evisceration stages of chicken processing.

6. In 1961, Buxted sold a ten per cent block of shares to Spillers, a leading British feed manufacturer, with a controlling stake in the company being acquired three years later by Nitrovit, the Yorkshire-based feedstuffs company, seeking to create a wholly integrated business 'from a day-old chick to the shop counter' (Godley & Williams 2007: 20).

7. Coccidiosis is a disease caused by intestinal parasites, transmitted via chicken droppings.

8. The remainder of this chapter draws on a series of life history interviews with employees at Marks & Spencer and their suppliers, conducted by Dr Polly Russell, as part of our project on 'Manufacturing meaning along the food commodity chain' (2003–7), funded via the AHRC-ESRC *Cultures of Consumption* programme.

9. Norman Robson, interviewed May 2004.

10. Fresh chicken is still regarded as a 'short life product – kill plus ten days', according to an anonymous chicken processor, interviewed July 2004.

11. David Gregory, interviewed April 2004.

12. Anonymous product developer, interviewed July 2004.

13. Category manager Andrew Mackenzie (interviewed April 2004) recalls how Marks & Spencer were first to market with iceberg lettuce, ready-made sandwiches and avocadoes, as well as fresh chicken.

14. Fred Duncan, interviewed June 2004.

15. Andrew Mackenzie, interviewed February 2004.

16. Andrew Mackenzie, interviewed February 2004.

17. Two Sisters also undertook to build a new processing facility, costing £15 million.

18. According to the company's website, 'The Ross 508 parent stock has been developed to maximise breeder performance without compromising the efficiency of meat production': http://www.aviagen.com (accessed 28 July 2005).

19. Mark Ranson felt that breeder companies were only interested in feed-conversion ratios, breast-meat yield and growth speeds: 'Succulence, tenderness and flavour were not on their agenda at all' (interviewed January 2004).

20. It can also be argued that the development of the Oakham brand was an attempt by a 'mainstream' food retailer to appropriate the discourse of 'alternative' (free-range and organic) farming methods (see Jackson et al. 2007).

21. Catherine Lee, interviewed February 2004.

22. The labelling is actually more complicated than this. Each package is stamped with the name of the farmer who produced this specific chicken alongside a generic photograph of 'a typical Marks & Spencer farmer' who is quoted as saying that they are 'proud to produce quality chicken for Marks & Spencer'.

23. Ray Moore, interviewed November 2003.

24. Audrey Kley, interviewed September 2003; Mark Ranson, interviewed January 2004.

25. Oakham chickens were originally called 'Oakham White', with a different designation (Oakham Gold) reserved for the free-range variety.

26. Market-driven supply chains are characterized, among other things, by deriving profits from control of marketing and research rather than relying entirely on economies of scale (Gereffi 1994).

27. A similar approach was subsequently taken to the branding of Marks & Spencer's 'Lochmuir' salmon, chosen because of the name's 'Scottish resonance'. When the company was criticized for the product's lack of connection to a specific location in Scotland, they referred to their previous experience with Oakham chicken ('Marks & Spencer fakes loch to launch salmon', *Sunday Times,* 20 August 2006).

28. Interview with Mark Ransom and Andrew Mackenzie at Marks & Spencer head office (29 November 2006).

29. In the discourse of animal rights, considerable attention has been paid to the question of whether animals can be considered as 'sentient beings', a concept that was written into the basic law of the European Union in 1997 (cf. Singer 1985, Cochrane 2012).

30. One free-range grower (interviewed in June 2004) held similarly ambivalent views, suggesting that 'happier chickens are healthier chickens' but going on to remark on the lack of individuality among his flock: 'There's no personality there, you don't interact with a chicken the same way you do with a cow . . . A cow's got character but a chicken's brainless really . . . There's no individuality there'.

31. Smith and Daniel make a similar point about the confinement of battery chickens (kept for egg production): 'Chickens confined, and especially chickens confined in large numbers . . . are at their least appealing [giving] off offensive odors; [behaving] badly to each other, bedevilling and pecking each other in boredom and frustration; [becoming] neurotic and susceptible to various diseases of the body and the spirit' (1982: 272).

32. Paul Willgoss also argued that customers 'have become far less connected to the way food is produced' than 20 years ago.

33. Current food safety advice warns consumers against washing raw chicken prior to cooking in order to reduce the risk of cross-contamination: 'Don't wash raw chicken – Food Standards Agency': http://www.food.gov.uk/news-updates/campaigns/campylobacter/fsw-2014/#.U8A9fmBOVjo (accessed 11 July 2014).

34. According to one company history, Marks & Spencer have a reputation as relentless innovators. Their establishment as a national institution and leading British retailer was based on the principle of 'quality first', developing long-term partnerships with suppliers, exacting standards of supply chain management and the application of science and technology to product development (Seth & Randall 1999: 116–20, see also Bevan 2001).

35. Before joining Marks & Spencer, Mark Ranson worked as an animal welfare officer for the RSPCA.

36. Mark Ranson's inability to express himself clearly in this extract ('it's lost . . . ', 'it's lost what it was . . . ') might be taken to reflect the difficult ethical issues he is attempting to address but finds hard to articulate in simple terms.

37. Andrew Mackenzie, interviewed February 2004.

38. Reflecting on whether chickens are creatures or commodities, geographer Michael Watts describes how he sometimes brings a freshly dressed oven-ready chicken into his undergraduate classes, challenging his students to identify the 'cold and clammy creature that I've tossed upon the lectern'. After five minutes, he reports, when students have exhausted their ideas ('It's a chicken', 'a dead bird' or 'a virtual Kentucky Fried Chicken'), he solemnly pronounces on its commodity form as 'a bundle of social relations' (Watts 2014: 394).

39. Critics have suggested that access to outdoor space can be a mixed blessing for free-range chickens, exposing them to adverse weather conditions (cold and rain) and making them more vulnerable to predators (Miele 2011: 2080).

40. Recent evidence from the UK FSA suggests that more than half (59%) of fresh shop-bought chickens are infected with Campylobacter ('Campylobacter survey results published', http://www.food.gov.uk/news-updates/news/2014/aug/campylobacter-survey, accessed 21 August 2014). Shortly before the evidence was published, the FSA Board voted not to release the figures for individual suppliers, waiting until further evidence was available beyond the initial 853 samples. Subsequent results released by FSA on 26 February 2015 showed that 73 per cent of chickens tested positive for the presence of Campylobacter, ranging from 79 per cent at Asda to 68 per cent at Tesco.

41. Joanna Blythman, 'The food chain is almost broken: who will reforge the links of trust?' (*The Observer*, 5 June 2011).

42. So, for example, the former head of agricultural technology at Marks & Spencer described his job as having moved on from a concern with food safety, in an absolute sense, to risk management in relative terms: 'No longer do people . . . aspire to make safe food, they manage risk' (David Gregory, interviewed March 2004).

Chapter 5

'Food scares' and the regulation of supply chains

This chapter focuses on a recent food 'incident' concerning the widespread adulteration of beef products with horsemeat that occurred throughout Europe in 2013.[1] The chapter focuses on the UK where inquiries revealed that the incident had resulted from fraudulent behaviour rather than from accidental contamination, with food producers deliberating reducing costs by substituting horsemeat for beef. The incident caused significant consumer disquiet and had severe commercial repercussions in terms of loss of sales and reputational damage. It also had a significant, though largely short-term, impact on consumer trust as food manufacturers and retailers were widely thought to have lost control of their supply chains. Although it led to the recalling of multiple food products, it was not a conventional 'food scare' in the sense that it did not pose a direct threat to human health. The incident does, however, provide a valuable opportunity for tracing the contours of a range of other food-related anxieties as they waxed and waned over several months, posing serious questions in terms of the governance and regulation of food supply chains and in terms of consumer confidence and trust in food.

The chapter provides an account of the 2013 horsemeat incident, focusing mainly on the UK, showing the relevance of the 'social anxiety' framework outlined in Chapter 3. It discusses what the incident revealed about the length and complexity of contemporary food supply chains, charting the extent of consumer concerns about these issues and considering their implications for food governance and regulation. The chapter is based on a range of documentary sources and official inquiries including reports by the UK FSA, the UK Environment, Food and Rural Affairs (EFRA) Committee on the contamination of beef products, the Irish Department of Agriculture, Food and the Marine (DAFM), and the interim and final reports of the Elliott Review into the integrity and assurance of UK food supply chains.

'Food scares' and related crises

While food adulteration has a long history (Atkins 2013), the concept of 'food scares' is of more recent origin. According to Miller and Reilly (1994), the term first appeared in the mid-1980s and has been applied to a variety of food safety and related concerns that cause public anxiety and are subject to escalating media attention. The UK has experienced many such incidents, from Salmonella in eggs in the 1980s to BSE in the 1990s (Van Zwanenberg & Millstone 2003). Similar 'scares' have occurred throughout Europe (Knowles et al. 2007), in North America (Blay-Palmer 2008) and elsewhere (see Chapter 6 on China). Closely related to the 'food scares' of the 1980s and 1990s were UK farming crises such as Foot-and-Mouth Disease (FMD), whose management was widely criticized, leading to the large-scale slaughter of livestock with significant consequences for the rural economy (Policy Commission on the Future of Farming and Food 2002; Ward et al. 2004).

While most 'food scares' are defined in terms of the potential threat they pose to human health, this was not the case with the horsemeat crisis as the contamination of beef products with horsemeat and pig DNA did not itself constitute a significant threat to public health. Except where horses have been treated with the veterinary drug phenylbutazone (or 'bute'), consumption of horsemeat poses no significant threat to human health, even among those with prior medical conditions whose immune systems might be compromised. Soon after the onset of the horsemeat crisis, the UK's Chief Medical Officer, Professor Dame Sally Davies, confirmed that horsemeat containing phenylbutazone presented a very low risk to human health, adding that 'A person would have to eat 500 to 600 burgers a day that are 100% horse meat to get close to consuming a human's [safe] daily dose' ('Bute in horsemeat: statement from Chief Medical Officer', 14 February 2013: https://www.gov.uk/government/news/bute-in-horsemeat-statement-from-chief-medical-officer, accessed 11 July 2013). This position was maintained throughout the crisis, even when, in April 2013, very low levels of phenylbutazone (around four parts per billion) were found in tins of Asda Smart Price Corned Beef, leading the company to recall the product ('FSA reassures public after horse drug found in Asda corned beef', *The Telegraph*, 10 April 2013). The fact that the horsemeat incident did not raise immediate food safety concerns had implications for the way it was managed in terms of departmental responsibilities within the UK government as will be discussed later in the chapter.

The 2013 incident led some observers to recall an earlier UK 'horsemeat scandal' during the period of food rationing shortly after the Second World War.

In 1948, a Pathé News bulletin reported on the 'sordid market' in horsemeat, a 'sinister trade' by which 'backstreet restaurants' were alleged to be selling horsemeat, mislabelled as beefsteak or veal, to millions of customers each week (http://www.youtube.com/watch?v=7gaZdHLB5tY, accessed 9 December 2013). Referring to this incident, BBC Radio 4's Food Programme ran a feature on horsemeat in April 2004, asking 'Why Don't We Eat Horse?' The programme compared the UK with France, Belgium and Italy where human consumption of horsemeat is popular and where prime cuts are significantly cheaper than similar cuts of beef. The programme reported that, while Britain exports around 10,000 horse carcasses to the continent each year for human consumption, eating horsemeat remains culturally taboo in the UK. Events in 2013 were very different from those in 1948, no longer confined to backstreet traders and disreputable restaurateurs, extending now to include major high-street retailers in Britain and across much of continental Europe.

The 2013 horsemeat 'incident'

Triggered by specific events in January 2013, the horsemeat 'incident' persisted over several months and had a lasting effect on public attitudes to food.[2] On 15 January 2013, the UK FSA announced that the Food Safety Authority of Ireland (FSAI) had found horse and pig DNA in a range of beef products on sale at several UK supermarkets including Tesco, Aldi, Lidl and Iceland, leading to the removal of some ten million burgers and other food products from public sale. FSAI's announcement followed a targeted survey of beef products purchased from Irish retailers in November 2012. The survey included 27 beef products of which 10 tested positive for horse DNA, with 23 of the 27 beef burgers and 21 of 31 ready-meal products testing positive for undeclared pig DNA. While most of the samples had very low levels of horse DNA, one sample (from Tesco's Everyday Value burgers) was found to include substantially higher levels, with horsemeat accounting for approximately 29 per cent of the burgers' total meat content. Acknowledging that these results were unlikely to have been uncovered through FSAI's regular inspection routine, journalists suggested that the Authority was responding to prior intelligence, with criminal activity suspected from the outset. In one British newspaper, Felicity Lawrence quotes a senior UK enforcement official's belief that the FSAI 'must have known exactly what it was looking for', also reporting that the UK Environment Secretary, Owen Patterson, had told Parliament that the Irish were acting on a tip-off and that he had been told this by Irish agriculture minister Simon Coveney – an allegation that he subsequently denied (*The Guardian*, 10 May 2013).

The FSA launched an urgent investigation, meeting with food industry representatives concerned with the integrity of the supply chain before announcing a four-point action plan on 18 January. The plan was:

1 To continue the urgent review of the traceability of the food products identified in FSAI's survey.
2 To explore further, in conjunction with the FSAI, the methodology used for the survey to understand more clearly the factors that may have led to the low level cases of cross-contamination.
3 To consider, with relevant local authorities and the FSAI, whether any legal action is appropriate following the investigation.
4 To work with the Department for Environment, Food and Rural Affairs (Defra), the devolved rural affairs departments and local authorities on a UK-wide study of food authenticity in processed meat products (FSA 2013a).

New events followed quickly, extending the crisis over several weeks, beyond the initial 'incident' reported on 15 January 2013. On 1 February, beef products that were certified as Halal and supplied to prisons in England and Wales were reported by the Ministry of Justice to contain pork DNA (http://food.gov.uk/news-updates/news/2013/feb/m-o-j, accessed 15 July 2013). Then, on 4 February, production at Rangeland Foods in County Monaghan, Ireland was suspended after 75 per cent equine DNA was found in frozen raw ingredients stored at that plant. The police were called in to investigate the possibility of food fraud. Three days later, samples of Findus lasagne were found to contain more than 60 per cent horsemeat, while Aldi lasagne and spaghetti bolognese products also tested positive, containing between 30 and 100 per cent horsemeat ('Tests reveal Findus frozen beef lasagnes contain "up to 100 per cent horsemeat"', *The Independent*, 8 February 2013; 'Lasagne taken off shelves amid fears of contamination', *The Guardian*, 7 February 2013). These incidents involved completely separate supply chains from those affecting Tesco's Everyday Value burgers, triggering a more comprehensive testing programme amid fears of widespread adulteration.

The UK-wide local authority testing regime, introduced on 6 February, was followed by a similar exercise, involving further tests undertaken by the food industry. The FSA announced on 8 February that the police had become involved in the investigations taking place in the UK and elsewhere in Europe since, in its view, the detection of significant levels of horsemeat in beef burgers and lasagnes indicated either gross negligence or deliberate adulteration rather than accidental contamination (http://food.gov.uk/news-updates/news/2013/feb/

investigation-statement, accessed 15 July 2013). On 12 February, raids were carried out on a slaughterhouse in Todmorden, West Yorkshire which had sold meat to a cutting plant in Wales and was suspected of passing off horsemeat as beef. Three arrests were made. On 13 February, a meeting was held in Brussels under the auspices of the European Council of Agriculture and Fisheries, acknowledging that the crisis was now affecting food businesses across Europe. Food businesses were instructed to carry out authenticity tests on all beef products including burgers, meatballs and lasagne, the first results of which were published on 15 February. Of the 2,501 samples tested, 2,472 (almost 99%) proved negative for the presence of horse DNA at or above 1 per cent (the pragmatic level set by the FSA to distinguish between accidental and gross levels of contamination). Twenty-nine samples, relating to seven products, were found to contain horsemeat at or above the 1 per cent level, all of which were in products that had already been reported and removed from sale. FSA's Chief Executive Catherine Brown confirmed that low levels of contamination can occur as a result of accidental 'carry over' from equipment previously used on another animal species but higher levels are likely to indicate deliberate food fraud. While 1 per cent was generally considered an acceptable threshold of accidental contamination by the public (according to FSA's consumer panel research), any level of cross-contamination may pose concerns for specific faith communities who wish to be religiously observant (EFRA 2013a: 3.36).

A second set of results was received from food industry tests on 22 February, with over 99 per cent of the 1,133 samples found to contain no horse DNA at or above the 1 per cent threshold. A further six samples were found to contain higher levels of horse DNA, all of which had already been withdrawn from sale. In several other cases, retailers withdrew products for precautionary reasons (such as where products had been supplied by manufacturers of other products that had been found to be contaminated). One such example was the withdrawal of meatballs by the Swedish retail chain Ikea after an inspection in the Czech Republic found horsemeat in a consignment of meat from Poland ('Ikea withdraws meatballs from UK stores after discovery of horsemeat', *The Guardian*, 25 February 2013).

A third set of results was received on 1 March that found four further products with levels of horse DNA above the indicative 1 per cent level all of which had been withdrawn from sale. On 13 June 2013, the FSA announced a further 19,050 test results that showed that three more beef products contained horse DNA at or above the 1 per cent threshold level ('More results of beef product testing published': http://food.gov.uk/news-update/news/2013/jun/beef-product-testing, accessed 11 July 2013). Shortly afterwards, the FSA reported that the initial phase of the horsemeat incident was drawing to a close, though news stories continued to occur throughout the remainder of the year as various reports on the issue were published.

Applying the 'social anxiety' framework

How might the theoretical framework, outlined in Chapter 3, be applied to the horsemeat incident? The framework seeks to trace how particular events rupture the fabric of everyday life, disturbing established routines and causing anxiety even for those who are not directly affected, persisting until such time as the object of anxiety is eliminated or until new ways of understanding and making sense of events are established. The theory also charts how food-related anxieties circulate within society, how they spread and/or are contained, how they move across different social fields, and how they are shaped by different 'communities of practice' (cf. Jackson & Everts 2010). While this was not a conventional 'food scare' in the sense that the horsemeat incident posed little direct threat to public health, the theory is still useful in tracing the wider ramifications of the incident.[3]

Consistent with social anxiety theory, the horsemeat incident had an impact on society at large through widespread media coverage of these events, whether or not individual consumers were themselves anxious about eating horsemeat. Familiar products were withdrawn from supermarket shelves, drawing consumers into a state of anxiety, whether or not they would have purchased such products. Fearing a crisis of consumer confidence, supermarkets took out full-page advertisements in national newspapers, apologizing to their customers and explaining the changes they proposed to introduce to remedy the situation. Government departments undertook official investigations and the police arrested those who were suspected of criminal activity.

The crisis was framed in contrasting ways by different 'communities of practice' including the media, government agencies and other interested parties. Different actors deployed a diverse vocabulary to describe the unfolding events. For example, the FSA referred to the horsemeat 'incident', food retailers referred to a 'problem' (which they sought to demonstrate was systemic in nature rather than specific to any particular company) while the Irish Department of Agriculture referred to the horsemeat 'saga' (DAFM 2013: 7.2.5). The Irish Minister for Agriculture talked about the horsemeat 'controversy', while newspapers commonly referred to a 'scandal' as did the UK Environment, Food and Rural Affairs Committee (EFRA 2013a: 4.43). As Miller (1999) notes in the context of his work on BSE, 'food scares' often give rise to definitional struggles among the various authorities who have a stake in resolving the issue, especially if there is any doubt about who has 'ownership' of the issue.

It is also clear that different parties interpreted events in ways that served their particular interests. So, for example, environmental health inspectors used the incident to highlight the adverse consequences of recent budgetary cuts in the service they provide while animal charities such as the RSPCA highlighted the need for changes to the passport system that governs the international trade in horses. Meanwhile, the National Farmers' Union (NFU) interpreted the crisis in terms of the political and economic interests of British farmers whose competitive position the NFU seeks to protect. The NFU argued that complex supply chains were becoming increasingly common as food businesses sought cheaper sources of imported meat. Arguing that UK farmers were under increasing pressure from the major retailers to produce ever-cheaper food, they warned that the constant insistence on getting 'more for less' might compromise consumer health, promoting greater transparency in order to increase consumer confidence (EFRA 2013a: 2.6). NFU president Peter Kendall urged consumers to 'Buy British' to benefit from 'the high welfare standards and rigorous traceability met by UK farmers'. 'This whole system of quality', he continued, 'is being completely undermined by failures within the supply chain reinforce[ing] our call for clearer labelling and a commitment from retailers to British produce.' In the meantime, he suggested: 'shoppers should look for the Red Tractor logo on their fresh meat which shows the products they buy have been produced to world-class standards, which are independently inspected' (quoted in Abbots & Coles 2013: 541).[4]

Social anxiety theory explores how popular food-related concerns move between social fields, shifting from a crisis affecting public health, for example, to one affecting the environment or issues of animal welfare or consumer ethics. In this case, the crisis was largely confined to the management of the food supply chain but there were some initial concerns about public health as well as debates about the cultural appropriateness of eating horsemeat.[5] The crisis did not give rise to widespread environmental concerns and, while it affected consumer confidence, undermining public trust in food manufacture and retailing, there was no major outcry over animal welfare or other ethical concerns.[6] Nor was the crisis moralized to any significant extent, except in so far as it was thought to reveal deficiencies in corporate responsibility. The report by DAFM referred to 'management oversight' and failures in corporate governance at Silvercrest, the firm that supplied Tesco with burgers that contained 29 per cent horsemeat, describing these practices as an 'inexcusable failure' and 'a real concern' (2013: 3.1.13–14). They also made accusations of 'improper practices' and 'irregularities' relating to the use of horse passports at the Ossory Meats slaughter plant in Banagher, County Offaly, which they found 'deeply disturbing' (ibid.: 7.2.1–7.2.4). But a wholesale 'moral panic' (Cohen 1972) did not ensue.

Social anxiety theory seeks to account for the way public anxieties spread or are contained as events unfold over space and time. One striking feature of the horsemeat crisis was the way the story kept gathering fresh momentum as new events were reported over several months rather than subsiding quickly as other stories rose to take their place in the public imagination. If anxiety events persist until the object of anxiety is eliminated and a new consensus is firmly established, then it is significant in this case how a resolution of the crisis was repeatedly delayed by successive announcements and new discoveries. While the crisis began with the NFAI's initial announcements on 15 January 2013, it was given new life by reports of the contamination of Halal meat with pork DNA in prison food on 1 February and by the discovery of high levels of equine DNA in meat stored at Rangeland Foods on 4 February. This continued as horsemeat contamination was reported in a range of Findus and Aldi products on 7 February and again, on 12 February, when raids were carried out in Yorkshire and Wales. Moreover, while initial reports were confined to cheaper, frozen products, the crisis intensified when more 'upmarket' food retailers such as Waitrose withdrew a range of burgers from sale as a precautionary measure.[7] Media interest in the crisis was also prolonged by the way the FSA announced test results in three separate waves (on 15 February, 22 February and 1 March 2013) and by news stories following the publication of successive inquiry reports that extended until July 2013.[8] Publication of the interim report of the Elliott Review in December 2013 gave the story further impetus, with the delayed publication of the final report causing further media comment in August 2014.[9]

Having outlined the nature of the incident and shown how social anxiety theory might be applied to its analysis, the next section seeks to establish the level of public concern about the crisis, based on consumer research commissioned by the FSA.

Consumer reactions to the horsemeat incident

The level of public anxiety about the horsemeat incident can be gauged from a survey of consumer attitudes undertaken by the market research firm Harris Interactive on behalf of the FSA. The survey was undertaken in two waves, at the height of the crisis in February 2013 and six months later in late July–early August, allowing inferences to be drawn about the persistence of consumer anxiety after the event as well as the immediate public response.[10] The initial survey found that almost two-thirds of respondents (64%) were concerned about the incident, with higher levels of concern reported by women (67%) and by older people (above 70% for those aged 55–64 and 65+). Almost three quarters of respondents (73%) felt less confident about the safety of processed meat than before the incident and almost half (49%) reported that they would buy less red meat, processed meat and/or ready meals than prior to the incident. Two-thirds (67%) of those who intended to buy less of these products reported basing their decision on a lack of trust. Respondents claimed to be exasperated at the 'sheer fraud' involved in these events. One person said: 'I feel let down by people trusted to provide what I expect. I don't think I can shop without concern about what is in my food anymore' (female respondent, aged 36, England), while another declared: 'It's appalling that one cannot confidently rely on the information on a label! It is not a matter of caring what I am sold, as much as KNOWING what I'm sold, and to mislead the public in this respect is sheer fraud, whether or not one would willingly eat the product if one did know' (female, aged 81, England).

Public feeling in the UK was no less strongly felt when confronted with the argument that similar events had occurred elsewhere in Europe. Interviewees objected vehemently to being lied to, feeling disgusted at what had happened and regarding recent events as immoral. As one person argued: 'It doesn't make any difference how many countries, it doesn't change the morality, if it says beef [on the label] it should be beef' (female, 23, England), while another felt that 'the public has been lied to about what they are eating' (female, 37, England) and another was 'disgusted that it's happening in most of Europe and not just the UK' (male, 17, England).

Over three-quarters (79%) of respondents thought that the mislabelling of horsemeat had been going on for years. Almost half (47%) felt much less confident about buying processed meat than before the crisis, with 52 per cent reporting that they expected to buy less processed meat in the short term and 46 per cent in the long term. Six months later, the wave 2 survey results showed that over one-third of consumers maintained that they had reduced their purchasing of processed meat (39%) and ready meals (36%). Lack of trust remained the main reason for buying less of these products (at 66%), though the proportion who intended to buy meat products from UK suppliers in future had declined from 36 per cent in wave 1 to 28 per cent in wave 2. While this suggests that consumer trust was starting to return within six months of the incident, significant concerns persisted. One-third (33%) of consumers anticipated buying less food from supermarkets in wave 1, falling to 21 per cent in wave 2, with 46 per cent anticipating buying fewer 'value' products in wave 1, falling to 32 per cent in wave 2. There had also been a slight decline in those expecting to eat fewer ready-meals in wave 2 (31%) than in wave 1 (39%), possibly reflecting the socially embedded nature of such routinized consumption practices (discussed further in Chapter 9).

In both waves of the survey, consumers placed most blame for the crisis on food manufacturers and their suppliers (50% in wave 1 and 48% in wave 2), with over 10 per cent locating ultimate responsibility with the FSA. Again, the vehemence of consumer attitudes is noteworthy. Asked how they felt about the issue, one consumer responded: 'Betrayed. It is not right that this was okay on a large scale' (female, aged 24, England), while another declared: 'If it is horsemeat then label it as horsemeat. I have no problem with that. I may even try it and like it, but don't deceive me' (male, 48, Scotland). Besides feelings of betrayal and deception, issues of trust and allegations of corruption also featured strongly. As one person said: 'I cannot trust the meat industry or the food industry in general' (male, 70, England), while another felt that: 'It shows how corrupt the industry is' (male, 53, England).

One of the critical issues contributing to this loss of consumer confidence was what the horsemeat incident revealed about the length and complexity of contemporary food supply chains.

Contemporary food supply chains

In February 2013, Britain's largest food retailer, Tesco, took out full-page advertisements in several national newspapers, admitting that their supply chain had become too complicated. While they argued that the problems affected the whole industry, they acknowledged the need to 'go further' and 'move quicker' (see Figure 5.1). Announcing plans to work more closely with British farmers, Tesco assured their customers that, in future, all their beef would be sourced from the UK and Ireland, with similar plans for fresh chicken, all of which would come from UK farms by July 2013. Other supermarkets issued similar statements, with Waitrose contacting customers to offer reassurances about the provenance of their meat. In a letter dated 1 March 2013, Waitrose claimed that 'All the meat in our own-label products is British – that's all our pork, chicken and beef – the only exceptions are the New Zealand lamb which we use to fill the gap between British seasons and our authentic continental meat ranges.' Waitrose reported an 11 per cent increase in sales in the quarter following the horsemeat incident having been relatively unscathed by recent events ('No horse-trading: Waitrose sales surge', The Guardian, 4 May 2013).

Tesco took a much harder hit, a consumer report in February 2013 finding that they were now the lowest-rated UK supermarket chain, 'caring least' about their customers and considered 'least trustworthy' (http://www.which.co.uk/news/2013/02/best-and-worst-supermarkets-revealed-by-which-311258/, accessed 13 May 2013).

Tesco had issued a previous statement, designed to restore consumer trust. Promising 'nothing less than the highest possible standard', the statement took the form of another full-page newspaper advertisement that was titled 'Our responsibility and our promise'. Customers were informed that 'We are reviewing our approach to our supply chain and building a thorough traceability system

---

The problem we've had with some of our meat lately
is about more than burgers and Bolognese.
It's about some of the ways we get meat to your dinner table.
It's about the whole food industry.
And it has made us realise, we really do need to make it better.
We've been working on it, but we need to
keep going, go further, move quicker.
We know that our supply chain is too complicated.
So we're making it simpler.
We know that the more we work with British farmers the better.
We've already made sure that all our beef is from the UK and Ireland.
And now we're moving on to our fresh chickens.
By July, they'll all be from UK farms too. No exceptions.
For farmers to do what they do best,
they need to know they've got our support.
We know this because of the work we've been doing
with our dairy farmers to make sure they always get paid
above the market price.
We know that, no matter what you spend,
everyone deserves to eat well.
We know that all this will only work if we are
open about what we do.
And if you're not happy, tell us.
Seriously.
This is it.
We are changing.

Figure 5.1 Tesco's public apology.
source: *London Evening Standard* (28 February 2013).

that includes DNA testing' which 'will help set new standards for the industry' (*The Guardian*, 16 February 2013). Such claims seem to equate shorter and more transparent supply chains with safer food which may not always be the case as well-regulated longer chains may be safer than more poorly regulated shorter chains. A similar case can be made in terms of the sustainability of food supply chains, where shorter chains are not necessarily more energy-efficient than longer ones, depending on the mode of agricultural production.[11]

For many food products today, supply chains are increasing in length and complexity, reflecting the increasingly globalized nature of the industry. This issue was referred to in all of the reports on the horsemeat crisis, including the extent to which food suppliers subcontract intermediaries to fulfil their orders. Professor Troop's independent report to the FSA Board drew attention to the intermediating role of 'food brokers' within the supply chain (Troop 2013: 44.7), while the Elliott Review described meat traders and brokers as 'highly vulnerable links' in the meat supply chain (2013: 37). The Irish Ministry of Agriculture report referred to 'traders and agents' (DAFM 2013: 3.1.11), many of whom, it transpired, were not registered as Food Business Operators (FBOs) and so were not covered by the relevant food safety controls, designed to protect consumers from mislabelling and other forms of fraudulent behaviour. The DAFM report found that processing companies secured their meat from numerous sources, including one company (QK Meats) that had used 19 different Polish suppliers, several of which were found to have supplied meat that tested positive for equine DNA (ibid.: 3.4.2). Responding to what it described as 'a complex traceability challenge', the report recommended that all meat traders operating in Ireland should henceforth be registered by the Department of Agriculture as FBOs (ibid.: 5.2).

An interactive map, reproduced on the BBC News website (14 February 2013), showed the complicated route by which it claimed horsemeat had entered the UK food supply chain (see Figure 5.2). The chain started with Comigel, a food processor in North-East France and its subsidiary, Tavola, who made beef lasagne and other food products for Findus. Tavola then contacted the French meat processor Spanghero, who liaised with their subcontractors in Cyprus, who supplied the meat via a Dutch trader, who ordered the meat from a Romanian abattoir. The abattoir insisted that the meat was properly labelled (as horsemeat) but it ended up in frozen beef lasagne in UK supermarkets. Similarly, the Silvercrest factory in County Monaghan that supplied Tesco's Everyday Value burgers used multiple ingredients from some 40 suppliers, the precise mix of which in each production batch could change as frequently as every half-hour (DAFM 2013: 2.7).

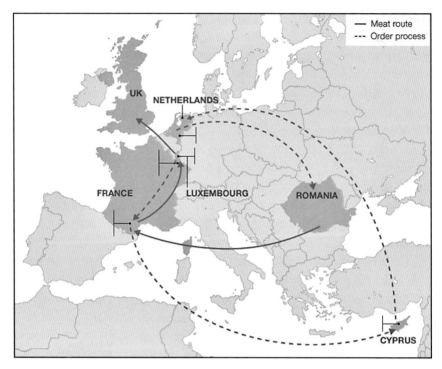

Figure 5.2 How horsemeat entered the UK food chain.
Source: French investigators, FSA and news agencies; redrawn from BBC News Online.

Existing measures for tracking horses as they are bought and sold across Europe were also found to be inadequate. The DAFM report confirmed that equine identification systems are open to abuse and significant reform of the horse passport system was required. In evidence presented to the EFRA inquiry, the RSPCA suggested that the scale of unregulated horse-breeding and trading had made horses entering the slaughter chain vulnerable to mislabelling and traceability problems (EFRA 2013a: 2.2.13).

The horsemeat incident revealed several other weaknesses in contemporary food governance arrangements, highlighting some of the current challenges of regulating an increasingly globalized industry. Even though there was no immediate threat to public health, the discovery of widespread adulteration raised questions about the integrity of food supply chains including concern that cheaper meat was being substituted for beef in order to reduce costs and increase profits. In evidence presented to the EFRA inquiry, for example, representatives of the Chartered Institute of Environmental Health argued that 'an inability to properly account for the ingredients of any foodstuff might reasonably be suggestive of other shortcomings, any of which might endanger health'

(EFRA 2013a: 3.21). The EFRA Committee concluded that 'It seems improbable that individuals prepared to pass horsemeat off as beef illegally are applying the high hygiene standards rightly required in the food production industry' (ibid.: 3.21).

The length and complexity of contemporary supply chains was identified as a critical challenge to the effective regulation of the food industry. For example, the EFRA Committee report suggested that 'In simple terms the supply chain for a beef burger consists of the farmer, abattoir, processor and retailer' (EFRA 2013a: 2.5). In practice, however, contemporary supply chains are significantly more complex. This complexity applies to the multiple ingredients that go into many present-day food products as well as to the multiple links that make up the supply chain. In evidence presented to the EFRA inquiry, FSA Chief Executive Catherine Brown confirmed that economy beef burgers sold in the UK may contain less than 50 per cent beef including added bovine collagen and fat. Other permitted ingredients include water, additional protein – often referred to as 'filler' – starches, additives and seasonings (EFRA 2013a: 2.8). As reported in several newspapers, 'filler' can include skeletal muscle with adherent fat and connective tissue, defined as meat under European law ('The secret of the special offer economy burger', *The Guardian*, 25 January 2013; 'Supermarkets can sell mince with 50 per cent fat and collagen', *The Telegraph*, 7 February 2013). Irish authorities later reported that 'filler product', imported from Poland, was the most likely source of the horsemeat found in contaminated burgers (*The Guardian*, 15 February 2013).

Some newspapers suggested that the reclassification of minced meat by EU authorities may have played a significant part in prompting the horsemeat crisis. Desinewed meat (DSM) had been a key ingredient in low-cost products such as burgers, pies and lasagnes but it was reclassified as mechanically recovered meat (MRM) following an EU ruling in April 2012. Under EU law, food manufacturers are not allowed to use MRM in meat products for human consumption. The reclassification of DSM encouraged manufacturers of low-cost food products to seek cheaper sources of meat from abroad, lengthening supply chains and providing more incentives for adulteration.[12]

One response to the threatened integrity and lack of transparency of contemporary food supply chains is to 'territorialise' the risks by insisting on the inherent safety of British food compared to imported produce. In its evidence to the EFRA Committee, the British Meat Processors Association urged British consumers to rely on domestic rather than imported produce, arguing that 'modern food supply chains can be complex, particularly in the case of more highly processed products, and raw materials, ingredients and final products are increasingly traded internationally' (EFRA 2013a: 2.7). Similar arguments were made by the Irish authorities in defence of the Irish meat industry, promoting the quality of 'Brand Ireland' (as discussed in more detail below).

These issues are significant in terms of the current structure of food regulation in the UK where the major supermarket chains have won the right to a high degree of self-regulation based on the promise that they can be relied upon to provide safe, healthy food at affordable prices. This process has been described by Marsden et al. (2000) as a system of 'retailer-led' food governance whereby the major supermarkets have become increasingly self-regulating, defending their reputation by imposing food safety and quality standards on their suppliers over and above the levels required by law. Marsden et al. show how the supermarkets developed their own quality and safety procedures, exerting power over the supply chain and claiming to represent the consumer interest (ibid.: 192–93). This was an argument advanced by Tesco's Technical Director, Tim Smith, in evidence presented to the EFRA enquiry where he outlined the procedures they had put in place to ensure the quality and safety of their merchandise:

> Once a supplier has been approved to supply us, we have an ongoing programme of site visits, audits and product surveillance to ensure our standards are being maintained. These processes are in addition to those carried out by the relevant food authority, and the suppliers themselves. (EFRA 2013a: 2.11)

In the case of the contaminated Everyday Value burgers, Tim Smith confirmed that Tesco had approved seven suppliers to their manufacturer (Silvercrest) but that the firm had used other suppliers that Tesco had not approved or audited (ibid.: 2.11).

As events unfolded, the horsemeat crisis threatened to undermine public confidence in the ability of supermarkets to regulate themselves. One commentator noted: 'We can't have the industry policing itself, that's what's gone wrong. The big food companies didn't actually have the control they said they have' (Tim Lang, Professor of Food Policy, City University: www.bbc.co.uk/news/uk-21455060, accessed 2 July 2013). While most food regulation is designed to detect *accidental* contamination, on food safety grounds, the horsemeat incident highlighted the need for policymakers to reframe their current procedures in order to detect *deliberate* adulteration and identify food fraud. For example, most industry-led food assurance schemes are designed to certify trusted suppliers and to mitigate the risks of unintentional errors rather than to detect deliberate deception. The horsemeat incident demonstrated the need for food regulators such as the FSA, as well as food retailers, to adjust their mind-set to be more aware of the potential for food fraud and other kinds of criminal behaviour. Despite its routine use of horizon scanning, for example, the FSA could be criticized for being insufficiently prepared to identify food fraud as a significant threat to the integrity of food supply chains. Likewise, had the Agency's foresight activities been more focused on the prospect of criminal activity affecting food supply chains rather than on specific food safety issues, it might have been better prepared to predict and prevent the horse-meat incident.

The current economic context had certainly made this kind of criminal activity more likely. For example, the Irish Agriculture Ministry reported that the contaminated meat that QK Meats had purchased from Poland cost €400 per tonne less than the price of beef trimmings available in Ireland (DAFM 2013: 3.4.4). Journalist Felicity Lawrence also claimed that 'it was very clear why someone might want to substitute cheaper ingredients somewhere in the supply chain', arguing that the cost of a quarter-pound burger using lean beef amounted to around 43 pence, while frozen economy burgers sold for around 25 pence (*The Guardian*, 11 May 2013). The opportunities for fraud, she concluded, were 'glaringly obvious'. Felicity Lawrence quotes senior figures within the UK food industry, including Paul Willgoss at Marks & Spencer, who had reached similar conclusions, arguing that 'It's a question of being vigilant about where the incentives for fraud might be'.

The interim report of the Elliott Review into the integrity and assurance of UK food supply chains highlighted a 'worrying lack of knowledge' of the extent of criminal activity in the food industry, calling for 'a significant change in culture' in terms of how threats of fraudulent activity are dealt with along increasingly complex supply chains (2013: 3). In the wake of the horsemeat crisis, the FSA is placing more emphasis on systemic issues affecting the food supply chain including a £1.5m joint programme with the Economic and Social Research Council on the current challenges facing the food system (http://www.esrc. ac.uk/funding-and-guidance/funding-opportunities/29283/understanding-the-challenges-of-the-food-system.aspx, accessed 11 December 2013). The FSA will also include more socioeconomic data in its future intelligence-gathering exercises in order to improve the potential for detecting food fraud as recom-mended by the Troop review which called on the Agency to strengthen its Emergency Risks Programme and food fraud teams, including the develop-ment of a more systematic intelligence management system (Troop 2013: 4.2). There is a degree of post hoc justification in some of these arguments and the FSA might feel that other explanations for the horsemeat 'incident' should also be explored including the nature of the regulatory landscape and the recent changes to their remit which arguably hampered the Agency's ability to meet their statutory obligations to protect the consumer interest.

The 'crowded landscape' of UK food governance

As well as revealing the length and complexity of contemporary food supply chains, the horsemeat incident also drew attention to the complex geography of food governance and regulation in the UK. Managing the incident highlighted the fragmented way in which food issues are governed, with responsibilities spread across several different departments and with different arrangements applying in different parts of the UK. In evidence presented to the EFRA inquiry, the consumer organization *Which?* argued that 'Food issues in practice do not break down into simple delineations that are made between government departments' (EFRA 2013a: 3.17). The present arrangements involving shared responsibility between the FSA, Defra and the Department of Health came into force in 2010 when the FSA's remit in England was changed by the Coalition Government, moving responsibility for food authenticity and most aspects of food labelling (except where related to food safety) to Defra and responsibility for diet and nutrition to the Department of Health. FSA's remit in England is now largely restricted to food safety. Different arrangements apply in the devolved administrations where the FSA retains its responsibility for human nutrition as well as food safety (except in Wales where nutrition policy transferred to the Welsh Government). The Scottish government is in the process of setting up its own integrated food body under arrangements outlined in the Scudamore review (http://www.scotland.gov.uk/Resource/0039/00391041.pdf, accessed 10 December 2013).

Giving evidence to the EFRA inquiry, the FSA's former Chair, Lord Rooker, reflected on the way in which the remit changes were introduced, recalling how he was called to a meeting at Defra on 8 July 2010, along with the FSA's then Chief Executive, Tim Smith (who now works for Tesco), to meet the Secretary of State and Minister of State:

> They informed us, at that date, they were taking from us all that they could without legislation, because this was a machinery-of-government change on the back of the diet and nutrition changes. There was no discussion . . . We lost 23 civil servants on food labelling aspects, composition and authenticity, who went from the FSA to Defra. Some 86 on diet and nutrition went to the Department of Health. We lost people and we lost the facility . . . The Board did

not like it but, because it was not food safety, it was not something you go to war on. (EFRA 2013a: 3.18)

The EFRA inquiry concluded that the FSA's 'diminished role' had led to a lack of clarity about where responsibility for food incidents such as the horsemeat crisis lies. This had, in the Committee's view, weakened the UK's ability to identify and respond to food standards concerns (ibid: 3.19). The horsemeat incident, it went on, had 'caught the FSA and Government flat-footed . . . unable to respond effectively within structures designed primarily to respond to threats to human health' (ibid.: 3.19).

The Coalition Government rejected the Committee's suggestion that the machinery of government changes had weakened the FSA's ability to respond to the incident, arguing that 'the response from Government was swift and effective, with clear, joined-up working between government departments, local authorities and the European Commission' (EFRA 2013b: 5). But the EFRA Committee returned to the issue in a later report, citing further evidence in support of its view that the Government should consider reverting to the pre-2010 position in order to strengthen the FSA's independence and operational effectiveness (EFRA 2013c: 58).

The question of remit (determining where responsibility for managing the horsemeat incident lies) was not straightforward. Although the incident was not primarily a food safety issue, the Cabinet Office assigned lead responsibility to the FSA. The Troop review confirmed that, despite the 2010 remit changes, the Agency retained responsibility for 'food safety incidents, including misleading labelling and food fraud *with possible food safety implications*' (Troop 2013: 4.3, *emphasis added*). There was, however, a degree of ambiguity over whether this was, in fact, a food safety incident. The Troop review also noted that there was 'some hesitancy' in the activation phase of the FSA's response regarding whether it should be treated as a one-off incident with no major health implications, suggesting that it might have been wiser to invoke the precautionary principle and to scale down at a later date if necessary, rather than trying to scale up once the severity of the crisis had been recognized (ibid.: 4.3).[13] Commenting on this issue, the Agency's Chief Executive, Catherine Brown, noted: 'It is striking that there was a large degree of agreement among other Government departments, and among senior staff here, that the role of the FSA was to lead the investigation of this national food incident, regardless of the extent to which there was any food safety risk' ('Horse meat review – key findings', http://www.food.gov.uk/news-updates/news/2013/jun/horsereview#. Ud8eKxVwb4g, accessed 11 July 2013).

The complex geography of UK food governance goes beyond the issue of the FSA's remit. The Agency's four-point action plan (referred to earlier) underlined the need for the FSA to work with other government departments, local authorities and food businesses including the FSAI, Defra and the devolved rural affairs departments, together with UK local authorities and representatives from the UK and Irish food industry (and subsequently with various European partners including EFSA). Working across government departments and in other multi-agency partnerships can be challenging. For example, the FSA does not itself carry out food tests. Although it is the UK's Competent Authority for food safety, the official testing regime is carried out by environmental health officers, trading standards officers and public analysts employed by local authorities. The FSA provides grant funding and national coordination for surveillance and surveys on priority issues but local authorities are responsible for inspecting the UK's 600,000 food businesses. Food companies also conduct their own testing and audit procedures (using Hazard Analysis and Critical Control Point procedures and similar risk management techniques), designed to impose control along the supply chain and to enable problems to be traced to their source. The horsemeat incident revealed that the focus of official controls might need to change. As the Irish Agriculture Minister, Simon Coveney, admitted: 'the focus of controls which hitherto was on food safety will henceforth have to encompass checks on food authenticity' (DAFM 2013: 6).

The Elliott Review also highlighted the complexity of the current regulatory landscape, noting how, at local authority level, food hygiene is enforced by District Councils in England, with composition and labelling being enforced by County Councils (2013: 40). In what Professor Elliott described as a 'crowded landscape', local authority trading standards and environmental health services operate without ring-fenced funding from Government which, in the current economic climate, has led to 'a steady reduction in staff' with the relevant skills for law enforcement (ibid.: 45–46). Rather than focusing on the specific remit of different agencies, however, the Elliott Review criticized the lack of clear responsibility for investigating and prosecuting food fraud. Detecting 'a lack of any wider sense of responsibility beyond the specific regulatory remit of each of the players' (ibid.: 52), the review concluded that there was no place for 'silos and boundary fights' during the process of crisis management (ibid.: 55).

The horsemeat incident also highlighted the problem of regulating processes that cross geographical and administrative boundaries. Writing in *The Guardian* (10 May 2013), Felicity Lawrence feared that the 'culprits will not face justice' because of political and jurisdictional issues. She quotes senior sources in law enforcement and the food industry who, she said, had accused the Irish authorities of being more concerned to protect the Irish beef industry than to expose all the links in the chain, referring to 'a wall of silence from the Irish'.

The DAFM report noted problems in tracing intermediaries and food businesses in Poland, the UK and the Netherlands, most of which operated outside its jurisdiction (2013: 37). It suggested that events at Silvercrest (the firm that supplied Tesco with adulterated meat) had put at risk 'the reputation of the entire agri-food sector in Ireland' (ibid.: 9.2). While the crisis had put pressure on 'Brand Ireland', the report argued that there was an important perceptual difference between Irish meats farmed in Ireland and processed convenience products that 'happen to be made in Ireland' (ibid.: 6.5, emphasis in original). In an ideal world, the report suggested, promoting 'Brand Ireland', enforcing food regulation and protecting consumer safety would be harmonious and consistent objectives with all parties benefitting from the maintenance of the highest food standards. But the horsemeat incident suggests that these high ideals may not always be achieved in practice.[14]

Felicity Lawrence pushed this argument further, drawing attention to the close links between Irish politicians and leading figures in the Irish food industry (The Guardian, 11 May 2013), highlighting how, for example, Patrick Coveney, chief executive of Greencore (the Irish food processing company that supplied Asda with bolognese sauce which was found to contain 5% horsemeat), is the brother of Irish agriculture minister Simon Coveney. She also suggested that enforcement agencies faced particular problems where supply chains cross jurisdictions, with prosecutions focusing on a company's immediate suppliers with whom they had legal contracts. Where more complex supply chains were involved, including subcontractors and other subsidiary arrangements, prosecutions were likely to be more difficult. Similar conclusions were drawn in the trade press (see, e.g., 'Horsemeat: scandal unleashes lawsuits across Europe', The Grocer, 10 February 2013).

An example of these complex and challenging arrangements is the ABP Group who supplied adulterated beef burgers to Tesco from its Silvercrest factory near the Irish border, as well as supplying contaminated frozen mince to Asda from its Dalepak plant in Yorkshire. ABP's Scottish factory was later found to have supplied beef meatballs to Waitrose that contained 30 per cent undeclared pork. The company's chairman, Larry Goodman, blamed 'rogue traders' at its Silvercrest plant for failing to follow the correct specification. Mr Goodman had faced previous allegations in 1994 when his company was accused of faking records, making fraudulent claims for European subsidies, commissioning bogus official stamps, cheating customs officials and practising institutionalized tax evasion during the 1980s. Declining to appear before the EFRA Committee in London, Mr Goodman claimed that he could not add to evidence that had already been given by the company (*The Guardian*, 15 February and 11 May 2013).

Arguably, the effectiveness of UK food regulation is also hampered by the FSA's limited jurisdiction (which is restricted to the UK) and legal powers (where the Agency has no authority to require industry testing or to force private companies to share the results of such tests). Professor Troop noted the FSA's limited powers of entry to food premises that could lead to the loss of valuable evidence (2013: 4.4). Questions of jurisdiction may have further limited the EFRA Committee's ability to summon witnesses to appear before it in Westminster. According to *The Guardian* (11 May 2013), for example, Martin McAdam, the Irish meat trader who was blamed by Silvercrest and another Irish firm for supplying contaminated Polish beef, declined the Committee's request to attend saying that he had cooperated fully with the FSAI, the authority which had jurisdiction over his business. Mr McAdam was implicated in another incident where a meat processor (Freeza Meats from Newry, Northern Ireland) was found to have a consignment of frozen meat in its cold store comprising 80 per cent horsemeat. The owner of the company and a senior executive claimed to be holding the meat as a goodwill gesture for Mr McAdam. Pursuing these issues across national boundaries, involving different jurisdictions, is likely to frustrate law enforcement officials in undertaking their investigations and upholding the public interest.

The increasingly global organization of the food industry appears to offer fraudulent traders protection from prosecution for crimes and misdemeanours that occur elsewhere in the chain. So, for example, the Irish Department of Agriculture blamed foreign suppliers for the contamination of meat products in Ireland, including the raw material that led to the contamination of beef burgers produced by Silvercrest Foods which came from frozen beef trimmings, labelled as originating from Poland. While Silvercrest could be blamed for a lack of vigilance in managing its suppliers, the DAFM report insisted that 'the integrity of Irish produced ingredients remained intact' (2013: 2.10). Arguing that events at Silvercrest were 'systemic in nature' (3.1.2), the report insisted that 'Nearly all [EU] Member States have been affected to some extent by the mislabelling of meat products' (2.14). The crisis revealed 'a fundamental issue of trust', the report concluded, resulting from 'a systemic failure rather than a failing by any one country' (6.4). In Abbots and Coles's analysis, this line of argument seeks to separate 'good' producers (and 'good' food) from 'bad' ones, laying the blame on one or two 'dodgy' producers (2013: 537–38). Where systemic issues are identified, the precise responsibility is hard to define and blame is difficult to ascribe. Where specific failings are detected, they tend to be located in the social, economic and discursive margins of Europe, such as in Poland or Romania, rather that responsibility falling closer to home (ibid.: 541).

Advocating a 'systems approach', the final report of the Elliott Review identified eight pillars that needed to be addressed in order to achieve greater integrity and assurance of UK food supply networks. These included specific recommendations about putting consumers first, zero tolerance of fraud, intelligence gathering, laboratory services, auditing, government support, leadership and crisis management (Elliott 2014). While it is hard to identify the current direction of travel in UK food policy, the Elliott Review encouraged greater emphasis on the prevention and detection of food fraud including the establishment of a new Crime Unit within the FSA. Its current funding of £2 million per year has to be met from existing resources and is likely to lead to reduced capability in other areas of the Agency's work. This is consistent with the Government's emphasis on reducing the 'regulatory burden' on UK businesses but may be in tension with the Agency's renewed pledge to 'put consumers first in everything we do'. This phrase appeared in a draft of the Agency's new Strategy for 2015–20, discussed by the FSA Board in September 2014 (https://www.food.gov.uk/sites/default/files/fsa140904a.pdf, accessed 6 November 2014). With limited regulatory powers and a reduced budget, the FSA is likely to place less emphasis on direct enforcement and more on what it calls 'facilitated compliance', encouraging businesses to conform to food safety and related standards. The Agency's Strategy also identifies three specific areas where consumer rights should be prioritized: the right to be protected, the right to make choices knowing the facts and the right to the best future that can be delivered. The emphasis on 'informed choice' might be criticized (with its simplistic understanding of the relationship between knowledge and behaviour) as might the discussion of the rights and responsibilities of different players in the UK's agri-food system (among whom power is very unequally distributed). The Elliott Review also called for a more proactive FSA, emphasizing the need for a coordinated approach, working across a number of government departments which, it acknowledged, 'will require a culture change' (Elliott 2014: 2).

Conclusion

Using the 2013 horsemeat 'incident' as a specific example, this chapter has reflected on the regulatory and governance issues that arise when food companies fail to manage long and complex supply chains. The complexities of the regulatory landscape, as well as the extended nature of food supply chains, have given rise to legitimate public concern, although survey evidence suggests that specific issues such as the horsemeat incident may have a relatively short-term impact on consumer behaviour. The chapter has also demonstrated the effectiveness of the social anxiety framework, introduced in Chapter 3, for analysing such incidents. While it did not pose an immediate threat to human health, the horsemeat incident led to significant public anxiety and a decline in consumer trust, as food manufacturers and retailers appeared to have lost control over their supply chains. The underlying assumption was that if suppliers were prepared to engage in fraudulent behaviour over the content of particular products, the integrity of their behaviour in other respects might also be questionable, including practices that have a direct bearing on food safety.

The horsemeat incident raises questions about the extent to which 'retailer-led' regulation is adequate to the task of governing what is an increasingly globalized industry (cf. Goodman & Watts 1997). Contemplating the possible occurrence of 'fraud on a massive scale', the EFRA Committee concluded that 'This scandal has . . . raised broader food policy questions about cheap food production, transparency, consumer confidence and pressures within the supply chain' (EFRA 2013a: 4.43). It also warned of the danger that consumers might be left to pay the costs of enhanced traceability, improved labelling and higher testing standards – or to accept that they will not be provided with adequate information about the provenance and composition of food products.

The interim report of the Elliott Review called for a 'more robust' FSA, capable of dealing with the complex, widespread and organized nature of food crime (2013: 3). While UK consumers have access to 'perhaps the safest food in the world', the Review concluded that there is 'very limited intelligence' on the current scale of food crime in the UK (ibid.: 7), with the FSA having become 'a rather isolated and inward-looking organisation' (ibid.: 43). An editorial in *The Guardian* echoed this view, describing the Agency as 'a small demoralised body' that was 'hopelessly out of its depth' in terms of its ability to investigate and prosecute food fraud (12 December 2013).[15]

Responding to these challenges at the European level, the European Commission announced a 'landmark package' of legislative reforms in May 2013, designed to modernize, simplify and strengthen the agri-food chain in Europe ('Smarter rules for safer food', http://ec.europa.eu/dgs/health_consumer/animal-plant-health-package, accessed 3 January 2014). The package, which is unlikely to come into force until 2016, includes measures to sharpen testing regimes, including mandatory spot-checks, with greater financial penalties for those found guilty of food fraud. Commenting on the proposals, European Health and Consumer Commissioner Tonio Borg confirmed the economic value of the European Union's agri-food industry, claiming that Europe has the highest food safety standards in the world, while admitting that the recent horsemeat incident had shown that there was still room for improvement.

While the immediate causes of the horsemeat incident may be attributable to the criminal behaviour of a small number of fraudulent traders, the evidence presented in this chapter suggests that the underlying issues are more profound, including the increasing length and complexity of food supply chains, the ineffective nature of contemporary food regulation and the confused and confusing current landscape of food governance within and between nation-states. This analysis of the 2013 horsemeat incident also reinforces the conclusion of earlier research which found that consumer confidence and public trust in food across Europe have deeper institutional roots than individual concerns that focus on a handful of 'rogue traders' (cf. Kjaernes et al. 2007). As food governance is stretched across the boundaries of several government departments, involving diverse agencies and multiple jurisdictions, such crises are likely to become more common. Viewed over the longer term, the 2013 horsemeat 'incident' is unlikely to be an isolated event, raising important questions about the regulation of contemporary agri-food systems.

Notes

1. As will be discussed later in the chapter, referring to the horsemeat 'incident' implies a particular way of framing these events, in contrast to other possible designations such as 'scandal', 'scare' or 'crisis'. Thanks to Angela Meah, Patrick Miller, Charles Pattie, Sian Thomas and Neil Ward who each made helpful comments on earlier drafts of this chapter.
2. The UK FSA website has a useful timeline of the crisis at http://www.food.gov.uk/enforcement/monitoring/horse-meat/timeline-horsemeat/ (accessed 5 July 2013).
3. As well as causing significant public anxiety, the horsemeat incident also became the subject of humour and ridicule. Besides frequent puns and other comic allusions in the press and on social media, whole websites were devoted to sharing jokes about the crisis. See, for example: http://www.horsemeatjokes.com/ (accessed 10 December 2013).
4. In their analysis of the horsemeat crisis, Abbots and Coles (2013) identify a series of moral framings including a discourse of 'failings', a discourse of 'good and bad food', a discourse of 'invisibility' (regarding food's geographical provenance) and a discourse of 'irresponsible consumers' – all of which, they claim, were shaped by a deeper, class-based, moral framework.

5. On the 'taboo' nature of eating horsemeat, see 'What's so bad about horse meat, anyway?' (*Business Week*, 12 February 2013).

6. Compare Fuentes and Fuentes (2014) on competing framings of the recent pig-meat scandal in Sweden and how, as the crisis progressed, the central issue shifted from a concern about animal welfare, prompted by animal rights activists, to a defence of national farming standards, prompted by Swedish agricultural interests.

7. 'Horsemeat scare: Waitrose pulls burgers from shelves as Tesco apologises after one store is found still selling withdrawn items' (*The Independent*, 25 January 2013).

8. See, for example, 'Horsemeat: FSA "hesitant" on horsemeat review, says review' (*Meat Trades Journal*, 8 July 2013); 'Slow, badly executed, indecisive and poorly communicated – watchdog rapped for "wait-and-see" handling of horsemeat crisis' (*The Independent*, 9 July 2013); 'Horsemeat food scandal inquiry's "slow pace" criticised by select committee' (*The Guardian*, 16 July 2013).

9. 'Row as horsemeat file shelved', *The Guardian* (15 August 2014). The delay followed a Cabinet reshuffle, with government officials suggesting that the new Environment secretary needed more time to consider the report fully prior to publication. Initially dated July 2014, the final report was published on 4 September 2014.

10. The online survey claimed to be representative of the national population, with a sample size of 1,527 in wave 1 (Harris Interactive 2013a) and with 1,928 new interviews in wave 2, plus an additional 're-contact' sample of 568 respondents in wave 2 who had already taken part in wave 1 (Harris Interactive 2013b). These data were presented to the FSA Board at its open session on 21 January 2014.

11. See, for example, Defra's (2005) critique of 'food miles' as an indicator of environmental sustainability.

12. This argument was advanced by a former FSA scientist, Dr Mark Woolfe, as reported by the BBC ('Mince ban "linked to horsemeat scandal"', http://www.bbc.co.uk/news/science-environment-2430329, accessed 16 August 2014).

13. The Agency's review of the use of scientific evidence in emergencies shows that establishing lead responsibility is often a critical issue in the first few hours and days of managing such incidents: http://gacs.food.gov.uk/gacsgroups/wg-science-emerg (accessed 30 July 2014).

14. For an analysis of the tensions between neoliberal and biosecurity logics in the work of the FSAI, see Devaney (2013).

15. The right-wing press was even more outspoken in its criticism of the FSA with one report describing the Agency as 'hopelessly bureaucratic', prone to 'navel-gazing and politically correct ideology' ('What's the point of a food safety quango that couldn't save us from eating stallion burgers?', *Daily Mail*, 13 February 2013).

Chapter 6

Mediating science and nature: parental anxieties about food

Expanding on the previous chapter which explored the impact of a recent food 'incident' in the UK and more widely across Europe, this chapter examines the recent experience of 'food scares' and adulteration scandals in China, highlighting further systemic weaknesses in the governance and regulation of the agri-food sector. In a three-month period in 2013, for example, over 900 people were arrested for 'meat-related offences' in China (*The Guardian*, 3 May 2013). A few months later there were similar reports about the illegal use of discarded animal parts in cooking oil and the sale of meat products made from animal waste (*The Guardian*, 11 October 2013). The extent of the problem can be gauged by quoting at more length from one of these news reports which began:

> Since January, authorities have seized 20,000 tonnes of illegal products and solved 382 cases of meat-related crime – primarily the sale of toxic, diseased and counterfeit meat.
>
> One suspect, named Wei, earned more than £1m over the past four years by purchasing fox, mink and rat meat, treating it with gelatin[e], carmine (a colour produced from ground beetles) and nitrate, then selling it as mutton at farmers' markets in Jiangsu province and Shanghai. Authorities raided Wei's organisation in February, arresting 63 suspects and seizing 10 tonnes of meat and additives.

The report continued:

> Suspects in . . . Baotou city produced fake beef and lamb jerky from duck meat and sold it to markets in 15 provinces. Levels of *E coli* in the counterfeit product 'seriously exceeded standards', the [public security] ministry said.
>
> Hao, another suspect, from Fengxiang city, Shanghai province, last year sold mutton that had turned black and reeked of agricultural chemicals to a barbecue restaurant, killing one customer and poisoning a handful of others.

In Fujian province, five suspects were arrested and two factories shut for butchering disease-ridden pig carcasses and selling their meat in nearby provinces . . .

Authorities closed two factories in the south-western province of Guizhou for soaking chicken feet in hydrogen peroxide before shipping them to market. And in Zhenjiang city, Jiangsu province, two people were arrested for selling pork products that were made with meat from 'poor quality pig heads'. (*The Guardian*, 3 May 2013)

This catalogue of criminal activity is part of a long history of food fraud and adulteration in China, the scale of which is deeply disturbing. A couple of months earlier, thousands of pig carcasses were dredged from rivers in and around Shanghai having been dumped there following a clampdown on the illegal trade in contaminated pork (*The Independent*, 22 March 2013). Food safety is clearly a pressing issue in China, the source of widespread media concern and a cause of persistent consumer anxiety.

This chapter focuses on one specific incident, tracing public attitudes, government reactions and commercial responses to the contamination of infant formula (powdered baby milk) with the poisonous chemical melamine in 2008 that led to the death of six infants and the hospitalization of hundreds more with kidney problems (Xin & Stone 2008, Xiu & Klein 2010, Pei et al. 2011). While the incident might be explained in terms of the criminal behaviour of a few unscrupulous merchants, watering down milk in order to increase its volume and adding melamine to enrich its protein content, its underlying causes are more deep-seated. The chapter suggests that the incident was a consequence of rapid urbanization, the changing consumption patterns of China's growing middle classes, an imbalance in the supply and demand of dairy products, lax governmental regulation and municipal corruption. The chapter also explores consumer reactions to the incident in terms of parental anxieties about the safety and security of milk supplies for their children in the context of increased female labour-force participation, the medicalization of childcare and the ideology of 'scientific motherhood'. The chapter examines how the major dairy companies responded to the incident in terms of the marketing of infant formula and how they sought to reassure consumers and regain their trust through television advertisements which artfully combined images of nature with an appeal to the authority of science.[1]

The 2008 infant formula crisis

In 2008, consumer confidence in China was undermined by a major 'food scare' concerning the contamination of infant formula. Unable to keep up with a rapid increase in demand from urban consumers, unscrupulous merchants encouraged producers to dilute their milk supplies, adding the poisonous chemical melamine as an artificial means of boosting the product's protein content. Failing to test for melamine, dairy companies passed on the nitrogen-rich chemical through their processed milk products to consumers. It soon became apparent that this was an act of deliberate adulteration rather than a result of accidental contamination. The level of melamine in contaminated infant formula produced by one company (Sanlu) was reported to be as high as 2560 mg/kg body weight compared with the US Drug and Food Administration (DFA) maximum tolerable daily intake (TDI) of 0.63 mg/kg and EFSA's recommended TDI of 0.5 mg/kg (cf. Hilts & Pelletier 2008).

As a direct result of the incident, nearly 300,000 babies suffered kidney problems, hundreds were hospitalized and 6 died. Twenty-two Chinese dairy companies were implicated in the scandal, with the Shijiazhuang-based company Sanlu attracting most criticism and later being declared bankrupt. When the problem was detected (which coincided with China's hosting of the Beijing Olympic Games), the government was slow to respond, only taking serious action once political pressure had been exerted by foreign governments (notably New Zealand, home to the dairy company Fonterra which had a part-share in the Sanlu corporation and who risked serious reputational damage from their association with the incident).[2] In the aftermath of the crisis, several companies went out of business, numerous senior company executives and government officials resigned, others were prosecuted and imprisoned, two offenders faced the death penalty and were executed (Xinhua News Agency 2009). The incident also led to an increase in the sale of imported infant formula, despite the premium price of foreign brands.

Contextualizing the crisis

Before examining consumer anxieties more closely, it is important to understand the social context of the 2008 crisis, including China's recent urbanization, the rising demands of middle-class consumers, increased female labour-force participation, and the neoliberalization and medicalization of childcare. Since the 1980s, China has experienced a period of very rapid urbanization, with large-scale migration from rural areas to the towns and cities of the coastal south. The percentage of the population living in cities rose from 18 per cent in 1978 to 46 per cent in 2008, when the urban population numbered over 606 million (China Statistics Yearbook 2008; Zhang & Song 2003). The process of urbanization was accompanied by a rapid expansion of the middle classes as a result of China's economic reforms in the past 30 years (Zhou 2008). Despite the material deprivation and anti-consumerist movements of the 1960s and 1970s, rising affluence in China created new patterns of demand for consumer goods with per capita annual consumer expenditure rising from ¥1,278 in 1990 to ¥9,997 in 2008 (China Statistics Yearbook 2008) including more spending on food, leisure and consumer durables (Wu 1999, Latham 2006). Consumption of energy-dense protein-rich meat and dairy products grew significantly, with annual per capita consumption of liquid milk rising from 6 kg to 19 kg per household between 1995 and 2004 in urban China (Bai et al. 2008), actively promoted by several school milk programmes (Lai 2003).

China's 'modernization' was accompanied by increasing rates of female labour-force participation, now among the highest in the world. Women were claimed to 'hold up half of the sky' and were encouraged by the state to enter the workforce alongside their male peers (Li et al. 2006, Berik et al. 2007). Together with higher rates of paid employment, women in urban areas also gained improved social status, economic independence and improved employment prospects (Cai & Wu 2006, Faure 2008). Critics suggest that these changes were motivated by the need to increase the workforce and have only had a limited impact in improving gender equality (cf. Croll 1978, Cohen & Wang 2009). In particular, women receive little health and safety protection during pregnancy and little or no maternity leave after giving birth (Fang et al. 2005).[3] The lack of adequate maternity leave is also believed to be one of the social factors discouraging women from breastfeeding, with breastfeeding rates decreasing in both urban and rural China over the last 20 years. Despite increased awareness of the health benefits of breastfeeding, new mothers in urban China rarely breastfeed for more than one month (Guldan et al. 1995) and in North-West China, the rate of breastfeeding at one month was significantly lower in 2003–4 than in 1994–96 (Xu et al. 2006). In rural China, researchers also found a sharp decrease in the prevalence of exclusive breastfeeding at 2–4 months from over 60 per cent in 2002 to just over 4 per cent in 2008 (Shi et al. 2008).

Childcare practices have also been subject to a discourse of medicalization including notions of 'scientific motherhood', shaped by the wider context of neoliberalization that contributed to China's rapid economic growth in the late 1990s (Jing 2000, Berik et al. 2007). However, neoliberal policies have led to a rapid dismantling of the welfare system that had been established in socialist China. The state has withdrawn from managing pregnancy, birth and childcare, leaving individual parents to make their own decisions within a system that is governed by medicalized notions of childcare, operating on an increasingly commercial basis (Shi 2009). In a health promotional video produced by one dairy company, for example, parents are informed that pneumococcus, diabetes and blindness may threaten the health of their babies and they are urged to take a proactive approach to prevent these diseases by purchasing infant food, fortified with artificial nutrients.[4] Meanwhile, childcare professionals, both public and private, have become authoritative sources of information for new parents, significantly undermining traditional norms and practices of caring for young children. While these discourses may be less marked than in the United States (cf. Stearns 2003), the scientific or pseudo-scientific rationale behind such practices remains largely unchallenged among new parents in China.[5]

High levels of female participation in the workforce, accompanied by relatively poor maternity leave arrangements, have led to high rates of demand for Caesarean sections and low levels of breastfeeding, enabling women to return to work as soon as possible after childbirth. These social changes provide an important context for the exceptionally high demand for infant formula in China. Meanwhile, the neoliberal trend and discourse of medicalization have further shifted childcare towards 'modern' self-managed practices based on quasi-scientific principles.[6] The research reported here suggests that all these changes were relevant to the way parents reacted to the infant formula crisis in 2008.

Parental anxieties about infant formula

There has been very little research on the impact of recent 'food scares' on contemporary consumer anxieties in China apart from some survey-based research (Qiao et al. 2010). Our research (Gong & Jackson 2012, 2013) attempted a more in-depth investigation of parental attitudes to food safety, based on focus group discussions with parents and grandparents from different socioeconomic backgrounds, including carers (mothers and grandparents) of babies and young children aged three months to two years. Most of the participants relied almost entirely on infant formula to feed their babies. Rather than focusing exclusively on the melamine scandal, participants were asked open-ended questions about their best and worst baby-care experiences, their decisions on breast-feeding or formula-feeding, their feeding practices and perceptions of the safety of baby food before and after 2008.

Participants were recruited from different social backgrounds, using residential location as a way of accessing people of different ages, education and income. Those described as 'middle class and above' were recruited via kindergartens in relatively affluent neighbourhoods developed by commercial companies. Those described as from 'low-income' backgrounds came from government-subsidized neighbourhoods and were recruited from open-air markets and mini-parks in these areas. All but two of our 57 participants (one father and one grandfather) were women including mothers with babies under two years of age and their parents (the babies' grandparents). Twelve focus groups were conducted in Chengdu, the capital of Sichuan province.[7] The groups, which lasted between 40 and 90 minutes, were internally homogeneous in terms of role and social status (e.g. mothers from 'middle class and above' neighbourhoods, grandmothers from 'low-income' neighbourhoods etc.), with four to six participants in each group (see Table 6.1). One group consisted of both mothers and grandmothers in order to gauge the importance of cross-generational differences and in-law frictions.[8]

Anxieties about food were prominent in many of the focus group discussions, although the word 'anxiety' ('焦虑' in Mandarin) was not always mentioned. Instead, participants often used words such as 'worry' (担心), 'fear' (恐惧) and 'scares' (害怕) to describe their emotions. Often used interchangeably, these words indicate different degrees of intensity, with 'worry' (担心) the least severe and 'fear' (恐惧) the most. When asked if they were worried about the safety of baby food within the context of food safety standards in China, the answers were almost unanimously affirmative. Reflecting such worries, most carers had developed high levels of loyalty to particular foreign (imported) infant formula brands. Favoured brands included Abbott, Mead Johnson, Dumex and Nestlé, which were believed to be technologically innovative and highly nutritional.[9]

Table 6.1 Composition of focus groups

Group No.	No. of participants	Carer group	Social status
1	6	Mothers	Middle-class and above
2	4	Mothers	Low-income
3	6	Grandparents	Low-income
4	5	Grandmothers	Low-income
5	5	Mothers	Middle class and above
6	4	Grandmothers	Middle class and above
7	5	Mothers/ grandmothers	Middle class and above
8	4	Mothers	Middle class and above
9	5	Grandmother	Low-income
10	5	Parents	Low-income
11	4	Mothers	Middle class and above
12	4	Mothers	Middle class and above

The perceived premium value of infant formula is demonstrated in the following case where the mother had enough breast milk for her baby but used formula as a supplement. Explaining this, the baby's grandmother said: 'Breast milk isn't nutritional enough. Imported formula has all sorts of micro-nutrients, like DHA' (grandmother, group 6).[10] The popularity of foreign brands can be explained by the fact that many domestic brands were implicated in the infant formula scandal and that foreign brands are promoted in terms of their premium nutritional value. In her research in a Beijing maternity hospital, for example, Gottschang quotes one mother's arguments in favour of foreign-brand infant formula, noting its allegedly higher safety and nutritional standards and its perceived modernity in comparison with domestic brands:

> I wanted to raise my son in the most modern scientific way . . . The foreign brand of infant formula is expensive, but I don't believe that the Chinese formula companies are reliable – who controls them? The foreign companies have international standards that they have developed and they are more scientific. So, I feel foreign products are safer and have better nutrition. Some of them even have more nutrients than breast milk. (Gottschang 2000: 181–82)

Many of our participants supported this view, believing that foreign infant formula companies are better regulated and that they have higher safety standards.

Feeding babies with foreign formula for food safety reasons was supported by other concerns. Several participants had experienced difficulties with breast-feeding or anticipated such problems when they returned to work:

> I have been on leave since I was seven months pregnant . . . still on leave because I'm breastfeeding, and it's not convenient. I'm planning on returning to work after weaning. It's not possible to breastfeed at work with breast pump and other stuff. I suppose I can only do it in the toilet (Mother, group 1).

> My daughter returned to work three months after giving birth. She works as a manager in a restaurant and she worries about breastfeeding at work. The doctor asked her to, but there is nothing she could do. (Grandmother, group 4)

Unlike many women in advanced industrial societies (Marshall et al. 2007), our participants do not seem to associate formula-feeding with being a 'bad mother'. Supporting this observation, Gao et al. (2010) report many other conditions (physical and emotional exhaustion, dissonance between modernity and tradition, relations with in-laws, the gender of the baby) that contribute to women's postpartum depression in China in addition to failure to breastfeed. Several of our participants also referred to the traditional Chinese practice of 'doing the month' which is thought to ensure a quick recovery from childbirth for new mothers (Pillsbury 1982). It includes special postpartum food and a full month's confinement at home, usually accompanied by the mother-in-law or mother.

While the state officially promotes breastfeeding in China, pregnant women continue to receive nutritional information in the form of glossy pamphlets produced by Western formula companies. In one study of a Beijing maternity hospital in the mid-1990s, for example, all of the women interviewed had received such promotional leaflets (Gottschang 2000: 237). In our study, most mothers had received numerous calls from infant formula companies, life insurance firms and childcare hospitals. Many believed that the presence of infant formula companies in hospitals counteracted official support for breastfeeding initiatives. However, within the context of the medicalization of childcare, the presentation of infant formula in medical settings was very appealing to new mothers, especially among those who worried that their breast milk was not adequate for their babies.

Price is also used as a guide to ensure the safety of formula milk where more expensive brands are assumed to be safer. Those who lose confidence in infant formula, frequently switch brands. As one mother explained:

> We always change the brands. Even if one formula has a problem, the baby shouldn't suffer too much [laughs] . . . You remember the Sanlu babies? Some of them have been drinking the formula for too long, and they [parents] had no idea that the formula is poisonous. (Mother, group 2)

In addition to worries about the safety of infant formula, the place where it is bought has also become a concern. According to our participants, retailers were under close scrutiny in terms of their ownership, location and reputation. Customer loyalty to foreign supermarkets and department stores such as Carrefour, Metro and Ito Yokado is growing. Some big domestic chain stores were acceptable, but corner stores were avoided by most of the participants. Infant formula is often brought back from trips abroad by those families with relatives who visited other countries on business. Others purchased foreign infant formula online. In total, only three babies out of the 58 in this study (including one mother with twins) were given domestic formula.

Parental anxieties about food safety also reflect contending relations within the family, especially between young mothers and their in-laws, many of whom are now primary care-givers, while their daughters are at work outside the home. Such anxieties were aggravated when different opinions about baby food were expressed. In the following quotation, it is clear that although grandmothers are extensively involved in childcare, they have very little power in deciding what to feed the baby:

> It's difficult to communicate with my own daughter, let alone my daughter-in-law . . . I do whatever she tells me. Whatever she wants to give to the baby, I don't argue, I just do it . . . When the baby is unwell, she [daughter-in-law] searches the internet and decides what to feed the baby. She doesn't listen to me. She wouldn't give the baby what I suggested anyway. (Grandmother, group 6)

The Internet is mentioned more often as a source of information for the younger generation. Many younger mothers believed that the Internet provides better 'information on-demand' than other relatively trustworthy sources such as childcare books or magazines. The older generation's advice on childcare is occasionally sought. But most of the time their practices (e.g. using washable nappies rather than disposable diapers) are considered outdated, unsanitary or unscientific. As is common elsewhere, young parents complain about the child-care practices of the older generation:

> We have different opinions about what food baby can eat at the moment. We believe there are certain things the baby can try . . . From time to time my mother spoils my son by giving him lollipops or biscuits. I don't think he should be given these because they affect his appetite. (Mother, group 8)

The mothers' generation also seems very well disposed to medicalized baby-care advice:

> I think this is very necessary. I think it's a lot better to get dietary advice from pediatricians than to muddle through the dangerous water by ourselves. They tell us what to feed, how to feed, how much to feed and what is normal from a medical point of view. (Mother, group 5)

When medical advice is not followed, young mothers are prone to worry. They complain about their mothers for not following the doctor's advice, for example with respect to the level of salt in their baby's food:

> My mum thinks the baby food is too bland, so she secretly adds a little more salt . . . Of course I know, I taste the baby food. This is not very nice . . . Doctors told us it should be low sugar and salt level in baby food. (Mother, group 8)

One grandmother openly challenged medicalized doctrines about steriliz-ing feeding bottles. She believed that those of a younger generation were too squeamish about bacteria, also arguing that oversterilization would not help the baby develop his immune system:

> I think it's OK to just wash the feeding bottle, spoon and bowls with washing liquid and hot water. They [her daughters] insisted on sterilizing by putting these things in boiling water, over and over again. There are some good bacteria. Besides, having a little bacteria is good for the baby to develop his immune system . . . I didn't go to the university like them, but I know this . . . I really want to ask them how come they grew up just fine without having their feeding bottles sterilized three times a day? (Grandmother, group 6)

Pregnancy, child-birth and infant care are increasingly subject to medical control in China. This is reflected in regular pre-natal scans and post-natal examinations. Births are often subject to Caesarean sections which are intended for complicated births but are becoming much more widely used. According to our participants, conditions such as high blood pressure, myopia, older age, breech presentation, skinniness and overweight are all considered justifications for having a Caesarean. Data from hospital-based studies also indicate that rates of Caesarean section in urban China ranged from 26 to 63 per cent during the late 1990s (Guo et al. 2007). Voluntary Caesareans are also often sought to avoid pain. Here again, medical advice, as with the 'techno-scientific rationalities' regarding low salt intake and sterilization of equipment, diverges from lay understandings, providing fertile ground for the development of social anxiety (cf. Hier 2003). Moreover, conflicting information from medical professionals and childcare experts leads to further uncertainties over childcare practices, contributing to a general lack of parental confidence and increased anxiety:

> You know the jab for pneumococcus? The news says kids die from getting the jab. I'm petrified because my kid had it. But the expert says it's OK, and my kid seems to be alright. I don't know what to do. (Mother, group 11)

Given the lack of authoritative information from sources such as the Ministry of Health, many parents face a plethora of childcare advice from different sources including the media, doctors, others parents and in-laws as well as official government channels. Despite parental efforts to obtain impartial information, commercial sources often succeed in filling the knowledge gap:

> My [childcare] knowledge is from people who sell infant formula, childcare seminars, baby clothing shops, community hospitals, childcare hospitals, books etc. Infant formula people taught me how to distinguish foreign formulae from Chinese infant formulae – you look at the barcode and the ones that

start with '69' are Chinese products . . . But in the end it's my child . . . You can't entirely trust others. (Father, group 10)

Generational differences in attitudes to childcare can be reinforced by urban–rural differences, particularly where members of the parental generation have developed more urban attitudes than the grandparents' generation. While rural residents may be stigmatized as backward, provincial or inferior, foods from rural areas may be regarded as safer and more trustworthy:

Back home we grow fresh vegetables and there is no pesticide to worry about. In the city, we worry about everything. (Grandmother, group 3)

In the context of recent 'food scares', there is evidence of a revaluation of the 'rural' as part of what Griffiths et al. (2010) refer to as a 'romantic reappraisal', particularly among middle-class urban residents (cf. Farquhar 2002).

Our focus group evidence confirms that the 2008 infant formula crisis intensified a number of existing parental anxieties concerning child-feeding practices and that these need to be understood in terms of the dramatic social changes that have occurred in China over the last few decades. Whereas in many parts of the world there is a presumption that local foods are preferable to those from abroad, recent 'food scares' in China seem to have reversed this logic and to have established a preference for imported over domestic brands. Parental anxieties about food also have to be accommodated within existing ideologies of 'scientific motherhood' and an increasingly medicalized approach to childcare, predicated on the growth of neoliberal understandings of the power of market forces and the underprovision of maternal support and advice from the state.

The next section considers how the dairy industry responded to this gap in official advice and to uncertainties about where to turn for impartial information about parenting practices, seeking to restore consumer confidence and trust following the infant formula crisis.

Restoring consumer confidence

Consumer confidence in Chinese dairy products plummeted immediately after the melamine crisis in 2008, particularly in Hohhot, the dairy capital of China, though it was reported to have been restored quite soon afterwards (Qiao et al. 2001), with fundamental long-term changes in behaviour affecting only a minority of consumers. In order to restore trust in domestic brands and to effect as quick a recovery as possible, Chinese and international dairy companies engaged in a series of marketing drives, including the use of television advertising to promote their brands. Examining these advertisements provides a fascinating window on parental anxieties about infant formula in China.

Infant formula advertisements were collected from Adtopic.net, the most comprehensive advertising video website for industry and academic use in China. The videos of infant formula advertisements were retrieved from a keyword search on the website search engine and filtered again through manual search.[11] In total 69 advertisements from 32 brands were collected, covering a two-and-a-half-year period from March 2008 to September 2010. Key themes were identified through repeated viewings and developed into a fuller coding scheme. Representations of nature and references to the authority of science were identified as prominent themes, particularly in the period after 2008, as illustrated here from the advertising campaigns for Wandashan (Wondersun), Firmus, Nanshan, Yili and Mengniu, including some comparative analysis with a leading international manufacturer (Dumex). In addition to analysing the content of selected advertisements, additional focus groups and interviews were undertaken with parents and grandparents in Chengdu to investigate consumer reactions to messages about 'science' and 'nature' in the advertisements.

In advertisements for some brands (e.g. Nanshan), staff members from the dairy company (including the firm's CEO, a lab worker and a buyer) testified to the safety of the company's products, claiming that they fed them to their own children. Other companies resorted to more conventional strategies, focusing on the scientific claims and alleged health benefits of their products. In many cases, idyllic images of 'nature' (including idealized images of dairy farms) were juxtaposed with images of 'science' (including white-coated scientists and their laboratories). For example, in a 15-second advertisement that Wandashan broadcast on a national television channel (CCTV 1) on 6 March 2009, a male voice-over asks 'With what to make good infant formula?'. While the voice-over spelled out 'location, milk source and formula', the screen showed a visual combination of all three elements (Figure 6.1). The voice-over continued: 'All these are very important, but what is more important is conscience.' The screen then switched to a group of Chinese and Western scientists in white lab coats, standing together with their hands across their chests (Figure 6.2). The advertisement finished by flashing up a series of pictures of smiling babies and showing several tins of infant formula, while the voice-over said: 'For 45 years, Wondersun has insisted on making good infant formula with conscience.'

The emphasis on 'conscience' ('良心') attempts to draw a distinction between Wandashan and other dairy companies that were implicated in the infant formula scandal and who were widely criticized for their lack of business ethics and conscience by the media. As one of the melamine-free brands, Wandashan benefited from the scandal and jumped from being a third-tier brand to a second-tier brand in the Chinese dairy market (interview with Wandashan sales representative, 2010). But even though the contamination occurred at multiple points in the production chain (milk collection at the farm, storage at milk stations and transportation to dairy manufacturers), this advertisement only addresses the first link in the chain (dairy farms). The farm in this advertisement is portrayed as an open green field, with sporadic grazing cows, adjacent to a lake and mountains under a blue sky. The complete absence of human figures or human-related subjects foregrounds conventional rural signifiers such as green grass and blue sky, invoking a romanticization of the rural and idealized representations of nature. This way of representing nature has its roots in the Western romantic tradition (Paterson 2006). Narratives of 'pure', 'natural' and 'green' have been present in Western food advertising since the early twentieth century (Domosh 2003) and have become more prominent in the context of contemporary agri-food systems with their characteristic separation of food production and consumption (Hollander 2003, Dimitri & Oberholtzer 2010).

The meanings of 'nature' in relation to baby food, as represented in these advertisements and in the focus groups, are quite diverse and internally inconsistent. While most urban baby-carers envision safer and higher quality food (such as free-range eggs and vegetables grown with less fertilizer) coming from more natural environments in rural areas, many parents also expressed their concerns that healthier diets based on natural ingredients may not be suitable for young children and that such diets may do more harm than good. Moreover, when asked if the images of nature in these advertisements would affect their decision to choose a particular brand of infant formula, participants considered the images a common feature of such advertisements with little impact on their

Figure 6.1 Wandashan screenshot I. Source: © Wandashan (reproduced with permission).

Figure 6.2 Wandashan screenshot II. Source: © Wandashan (reproduced with permission).

choice of a specific brand. For example, the members of one group reasoned as follows:

> I have seen this too much . . . Too much. They all have it, cows and meadows.
> Yili and Mengniu both have it. (Parents, group 10)

Other participants also found these images of nature unconvincing, reflecting widespread public distrust of deceptive and misleading advertisements in China (Hong 1994). The most influential factor in their decision-making, according to our participants, was their babies' experience of using different products. When asked to elaborate on this, participants talked about the physical condition of individual children when choosing between different brands, for example, brand X causes indigestion for this baby but not brand Y. This suggests that more complex criteria are at work in the selection of particular brands, beyond simple assertions of the superiority of 'foreign' over 'domestic' brands.[12] Their final selection is combined with other 'rules of thumbs' (e.g. whether the baby likes the taste, whether the formula causes dry mouth or constipation) (cf. Green et al. 2003). At this point, references to nature, although highly valued in relation to solid baby food, do not seem to be closely linked to images of nature in infant formula advertisements, creating no clear brand preference.

Although images of 'nature' in the advertisements were unlikely to have a direct effect on the selection of formula brands, parents referred to images of green pastures and blue skies in judging the location of food production in more general terms. These criteria were particularly applicable to foreign brands that were thought to be produced in truly unpolluted and natural environments. After expressing their distrust of images of 'nature' in the Chinese infant formula adverts, one father said:

> New Zealand has the best milk source in the world . . . It's less polluted there,
> and there are very few people too. (Parents, group 4)

Childhood experiences in rural villages influenced some parents' decoding of images of 'nature'. While most parents criticized the images used in Chinese infant formula advertisements as false representations of nature, some recalled similar images from their own village childhood experiences and used these images of rurality to support the safety and quality of local infant formula products:

> Look at that blue sky and white cloud in that ad . . .
> Chengdu has no blue sky and white cloud.

> My husband chose Hongya [a small county 120 km from Chengdu] infant
> formula for my little boy. He [husband] grew up there, and he knows the
> pasture there.
>
> The environment [there] is better and the air is fresher. (Parents, group 10)

Others parents were less influenced by such romantic and nostalgic sentiments.
One mother said the images promoted in the advertisements provided her with
a reference point, but other criteria such as having a safety certificate were also
relevant to her choice of a domestic brand which was considered risky and
almost unacceptable by most of the focus group participants:

> I use the images in the ad as a reference. I'm thinking about using Wondersun,
> because it is from Helongjian where there is good pasture and environment.
> I know for a fact that there is good, pure raw milk that doesn't have to travel
> thousands of kilometres to other parts of China. There should be plenty of milk
> sources for local dairy companies. If the formula was produced right next to
> the dairy farm, it should be safe. (Parent, group 8)[13]

This mother drew on her knowledge of the 2008 melamine 'scare' to interpret
the advertising message. Her explanation also demonstrates an understanding of how food safety risks are thought to increase as the length of the supply
chain increases. This knowledge helped her in critically decoding the advertising messages, reaching an alternative perspective on food safety, based on the
perceived location of milk production.

The above examples show an inconsistent understanding of the place of
'nature' in representations of the location of infant formula production among
parents and other carers. Similar inconsistencies are demonstrated in contexts
where nature is considered as a healthy environment for children to grow up.
Following the discussion of safer food in rural areas, grandmothers in one of our
focus groups explored the idea of raising their grandchildren there in order for
them to benefit from fresh vegetables and free-range eggs. The group expressed
mixed feelings about rurality: while they supported the view that the natural environment is associated with 'unproblematic' foods such as chicken, duck, fish
and meat, they also worried that some aspects of nature such as soil and water
may not be suitable for urban-born children:

> This kid was born in Chengdu. If he goes back [to the rural area] he'll get a rash.
>
> It won't work. He can't get used to the water and soil there . . . The water here
> [in Chengdu] is disinfected, but it's not there [in the rural area].
>
> That's why, he has no antibody.

My mum gets water from the foot of the mountain. It is cleaner than the tap water here. (Grandmothers, group 9)

As the most common materialization of nature, water is associated with purity (clean water 'from the foot of the mountain') and risk (giving a nasty rash to children). Parental perceptions relate to both the romantic side of nature that revitalizes and the dark side of nature that destroys.

Similar issues are apparent in the way that 'science' is represented in the advertisements and in consumer reactions to these representations which can be interpreted as part of the current medicalization of childcare in China. In a 30-second advertisement for Firmus infant formula, for example, the production process is shown in a sequence of frames made up of images and texts.[14] These frames are accompanied by gentle piano music. Unlike the Wandashan advertisement (discussed earlier), images of nature are in this case juxtaposed with images of science, even within the same frame, with the blue sky floating above images of an industrial processing plant (the text confirming that 300,000 purifying procedures are used in the production process, meeting the best international standards). After two shots showing lab-coated scientists and another frame of the green earth, the product itself appears in a beaker-like container. In this advertisement, a complex production process has been reduced to two key sites: farms and laboratories. The only humans involved in the production process are scientists. Nature and science coexist harmoniously, with no apparent conflict. First broadcast in November 2008, a few months after the melamine crisis broke out, the message contained in the advertisement is of a highly simplified production process with a reassuring combination of science and nature, leading inexorably to satisfied babies and contented mothers. Our focus group evidence suggests that consumer reactions to these idealized images of nature and simplified representations of science are often more ambivalent.

Resorting to the powerful discourse of science, infant formula companies are keen to draw attention to the alleged health benefits of their products. Companies highlight the importance of incorporating micro-nutrients such as vitamins in infants' daily diet, emphasizing the health benefits of their products and exploiting the lax regulation of health claims in China.[15] As noted previously, one grandmother in our focus group research believed that her daughter's breast milk was nutritionally inferior to imported infant formula because the latter contained micro-nutrients such as Docosahexaenoic acid (DHA) and Arachidonic acid (ARA) – and several of the TV advertisements refer to both DHA and ARA. While parents engage critically with the narratives of 'nature' employed in infant formula advertising, our research suggests that they are generally less able to make an informed judgement about the products' alleged scientific benefits.

There is, however, more evidence of consumer scepticism towards the companies' promotional tactics. As one mother reported:

> Abbott had this seminar . . . they flew a childcare expert from Shanghai to Chengdu to explain the advantages of Abbott products. It's said that he charges ¥300 per hour for consultancy. I went there because I really wanted to learn. I took my pen and notepad. The hall was full . . . He showed us a video like this, followed by a little quiz [about various medical risks] and the questions were all in the video . . . Those who got the questions right got some free infant formula. (Mother, group 9)

In this case, the mother's enthusiasm wore off as she attended more seminars and realized that they seemed to be more about promoting infant formula than about disseminating experiences and knowledge of childcare. Another young mother was equally unhappy about her experiences in peer-support group meetings organized by an online mothers' forum:

> I don't know. We have different levels of knowledge, so the conversation doesn't always flow . . . and the strangest thing is, all of a sudden, a participant turns into a sales representative and starts selling formula to us. (Mother, group 12)

While these mothers were sceptical about commercially motivated medical advice, many new parents felt uncertain about their childcare skills and were faced with a plethora of (sometimes conflicting) information from a range of unsanctioned sources.

The marketing of infant formula products in China also draws on a discourse of health risk and consumer protection. In a health promotional video produced by the infant formula company Dumex, for example, parents are told that pneumococcus poses serious threats to children under the age of two. According to the video, associated diseases include pneumonia, meningitis, otitis media, bacteremia, hypophrenia, deafness, epilepsy and paralysis. The video also claims that pneumococcus infection results in 700,000 to 1 million child deaths each year worldwide. In the course of the video, babies and young children are shown with a shining outline (or halo effect), evoking the enhanced protection provided by artificially added nutrients.[16] Such representations offer parents a form of psychological comfort in addition to the assurance of food safety through the representations of nature described earlier.

Parental confidence in commercial childcare advice has also been undermined by the recent neoliberal reforms of the Chinese medical system, exacerbated by 'food scares' such as the 2008 infant formula incident, leaving parents without independent and authoritative guidance on childcare issues. The frequency of post-natal health checks in China and the health warnings issued by doctors generate high levels of anxiety among many new parents. Our focus group discussions with young mothers revealed a pronounced sense of anxiety about the perceived threats to the well-being of their children which are reflected in the way the infant formula companies adopt the discourse of scientific motherhood and protective childcare in their advertisements. While some mothers made use of the Internet to search for impartial advice on childcare issues, others (such as the grandmothers in group 4) thought that this should be a responsibility of the government. In the absence of independent medical advice from official sources, infant formula companies have an opportunity to fill the information vacuum, employing dubious promotional tactics and making poorly substantiated health claims for their products.

That consumer rights in China do not receive adequate protection was demonstrated by the initial cover-up of the infant formula incident and by the long-unresolved compensation of victims. Nonetheless, public outcry over the incident and wider concerns about food safety may have helped speed up the passage of a new Food Safety Law with more comprehensive and stricter food safety standards (interview with official from the China National Centre for Food Safety Risk Assessment, 2010). The incidents reported at the beginning of this chapter suggest, however, that China still has a long way to go to meet international food safety standards.

Conclusion

The 2008 infant formula crisis might appear to be an extreme case, indicating China's exceptionalism in relation to the governance and regulation of food safety. But many of its features correspond to the theory of social anxiety outlined in Chapter 3. The detection of melamine in infant formula clearly ruptured the routines and rhythms of everyday life, puncturing the current consensus about the best way to feed young babies. The event involved a number of different 'communities of practice' including the media; municipal, national and international governments; the dairy industry and infant formula companies; health professionals and other experts. Clear gaps emerged between different sources of advice, provoking further anxiety, in a context of neoliberalizing healthcare systems and inadequate public health advice from official sources. While the incident itself was largely confined to anxieties about commercial food producers, exacerbated by lax governmental regulation, it drew on a longer history of 'food scares' in China and on associated ideologies of 'scientific motherhood' and medicalized childcare. These ideologies are themselves highly moralized in terms of the 'best' ways to care for children in situations where state provision for working mothers is poorly developed. These are fertile conditions for the genera-tion of consumer anxieties about food, where parents' relative powerlessness and the lack of reliable information are classic conditions for the development of anxiety as well as being defining features of the 'risk society' (Beck 1992, Wallace 1998, Nelson 2010). In the risk society thesis, individuals face invisible risks such as air pollution, radiological hazards and food contamination which cannot be eradicated and may even be exacerbated by scientific progress. High levels of uncertainty, ambiguity and conflicting information further undermine individuals' confidence in handling social and environmental risks, giving rise to growing anxieties.

The research reported in this chapter suggests that anxieties about food safety in China are entangled with a variety of other tensions: between parents and in-laws, between rural migrants and urban residents, between discourses of science and nature, between citizens and the state. While the scale of recent 'food scares' in China may be exceptional, there are many similarities with experiences in Europe and North America regarding ideas about 'scientific' child-rearing and threats to public health. One might, for example, point to recurrent debates about the merits of breastfeeding in various contexts or the politics of infant formula consumption in the developing world (cf. Greenaway et al. 2002, Nestle 2002, Hausman 2003). In the aftermath of the 2008 adulteration issue, new mothers in urban China did not resort to breastfeeding their children which might have been seen as a 'rational' choice, informed by both medical science and food safety concerns. Instead, those who could afford it managed their anxieties by purchasing more expensive foreign brands of infant formula while others accessed trustworthy food from friends and family in rural areas, resort-ing to more frequent post-natal health checks for their babies (allaying nutritional anxieties through the paradigm of medical science). Many factors contribute to the widespread use of infant formula in China including employment insecurity, poor maternity leave provision and the promotion of infant formula as a premium source of nutritious food.

Understanding parental anxieties about food requires a better knowledge of the wider social ecology of information and advice available to young mothers (cf. Brembeck 2011). This chapter has shown how qualitative evidence (from interviews and focus groups) can contribute to this understanding, together with media and documentary research (including an analysis of television advertising and commercially sponsored health advice). The next chapter provides further analysis of the blurred lines between public health campaigns and televisual entertainment in the context of Western 'celebrity culture' providing another source of consumer anxiety about food.

Notes

1. This chapter is based on fieldwork and media research in Chengdu, conducted by my colleague Qian Gong, a research associate on the ERC-CONANX project. The chapter draws on two of our previously published papers (Gong & Jackson 2012, 2013).

2. One of the ironies of this story occurred in September 2013, when China's President, Xi Jinping, challenged New Zealand's Prime Minister, John Key, over New Zealand's food safety record. President Xi's remarks followed the recalling of milk products by the New Zealand dairy company Fonterra after a botulism scare. Fonterra accounts for around 90 per cent of China's milk powder imports and the company had been instrumental in drawing public attention to the melamine crisis in 2008. Now, President Xi seized the opportunity to urge New Zealand to take tough measures to ensure the safety and quality of its food exports. The President's remarks provoked a backlash on Chinese social media (as reported in *The Guardian*, 11 October 2013) with citizens expressing incredulity and indignation at the Chinese government's effrontery in criticizing another country's lapses in food safety when their own record was so poor.

3. According to the Labor Act (1994), women should receive three months maternity leave, plus an extra month's leave if they give birth after 24 years of age. However, Fang et al. (2005) found that 50 per cent of the factories they surveyed in Zhejiang had no protection for pregnant employees and that 38 per cent of women workers received no maternity leave, with a further 39 per cent receiving fewer than 56 days.

4. The video can be viewed at http://v.youku.com/v_show/id_XMTM1NjY5NzAw.html (accessed 30 October 2013).

5. In fact, many so-called professionals lack proper qualifications and expertise. In Qian Gong's fieldwork (reported below), many child health professionals were encountered who had made a career change from nursing or kindergarten teaching without gaining further qualifications.

6. Compare Grant (1998) and Apple (1987, 2006) on the rise of 'scientific motherhood' in the United States.

7. Chengdu was the site of previous work on infant-feeding practices (Guldan et al. 1995), providing a useful point of comparison with our work.

8. It is also worth noting how the one-child policy may have impacted on the childcare experiences of first-time mothers in China (cf. Hesketh et al. 2005). In practice, most women who had a child after 1979 were first-time mothers with limited personal experience to use in evaluating medical advice or the opinions of older generations.

9. These companies are in foreign ownership but the formula is produced in China. Dumex, for example, has its production plants in Shanghai. The mid-market price of most foreign formula is around ¥ 200 per 900 g, while the price of similar formula from domestic companies such as Mengniu is around ¥ 110. In an earlier study in Beijing, one couple spent around 18 per cent of their monthly income on imported formula (Gottschang 2000: 180).

10. Docosahexaenoic acid (DHA) is an Omega-3 fatty acid, thought to be important for infant brain development and to reduce the risk of heart disease.

11. The keyword '奶粉' (milk powder) was used to search the videos. In Chinese, infant formula is usually called '(baby) milk powder'. During the manual search, milk formula advertisements for adults (e.g. pregnant women and seniors) were excluded.

12. The distinction between foreign and domestic brands is, in any case, becoming more complicated as foreign companies franchise the production of infant formula in China to local (Chinese) companies.

13. The relative merits of 'raw' and heat-treated (pasteurised) milk are debated in many other places too (cf. Mincyte 2014).

14. A video clip of this advertisement can be viewed at: http://v.youku.com/v_show/id_ XODA4NTU0OTI=.html (accessed 31 October 2013).

15. Claims about the health benefits of DHA are a good case. While the European Parliament only cleared the way for infant formula companies to make health claims about Docosahexaenoic acid based on scientific evidence following an application submitted by Mead Johnson Nutritionals in April 2011, the function of DHA in facili-tating brain development was already a central feature in advertising infant formula products in China in 2010 when the fieldwork for this chapter was carried out. As discussed elsewhere (Gong & Jackson 2013), the scientific basis of the European Union's resolution is contested.

16. The video can be viewed at http://v.youku.com/v_show/id_XMjczOTA3NjQw.html (accessed 31 October 2013).

Chapter 7

Celebrity chefs and the circulation of food anxieties

In the wider social ecology of information sources that consumers use to negotiate the pleasures and anxieties of food, celebrity chefs have risen to increasing prominence in recent years. Such figures now play a significant role in the lives of many consumers, providing televisual entertainment, culinary advice and a shared resource for social interaction with friends and family. They also, it will be argued, play a crucial role in mediating consumer anxieties about food and related issues. By focusing on the active role of audiences in appropriating these media figures, incorporating them within their everyday social discourse, this chapter examines the role of celebrity chefs in the circulation of consumer anxieties about food-related issues, including many concerns that are only indirectly connected with food.

There is an increasing volume of research on the relationship between media celebrities and food, including several studies which address their social and cultural significance. This body of work includes studies of the role of celebrity chefs in promoting sustainable fishing (Silver & Hawkins 2014), the 'celebrification' of tourism and culinary taste (Stringfellow et al. 2013), the production of campaigning culinary documentaries (Bell et al. 2014), the consumption of cookbooks, kitchen utensils and other merchandise associated with celebrity chefs (Abbots 2015), the construction of 'stranger fetishism' in travelogue cooking shows (Leer & Kjaer 2015), the role of celebrity endorsement in ethical branding campaigns (Lewis & Huber 2015) and the promotion of dietary products and advice by media celebrities (Rousseau 2015). Much of this work focuses on the circulation of ideas and images involving celebrity chefs on television, in the print media, on the Internet and in various forms of social media. While the work features a range of celebrity figures, the most prominent of them has been the British TV chef and cookbook writer, Jamie Oliver.

This chapter examines the way Jamie Oliver has harnessed his celebrity status to enhance his professional career and to pursue a variety of morally charged political campaigns. The chapter traces the historical emergence of 'celebrity chefs' and attempts to assess their contemporary social and cultural significance. Gauging their influence on everyday life is problematic, but it is hard to underestimate the reach of celebrity chefs such as Jamie Oliver in terms of their ability to attract large television audiences in many countries and to produce cookbooks which reach a mass readership, providing pleasure to millions of viewers and readers, and serving as a conduit for the communication of shared culinary values.[1]

Besides their success as popular educators and entertainers, this chapter will argue that the commercial success of celebrity chefs such as Jamie Oliver can be read as a sign of consumer anxiety where audiences and readers are turning to these figures to provide the kind of culinary guidance and lifestyle advice that may previously have been available from family and friends (and other more immediate sources). Addressing this alleged deficit in consumer knowledge is how Jamie Oliver positions himself, pointing to a generation of people who he feels no longer have the skills or knowledge to prepare even the most basic meals for their families, a deficit which he associates with the current rise in childhood obesity and other food-related health and social problems. Problematizing these claims, the chapter explores the wider social and cultural significance of celebrity chefs such as Jamie Oliver, following the 'tracks and traces' of his influence in the mediation and circulation of consumer anxieties about food.

Celebrity culture

According to Chris Rojek (2001), 'celebrity' involves the attribution of glamour or notoriety to an individual within the public sphere from which they come to have an impact on public consciousness. Celebrity involves the cultivation and social recognition of personal style to the point where it attracts a mass audience, undermining notions of democratic equality and meritocracy. True to its Latin roots, celebrity can be brief, acknowledging what Rojek calls 'the fickle, temporary nature of the market in human sentiments' (2001: 9). But celebrity status can also have a wide and lasting impact which goes beyond the sphere in which it was originally acquired. Through their personal fame, acquired wealth and public prominence, celebrities such as Jamie Oliver have been able to use their professional expertise as chefs to extend their sphere of influence, launching successful cookbooks and popular television series which have, in turn, enabled them to undertake political campaigns and other projects for which they have been identified as powerful cultural intermediaries (Rojek 2001), public pedagogues (Rich 2011) or moral entrepreneurs (Hollows & Jones 2010).

As Rojek and others have argued, celebrity culture has come to permeate everyday life and ordinary social relationships, including the development of what have been called 'para-social' relationships between members of the public and media personalities who viewers may have never actually met but who assume a virtual presence in their lives (cf. Turner 2004, Collins 2009). For some critics, celebrity chefs can play a more sinister role, 'delivering' captive audiences to feed the insatiable appetites of advertising and other forms of commerce, fashioning them as consumers with a desire to buy, cook and eat what they see on TV or to engage in more vicarious forms of consumption as viewing audiences (cf. Adema 2000, Hansen 2008).

In tracing the mediation and circulation of ideas from TV series such as *Jamie's Ministry of Food* and its American spin-off *Jamie Oliver's Food Revolution* (originally broadcast in 2008 and 2010 respectively), this chapter seeks to go beyond a focus on media representation to try and grasp its wider social significance. In doing so, the chapter follows Roger Dickinson's (2013) argument about the way television and other mediated images serve as important cultural resources which audiences use to help them make sense of their everyday lives. Advocating a socially situated understanding of the media's contribution to food-related behaviour, Dickinson seeks to uncover 'the complex and changing interdependencies between the personal experiences of people in different social groups and contexts' and their subjective readings of media outputs (ibid.: 452). Methodologically, this moves away from the kind of content analysis or focus on media representations that form the core of conventional media studies towards a more active engagement with audiences including what Abercrombie and Longhurst (1998) describe as the process of 'audiencing'. This approach positions audiences not as the passive consumers of media broadcasting but as active agents in the process of interpretation and 'making sense' of the media they consume. This understanding of the process of audiencing, where the media provide resources for the performance of everyday life, takes the analysis beyond those who are direct consumers of particular media content (such as the actual viewers of specific TV programmes), extending the concept to those for whom the media in question have a wider cultural resonance. Many people, for example, have views about Jamie Oliver and the issues he addresses through his television shows, and his social significance extends well beyond those who have seen any particular programme.[2] It is this wider social and cultural process that is addressed in the current chapter, seeking to understand the role of celebrity chefs in the mediation and circulation of consumer anxieties about food. First, though, it is necessary to account for the rise of celebrity chefs in general.

The rise of the celebrity chef

The category of 'celebrity chef' is an imprecise one which includes some figures, such as Gordon Ramsay and Marco Pierre White, who worked as professional chefs before gaining public prominence through their media careers, as well as others, such as Julia Child and Nigella Lawson, who achieved their status as celebrity chefs via other routes. The category therefore includes a diverse array of individuals who are famous for cooking or talking about food using various kinds of media (Piper 2013b: 40). It is uncertain when cooks and cookery writers first came to be recognized as 'celebrity chefs' though the term has been applied to figures such as Marie-Antoine Carême who worked in Paris in the early nineteenth-century (Kelly 2005). The label might also be extended to food writers such as Elizabeth David, in the UK, or Julia Child, in the United States, both of whom developed a significant presence beyond the print media in which they established their reputation.

Elizabeth David's *A Book of Mediterranean Food* was originally published in 1950, 'when almost every essential ingredient of good cooking was either rationed or unobtainable' (Preface to the Penguin edition, 1955: xiii). As one of the first trade paperbacks, the book reached a wide audience, though for many readers its recipes were consumed more as a form of fantasy than as a practical guide to home cooking. In her own words, Elizabeth David argued that 'even if people could not very often make the dishes here described, it was stimulating to think about them; to escape from the deadly boredom of queuing and the frustration of buying the weekly rations; to read about real food cooked with wine and olive oil, eggs and butter and cream, and dishes richly flavoured with onions, garlic, herbs, and brightly coloured southern vegetables' (ibid.: xiii). Although she provided details of places in Soho and off Tottenham Court Road in London where such elusive ingredients as Greek cheese and Kalamata olives, stuffed vine leaves from Turkey or Spanish sausages might be purchased, the book's essential purpose was to address a perceived lack in contemporary English cooking: 'variety of flavour and colour and the warm, rich, stimulating smells of genuine food' (ibid.: xiv). Offering an antidote to the 'bleak conditions and acute food shortages of immediate post-war England', Elizabeth David was acutely aware that many of her ingredients were out of reach for most home cooks who were forced to rely on such unappetizing staples as packet soups, dried egg powder and evaporated milk. She records how:

> Avocado pears and southern vegetables weren't yet available in England.
> Aubergines, peppers, courgettes and fennel had hardly been heard of. Even

garlic was hard to come by. If you'd mentioned basil or tarragon you'd have been asked who they were. (Introduction to the 1988 edition: xvi)

The world that Elizabeth David (re)created for her readers emphasized the warmth and pleasures of the Mediterranean, accessible second-hand through the author's recipes and recollections of her personal life (having spent most of the war years overseas). Her influence on British cultural life extended well beyond the provision of specific recipes and cooking advice.

Meanwhile, in the United States, Julia Child emphasized the practical skills that were needed to 'master' the art of French cooking (Child & Beck 1961, 1970). Besides her books, Julia Child's work reached a nationwide audience through her popular TV series *The French Chef* which was broadcast in the 1960s, famously 'demystifying' the classic dishes associated with the socially and geographically remote world of gourmet food and *haute cuisine* (cf. Trubek 2000). Consistent with the argument of this chapter, however, it can be argued that Julia Child's success depended on the receptiveness of her audience as much as on her own personal charisma or the style and content of her work. For, as Signe Rousseau argues, 'the story of modern celebrity chefs tells us more about consumers and their relationships to food than it does about the celebrities themselves' (2012: x).

Rousseau describes how celebrity chefs celebrate their audience's food fantasies and fuel their food anxieties (ibid.: xiv), filling a void created by consumers' alleged lack of culinary skill and confidence. In support of this argument, Rousseau quotes John Leland's commentary on Julia Child in a 2001 article in the *New York Times*:

> Mrs. Child, who first went on television in 1962, is often credited with bringing gourmet French cooking to a macaroni-and-cheese America, but this is an oversimplification . . . In fact, the culinary revolution was already taking shape: Jacqueline Kennedy had a French chef in the White House, piquing middlebrow interest in Parisian cooking; postwar Americans were traveling to the Continent, tasting French food for themselves. What Mrs. Child brought were not so much French techniques as American bluster and self-confidence, a willingness to overlook one's own mistakes and forge ahead. (cited in Rousseau 2012: 36–37)

Rousseau goes on to argue that the reception of Julia Child's work in the 1960s was shaped by wider social conditions, providing an escape from the realities of a contentious political climate, including public divisions over the Vietnam War that threatened the very coherence of the nation (ibid.: 37). Similar arguments can be applied to the popular reception of other celebrity chefs, including Jamie Oliver, whose work is discussed below.

Cookery programmes on TV have moved on rapidly since the instructional format favoured by Julia Child, in the United States, or Marguerite Patten and Fanny Cradock in the UK, though the genre remains popular in the work of 'practical' cooks such as Delia Smith. Cookery-as-entertainment became more prominent in the 1980s through the work of flamboyant chefs and raconteurs such as Keith Floyd who combined cooking with travel and tourism in series such as *Far Flung Floyd*, broadcast in 1993. Floyd was also significant in revealing the technical artifice of modern media representation, talking on screen to the cameraman and asking him to move between shots of the chef and his cooking.

But what kind of public anxieties about food are celebrity chefs addressing in their work and what can be said about their influence on consumer attitudes and behaviour (cf. Caraher et al. 2000)? Here, it is all too easy to reduce 'influence' to 'reach' and to quote the impressive sales figures of celebrity cookbooks (where it should be noted that book sales do not equate to actual readership or practical use in the kitchen) or to see a surge in sales of particular ingredients advocated by a particular celebrity chef as evidence of their wider influence as well as an immediate media 'effect'. While it is notoriously hard to establish direct or indirect measures of the 'influence' of television and other media, it is equally difficult to identify the specific personal or social anxieties that their work evokes, whether cast in terms of a general lack of confidence in culinary knowledge or skill, specific concerns about personal health or wider issues such as childhood obesity, worries about how best to feed the family or general concerns about gender, class and place, as refracted through anxieties about food and cooking – all of which are addressed below.

In the case of Nigella Lawson, for example, one might infer that her work addresses a range of anxieties about changing gender roles and relations, where cooking is reclaimed as a legitimate source of pleasure and enjoyment, as opposed to the more mundane aspects of women's conventional domestic work which is often represented in terms of drudgery and routine (cf. De Vault 1991). In the Preface to *How to be a Domestic Goddess* (2000), for example, Nigella Lawson writes about how many women have become alienated from the domestic sphere and how she wants to 'claim back some of that space' (ibid.: vii). In what she describes as an ironic dream, she contrasts a life of domestic drudgery with the fondly imagined 'familial warmth of the kitchen'. Compared to the 'skin-of-the-teeth efficiency' of much modern cooking– 'all briskness and little pleasure' – she wants women to feel like a domestic goddess 'trailing nutmeggy fumes of baking pie in our languorous wake', 'wafting along in the warm, sweet-smelling air . . . winning adoring glances and endless approbation from anyone who has the good fortune to eat in her kitchen' (ibid.: vii). This passage is written with playful irony, of course, and alternative representations of domestic life are clearly possible where kitchens become a site of violent and abusive relationships or are experienced as crowded, oppressive or uncanny places (cf. Meah & Jackson 2013, Meah 2014a).[3] But, as the back-cover of How to be a Domestic Goddess puts it, this is a 'deliciously reassuring' vision that 'feeds our fantasies' and 'understands our anxieties'.

Nigella Lawson's work invites the reader/viewer to indulge in the fantasy of culinary and personal fulfilment as represented on the page or screen. As fantasy, in the words of one of her critics, Nigella Lawson's work 'responds to the contradictions of the present' (Hollows 2003a: 190) and it is these contradictions that provide a key to the social anxieties that her work addresses.[4] In the United States, playful sexuality is also a key aspect of the culinary performance of celebrity chef Rachael Ray – and both Nigella Lawson and Rachael Ray have posed for photo-shoots in men's lifestyle magazines such as GQ and FHM. But Rachael Ray is very differently positioned in class terms from Nigella Lawson, the former described as cute, down-to-earth and with a girl-next-door appeal unlike the latter's more remote, upper-class allure. Neither celebrity has had any formal culinary training, but unlike Nigella Lawson, Rachael Ray focuses on no-nonsense, quick and convenient '30-minute meals'.

Discussing the cultural significance of Nigella Lawson, Signe Rousseau (2012) connects the sexualized language of fetish and glamour, envy and desire, salaciousness and innuendo with a politics of distraction and escapism. But Rousseau's key contribution in the current context is to ask what does it say about us (as viewers) that we derive such apparent pleasure from temporarily inhabiting someone else's fantasy world (ibid.: 86)? Rousseau deploys this argument in searching for a more critical engagement with popular food media, consistent with her view that such media 'interfere' with the exercise of our critical faculties as consumers, denying our sense of ethical and political responsibility by placing our trust in the authority of media celebrities who may have no training or expertise in the field over which their influence is exercised.[5] While this may be too bleak and overstated a view, it is to the wider social and political influence of celebrity chefs that the chapter now turns.

Celebrity chefs and the politics of food

While celebrity chefs such as Nigella Lawson and Delia Smith both eschew any direct engagement with the politics of food, focusing respectively on the sensual and practical aspects of food and cooking, other food writers and television chefs have used their media celebrity for more directly political purposes. Of particular interest here are those who have turned their attention to public campaigns calling for changes to current agri-food systems. They include campaigns about intensive poultry production and improved animal welfare such as *Jamie's Fowl Dinners* (2008) and Hugh Fearnley-Whittingstall's *Chicken Run* (2008); campaigns intended to promote more sustainable fishing, such as the *Big Fish Fight* (2011) involving Gordon Ramsay, Jamie Oliver and Hugh Fearnley-Whittingstall; and, in the United States, Rachael Ray's *Yum-O!* charity which deployed her famous catch-phrase to launch a non-profit organization in 2006 which aimed to empower children and their families to develop healthier relationships with food, teaching them to cook and offering educational scholarships.

But the outstanding example of a cross-over from TV entertainer and celebrity chef to food campaigner and political activist is Jamie Oliver whose series *Jamie's School Dinners* aired in 2005. The TV series was part of a longer campaign, outlined in Jamie Oliver's Manifesto for School Dinners, which urged people 'to get back to a proper diet' and 'make better choices' about what they eat.[6] As Hollows and Jones argue in their analysis of Jamie Oliver's moral entrepreneurship, Jamie Oliver's work 'provided a focus for debates around the "condition of England" that were circulating within the media and political rhetoric'. His willingness to 'get off his arse', they argue, 'resonated with the notion that Britain was a society in need of healing, and that local and national government were structurally and ideologically incapable of remedying this rupture' (2012: 316–17).

In contrast to the perception of state inaction and public apathy, Jamie Oliver's approach was characteristically direct. He began by deploring the current quality of school meals, using the infamous Turkey Twizzler© to epitomise the kind of junk food that he deplored. He then worked with canteen staff to devise alternative menus and to persuade school children to eat healthier lunches, eventually going to Whitehall to lobby the UK government about the need for significant policy change and financial investment. The outcome was impressive in both political and media terms. While some children rejected Jamie Oliver's healthier alternatives, with a rise in the number of children bringing packed lunches to school, the campaign was generally regarded as a great success, with the UK government pledging £280m to improve the nutritional quality of school meals. In 2006, Jamie Oliver won two British Academy of Film and Television Arts (BAFTA) awards for most outstanding presenter and best factual TV series and he was voted Channel 4's most inspiring political figure (Rousseau 2012: 47–48).

The use of the possessive term 'Jamie's . . .' in many of his projects is significant, according to Simon Hattenstone, signalling that Jamie Oliver thinks of himself in the third person, as a product rather than as a person ('Never before has a boy wanted more', *The Guardian*, 24 September 2005). Johnston and Goodman (2015) also emphasize how some celebrity chefs are sufficiently well known that they can be referred to in first-name terms (as Jamie, Nigella, Heston etc.), becoming 'intimate strangers' according to Schinckel (2000).[7]

After a second series of *Jamie's School Dinners* was aired in 2007, Jamie Oliver returned to this theme in 2008, launching *Jamie's Ministry of Food*: a TV series, cookbook and political campaign which included the establishment of physical 'ministries of food' (cafes and culinary training centres) in numerous British town centres, including Rotherham in South Yorkshire which had been a key site in the filming of *Jamie's School Dinners*. In a backlash to the changes that Jamie Oliver helped introduce, one school in Rotherham (Rawmarsh Comprehensive) became the centre of media attention when a group of mothers, dubbed 'Sinner Ladies' by a tabloid newspaper (*The Sun*, 16 September 2006), tried to circumvent the reforms by providing alternative food for their children. The women were photographed taking orders for burgers, chips and other 'junk food' from their children to whom they then delivered the food through the school railings. The details of the case are disputed (Fox & Smith 2011) but it became a *cause célèbre* in public debates about 'healthy eating'. Jamie Oliver was associated with these events because one of the mothers involved at the school in Rawmarsh, Julie Critchlow, had previously worked on *Jamie's School Dinners* while employed as a 'dinner lady' at that school. In choosing a location for his *Ministry of Food* initiative, which set out to 'teach a town to cook', Rotherham therefore seemed an obvious choice.[8]

Jamie Oliver's argument in this new series was that the UK needed to return to the war-time values of self-sufficiency, culinary simplicity and thrift. He used the iconography of the original (1940s) Ministry of Food, including its no-nonsense approach to simple cooking with limited ingredients. More specifically, Jamie Oliver argued that a generation of people had forgotten how to cook even the simplest meals and that this alleged deficit of skills could be overcome by the simple process of 'passing it on' – teaching small groups of people a handful of recipes and getting them to pass the skill on to their families and friends.

While there is an increasing volume of research on celebrity chefs, relatively few studies have undertaken empirical work with consumers (readers, viewers, audiences . . .) on how they engage with them. Recent exceptions include Emma-Jayne Abbot's work on the 'intimacies of industry' which used online questionnaires, group discussions, photo elicitation and informal interviews with UK consumers to explore their mediated interactions with celebrity chefs (Abbots 2015) and Christine Barnes's work on celebrity chefs as 'talking labels' which includes evidence from an online survey and a review of social media comments about Jamie Oliver's series *Save with Jamie,* broadcast in summer 2013, which sought to teach viewers 'how to cook tasty, nutritious meals on a budget' (Barnes 2014). The rest of this chapter explores audience engagements with *Jamie's Ministry of Food*, drawing on Nick Piper's PhD research, conducted as part of our European Research Council–funded CONANX (*Consumer culture in an 'age of anxiety'*) programme, which charts the way ideas about the series circulated among viewing audiences and the wider public. Piper based his work in two contrasting places, Rotherham, a working-class town in South Yorkshire (where *Jamie's Ministry of Food* was set) and Tunbridge Wells in Kent, an archetypally middle-class town in the South of England.[9]

The circulation of food-related anxieties

As previously argued, 'audiencing' involves the active appropriation of meaning by consumers from various media sources. Ideas and images are selected and reworked in different contexts and their meanings shift as they circulate within different social and spatial settings. In the context of their work on 'reality TV', Skeggs and Wood (2008) suggest that audience engagement is an 'extended social realm' whereby viewers identify with the apparent immediacy of the broadcast material to enhance notions of community and intimacy through the use of imaginary relationships with those whose lives they view on TV. Significantly, Skeggs's work includes an analysis of the role of specific formations of class and gender in television 'audiencing', leading viewers to engage in lively, sometimes highly moralized, commentaries on what has been viewed. Skeggs identifies different class positions in the 'audiencing' of reality TV whereby middle-class viewers employ a different cultural logic from working-class viewers when confronted with what might be regarded as 'shameful' viewing practices (such as the enjoyment of watching other people engage in 'disgusting' culinary practices) – ideas that are further developed below.

Jamie Oliver's own class and ethnic background is also relevant to how audiences position him socially in terms of his televisual presence.[10] Born in Essex, Jamie Oliver grew up in his father's pub and got his first job working at acclaimed chef Antonio Carluccio's restaurant in Covent Garden. Jamie Oliver was allegedly 'discovered' (in media terms) while a television crew was filming at London's River Café where he was subsequently employed. Shortly afterwards he was given his own TV series, *The Naked Chef* (first broadcast in 1999) which ran for several series. The title of the series refers to Jamie Oliver's ambition

of stripping food down to its bare essentials, rejecting the culinary preten-
sions of *haute cuisine*. These early shows, up to and including *Jamie's Great
Italian Escape* (2005), played on his 'cosmopolitanism' as well as on his 'Essex
boy' persona: riding around London on a Lambretta motor scooter and talking
fondly with his Italian mentor Gennaro Contaldo, while using trademark cockney
phrases such as 'pukka' and 'bish, bash, bosh' (cf. Bell & Hollows 2007). His
class position is now complicated by his considerable wealth, accumulated from
the sale of his popular cookbooks, the development of a series of successful
restaurants, and his commercial endorsements for the Sainsbury's supermarket
chain – a relationship which lasted for more than ten years.

Jamie's Ministry of Food is premised on a number of contemporary food
anxieties, with concerns about 'healthy eating' and childhood obesity providing the grounds for his proposed culinary intervention and the story-line for the
series. Through focus groups and interviews with consumers in Rotherham and
Tunbridge Wells, Nick Piper was able to show how the series provided a common
set of discursive resources for the expression of a range of opinions about food
and related concerns including stereotypical representations of class, gender
and place. So, for example, residents in Rotherham were clearly concerned
about the way their town was represented in *Jamie's Ministry of Food* raising
issues that go far beyond the series' ostensible focus on food. One focus group
participant (Martin from Rawmarsh) said he was embarrassed by the way the
town was depicted by Jamie Oliver because of the association of the area with
poverty and 'bad eating habits':

> That's probably why I was embarrassed, because I naturally associate bad
> eating habits and obesity levels of the kids and adults . . . with poverty and that
> embarrassed me, the fact that I would be associated with a poverty-stricken
> area.

While Martin was anxious that he might be associated (by other viewers) with a
'poverty-stricken area', he was clear that Rotherham should not be so compre-
hensively disparaged as 'there's good places and bad places in every town'.
Significantly, however, Martin did not credit other people with the same level of
understanding, seeing TV characterizations of places such as Rotherham as
dominating the national imagination. In particular, he was worried about how his
friends in London might see the show and jump to false conclusions, not just
about the place (Rotherham) but also about its residents and their perceived
deficiencies, including his own parenting skills and eating habits. While the TV
series, perhaps inevitably, focused on a few extreme cases, Martin and other
residents were adamant that 'we're not all like that', invoking comparison with

Skeggs's (1997) analysis of the way formations of class and gender involve processes of identification and dis-identification.

In another example, Sue (a 34-year-old charity worker from Rotherham) found herself denying her connection with the town while on holiday abroad, claiming to be from nearby Sheffield in order to avoid a perceived sense of 'guilt by association'. Asked if she was worried about how other people would see her, she acknowledged the media's need to distort and exaggerate in order to increase audience ratings, replying ambivalently:

> Yeah, but I'm in two minds . . . because I know why they did it, and I understand that they did it to get the ratings, you've got to be confrontational to get the ratings on TV nowadays . . . but I think for me I was a bit worried that everybody would think that 'Oh she's from Rotherham, she must be like them on TV', you know, 'she must be a bit dim' . . . I remember actually we went on holiday not long after [the series was broadcast] and er . . . I used to tell people I was from Sheffield which I've never done before. I don't know why, I just can't bear the thought of people thinking that about me.

Sue's sense of embarrassment was all the more pronounced as the interview took place in a coffee shop in Rotherham which she described as 'nice' and 'classy', underlining her uneasy sense of (dis)identification with the town and its perceived lack of culinary capital.[11] As this interview extract demonstrates, Sue was prepared to misrepresent where she came from in order to avoid the imagined sleight of being considered 'dim' through her association with the town. Whether other television viewers would actually have made this connection is beside the point: Sue's anxieties are premised on the fear that such connections might be made.[12]

Focus group participants rarely questioned Jamie Oliver's good intentions in trying to get people to eat more healthily. Apart from a minority of residents in Rotherham who campaigned against his presence in the town under the slogan 'Jamie Go Home', most people broadly accepted his positive intentions.[13] Asked his opinion, for example, Mark (a chef in his late thirties who worked with Jamie Oliver during the filming of *Jamie's Ministry of Food*) expressed his mild sense of discomfort:

> I don't know. It's a tricky one. I think overall his ethos for the whole thing about getting people eating and . . . cooking proper food is really good and I think his morals are proper and he is a really nice guy. He's definitely got everybody's best interests at heart. But, I don't know, it just came over on the telly a bit, a bit wrong I thought.

While such ambivalence was not uncommon, most focus group participants were prepared to give Jamie Oliver the benefit of the doubt, as signalled in the phrase 'at least he's doing something' (Hollows & Jones 2010). Other participants acknowledged that television shows may have to exaggerate to make their point. While they understood how these conventions worked, participants were less willing to trust other viewers to be equally reflexive or media-savvy, fearing that they might accept media stereotypes of Rotherham and its residents in an unquestioning manner.

The focus group discussions also demonstrate how food-related anxieties serve as a vehicle for a variety of other concerns, including anxieties about gender and class. In Tunbridge Wells, for example, some middle-class viewers appeared to enjoy the series as a form of voyeurism, allowing them to watch working-class families (and working-class mothers in particular) displaying what might be considered poor taste or a lack of good judgement.[14] In one iconic scene, Jamie Oliver visited a young woman (Natasha) in Rotherham and watched her children eating take-away kebabs on the kitchen floor.[15] The scene begins with a voice-over from the narrator saying that Natasha's family has 'just picked up their fourth takeaway of the week and it's only Tuesday'. Natasha lives on state benefits and although she has a high-end eight-burner cooking range she tells Jamie Oliver that she has never learnt to cook. She opens the fridge door and reveals a drawer full of sweets while her daughter tells the audience that her favourite drink is Dr Pepper. Natasha is worried that her daughter will end up 'being obesed' and all she wants is 'to learn how to cook and just be healthy'.

The scene was discussed by a focus group in Tunbridge Wells where one participant (Catherine) called it 'a bit freak-showy', wondering if that was part of its appeal for middle-class viewers such as herself.[16] Her friend Jess agreed, adding: 'because that's what we want to see and be shocked by'. Describing how Jamie Oliver is positioned within this scene, Catherine's friend Alec surmised: 'We all know what he's thinking, he's thinking you dirty bitch for feeding your kids takeaways . . . Yeah, you slag'.[17] Catherine went on, more reflexively, to wonder what the show implied in terms of the woman's education and lack of culinary skills, concluding that 'it's all about education though, isn't it'. While her friend Jess thought that the 'freak-show' element could be justified in terms of the social changes that the series might prompt, Catherine worried that working-class viewers would not see the show ('because nobody in that council estate is going to be watching Jamie Oliver'). The show's target audience, she felt, was '*middle class wankers like us*, sitting there going . . . that's shocking' (*emphasis added*).[18] The sexualized language of these extracts, with pejorative references to 'slags', 'bitches' and 'wankers', signals the operation of psychological processes of abjection, displacement and projection which are noteworthy in highlighting behaviour that participants find morally reprehensible while guiltily acknowledging their own voyeuristic pleasure. This parallels Probyn's (2000) analysis of public expressions of disgust which, she suggests, indicate both a drawing away from the object that is identified as disgusting while simultaneously drawing boundaries of community around those who share the same sense of disgust.[19]

These examples show how food-related anxieties are expressed by viewers of *Jamie's Ministry of Food*; how food anxieties are reworked in ways that are class- and place-specific; and how differently positioned audiences respond to such representations. Consistent with the theory of social anxiety outlined in Chapter 3, they also show how food-related anxieties circulate socially rather than functioning at a purely individual level. In these extracts and others like them, consumer anxieties about food blend into a range of other concerns about place, class and gender, often expressed in highly moralized language.[20] These examples also show how anxieties circulate in a complex fashion where residents in one place may be confident of their own ability to challenge regional stereotypes and to see through media contrivance, but do not trust viewers in other places to exhibit similar levels of reflexivity and media awareness. That their suspicions are well-founded is suggested by the way these programmes were viewed by middle-class viewers in Tunbridge Wells, where they provided a common resource for the expression of moral judgements, acting as a source of guilty pleasure, where participants could publicly express their disgust at watching other people transgressing the boundaries of good taste.

At one level, of course, viewers in Tunbridge Wells can be as critical as viewers in Rotherham, aware that TV shows such as *Jamie's Ministry of Food* are unlikely to provide a truly representative view of any town's residents. At another level, however, the series encourages viewers to suspend their disbelief and to enjoy the sense of shock that such scenes generate, taking pleasure in the experience of disgust and moral outrage, especially when such sentiments are shared with their peers.[21] In this sense, viewers' anxieties about food are readily displaced onto a wider set of anxieties about class, gender and place which circulate through their perceptions of how they may be seen by others who are credited with variable degrees of reflexivity in their viewing practices. As the conventions of reality TV demonstrate, shock and disgust are now well-established tactics for entertaining audiences (Andrejevic 2004, Hill 2005).

Other readings of the political and moral significance of *Jamie's Ministry of Food* are equally possible. Contemporary newspaper accounts suggest that the series prompted a range of reactions concerning the relationship between food and class in twenty-first-century Britain. Writing in *The Guardian* (1 October 2008), for example, Felicity Lawrence described *Jamie's Ministry of Food* as 'a powerful portrait of the socially excluded':

> Whether by intention or accident, the naked chef [Jamie Oliver] has entered the domestic life of a British town and captured a snapshot of the country's social health. The result is an indictment of the current political system as disturbing as any ideological tract. Food, and real people's experience of it, is still all about class.

But, as several critics have observed, such programmes also contribute to the de-contextualization and moralization of social inequalities, positioning individuals as uniquely responsible for their dietary choices and ignoring the wider social forces that shape their individualized decisions (cf. Fox & Smith 2011, Rich 2011). These are the more worrying repercussions of popular TV series such as *Jamie's School Dinners* and *Jamie's Ministry of Food*.

Conclusion

This chapter has focused on the cultural mediation and social circulation of consumer anxieties about food via an analysis of the public role of celebrity chefs. It shows how food-related anxieties circulate within society, reproducing the boundaries of class and gender and reinforcing place-based stereotypes. This is particularly clear with celebrity chefs such as Jamie Oliver who step outside their conventional media role as cooks and entertainers to engage more directly in the politics of food through public campaigns such as *Jamie's School Dinners* or projects such as *Jamie's Ministry of Food*. While such extensions of the role of celebrity chefs can be challenged (as an audience member of *Jamie Oliver's Food Revolution* did when she asked him why he felt qualified to advise professional nutritionists about public health issues), 'audiencing' more generally provides a source of entertainment rather than generating more sustained critique.[22]

The evidence presented in this chapter provides support for the argument that 'audiencing' is an active process where television viewers take their own meanings from media representations, making sense of it in their own ways rather than being 'duped' by what they see on TV. These meanings, which can be a source of pleasure or anxiety (or both), are then shared among their peers through a process of circulation that extends the boundaries of 'audiencing' well beyond the actual viewers of specific programmes (as discussed in Chapter 3 in terms of the social nature of consumer anxiety). The process of circulation can evoke a range of emotions from embarrassment to disgust (as elaborated more fully by Piper 2013a). Viewers also express ambivalence about what they see on TV, acknowledging its selectivity and exaggeration, aware of the contrivances that are used to promote audience ratings. But this level of media reflexivity does not prevent the circulation of damaging (class, gender and place-based) stereotypes where audiences indulge themselves in a sense of *schadenfreude*, revelling in the enjoyment of other people's misfortunes, openly expressing their disgust and sense of moral superiority at seeing others represented in a negative light. These expressions are sometimes qualified or subject to a degree of reflexivity (when such scenes are justified for their educational or political potential, for example). But it does not prevent them from having social consequences which may be damaging for those who are represented in this way.

It may be an exaggeration to see the success of celebrity chefs as a direct expression of contemporary anxieties about food and related issues. But the examples reported in this chapter suggest that celebrity chefs play an important role in everyday life, shedding light on contemporary consumers and their anxieties as much if not more than their work fulfils its ostensible purposes of education or entertainment. The influence of celebrity chefs can, of course, be overestimated. But it is in the mediation and circulation of contemporary anxieties, in the present context at least, that their cultural significance principally lies.

Notes

1. Jamie Oliver is reported to have sold over ten million cookbooks and to have earned over £100 million from book sales and related merchandizing (*Mail Online*, 8 September 2012). In 2010, one of his cookbooks, *Jamie's 30-Minute Meals*, became the fastest-selling non-fiction title of all time, selling 735,000 copies in ten weeks (*BBC News*, 9 December 2010).
2. This argument is based on the work that Nick Piper undertook as part of his PhD research on the 'audiencing' of Jamie Oliver, funded by the ERC-CONANX project and supervised by Matt Watson and me. The theoretical approach is further articulated in Piper (2013a) and in Jackson et al. (2013).
3. Nigella Lawson's own domestic life was revealed to have a darker side in June 2013 when her husband was accused of assaulting her outside a London restaurant ('Charles Saatchi cautioned for Nigella Lawson assault', BBC News, 19 June 2013). During the subsequent trial, she was accused of habitual drug abuse leading to a ban on her entering the United States (*The Guardian*, 20 December 2013).

4. Hollows (2003a) relates the irony and playfulness in Nigella Lawson's work to its 'post-feminist' politics.

5. Christine Barnes also questions the trust placed in celebrity chefs suggesting that they are simultaneously 'familiar, engaging and trusted' figures who are 'vulnerable to inconsistency and contradictions' (2014: 2).

6. The Manifesto can be read at http://www.jamieoliver.com/media/jo_sd_manifesto.pdf (accessed 30 July 2014).

7. Johnston and Goodman (2015) identify three further paradoxes in consumer relationships with food celebrities: authenticity and aspiration; accessibility and exclusivity; and responsibilization and empowerment.

8. A similar, though less elaborate, logic applied to the selection of Huntington, West Virginia as the initial location for the US spin-off series, *Jamie Oliver's Food Revolution*, chosen because of its high rates of obesity (Slocum et al. 2011). Each episode followed a similar pattern of initial hostility to Jamie Oliver's proposed interventions, gradually overcome by his naïve charm, cheeky personality and dogged persistence. Even when he was banned from filming in any school in the Los Angeles Unified School District, Jamie Oliver eventually succeeded in being invited to address the annual conference of the California School Nutrition Association.

9. The analysis in the remainder of this chapter draws on Piper's research including a co-authored paper with Matt Watson and me (Jackson et al. 2013).

10. The nature of Jamie Oliver's gender identity has been debated at length, his particular brand of 'domestic masculinity' embodying someone who embraces cooking as a leisure activity rather than as routine labour (Hollows 2003b).

11. The term 'culinary capital' is used as an extension of Bourdieu's (1984) classic work on cultural capital where he argues that judgements of taste function as markers of social class.

12. Indeed, Piper's research in Tunbridge Wells confirms that few residents outside Rotherham have strong memories of where the series was filmed.

13. Through the combination of his campaigning work and cooking programmes, Jamie Oliver has been referred to as a 'moral entrepreneur' (Hollows & Jones 2010), a 'lifestyle expert' (Lewis 2010) and a 'public pedagogue' (Rich 2011). See also Powell and Prasad (2010) on 'celebrity experts'.

14. Rousseau talks about 'authorised voyeurism' in relation to *Jamie's Ministry of Food*, where viewers are 'sanctioned by invitation' to observe other people's morally reprehensible domestic practices (2012: 53).

15. The scene can be viewed at: http://www.youtube.com/watch?v=x44WuD_qWsU (accessed 8 January 2014).

16. Compare Tyler and Bennett's (2010) analysis of the figure of the 'chav mum' whose morally transgressive behaviour provokes anxiety and disgust about female sexuality, reproduction, fertility and 'race mixing'.

17. Jamie Oliver has occasionally expressed exactly such sentiments. In *Jamie's Return to School Dinners*, filmed in 2006, he expostulates: 'I've spent two years being PC

[politically correct] about parents. It's kind of time to say if you're giving very young kids bottles and bottles of fizzy drink you're a fucking arsehole, you're a tosser. If you're giving them bags of shitty sweets at that very young age, you're an idiot' (quoted in Rich 2011: 16).

18. The self-deprecating reference to 'middle class wankers like us' also suggests a degree a moral discomfort and ambivalence concerning the participants' viewing practices, which could be described in terms of guilty pleasure.

19. See also Fox and Smith (2011) for an analysis of 'class disgust' in the context of *Jamie's Ministry of Food*.

20. The relationship between class and gender relations and social discourses of taste and value are pursued in more detail in Piper (2015) where he argues that media 'messages' are not simply transmitted but transformed and augmented in local contexts of consumption.

21. Compare Miller's (1997) analysis of the 'anatomy of disgust' that centres on such visceral reactions to food taboos as a means of establishing and policing social boundaries.

22. The audience criticisms arose in relation to the second season of *Jamie Oliver's Food Revolution* (reported in Rousseau 2012: 148). See Poppendieck (2011) for an extended account of the problems of school food in America and Slocum et al. (2011) for further criticisms of *Jamie Oliver's Food Revolution*. The problematic relationship between celebrity and science, where 'expertise' is conferred by popularity rather than knowledge, is further explored in Rousseau (2015).

Chapter 8

Consumer anxieties and domestic food practices

This chapter takes the analysis of consumer anxiety down to the household level and considers the anxieties that consumers experience in their own everyday domestic food practices (including shopping, cooking and eating). While previous chapters have considered the extent of reported anxieties about food, based on survey data, or used government reports to track the incidence and implications of particular events such as the European horsemeat incident or the infant formula scandal in China, this chapter is based on the observation of domestic food practices at the household level. It develops some of the ideas in the previous chapter about the social circulation of food-related anxieties within and beyond particular households and across several generations of the same families. These ideas are then picked up in the final empirical chapter that examines consumer anxieties about 'convenience' food and the generation of food waste.

The chapter is based on ethnographic fieldwork conducted by Angela Meah as part of our ERC-funded project on consumer culture in an 'age of anxiety'. The fieldwork was carried out in South Yorkshire and North Derbyshire and involved a multi-generational study of 17 households comprising a total of 23 participants across a wide age range (17–92).[1] The research included food-focused life history interviews, shopping 'go-alongs' (Kusenbach 2003), kitchen tours, photography and video recordings of meal preparation, and more informal conversation with household members. Seven focus groups were also conducted as part of the study in order to access more publicly expressed anxieties about food.[2]

One of the paradoxes of this ethnographic-style research was that it revealed much lower levels of anxiety than might have been expected from the survey data discussed in Chapter 2 where, it will be remembered, 79 per cent of respondents reported concerns about food safety. The ethnographic fieldwork, interviews and household observations found much less evidence of food-related anxiety than was reported in the survey data. In many cases, it can be hypothesized, the kind of anxieties that consumers reported in response to surveys such as those conducted by Eurobarometer have been 'negotiated into practice', in Watson and Meah's (2013) useful phrase. In other words, expressions of anxiety may be articulated in response to abstract questions about food-related issues but consumers' mundane domestic practices, observed 'on the ground', appear to be governed by a different logic where anxiety is less prevalent in everyday life than when consumers are called on to verbalize their feelings in response to direct questioning. This everyday logic by which consumer anxieties are negotiated into practice might involve technologies such as food labels, sensory judgements of taste, smell, touch or sight, or other 'rules of thumb' (Green et al. 2003), which enable consumers to cope with their potential worries about the safety and security of food to the point where few serious food-related anxieties were expressed in the course of the household research reported here. The remainder of this chapter seeks to establish the validity of this argument and to explore its significance in terms of more publicly expressed consumer anxieties about food.

Although the emphasis, here and throughout the book, is on consumer anxiety, the analysis begins by noting how food can serve as a source of both anxiety and pleasure. For example, one research participant (Ted Anderson, aged 66) notes: 'I have no worries with food . . . it's a very simple, every day, natural thing, food.' Expressing a preference for 'simple foods, uncomplicated cooking, great tastes', he enjoys spending time 'cooking and eating and having people round to join you'. Ted also notes that he found cooking to be a valuable form of therapy during the six years he suffered from ME (a form of chronic fatigue) when, he says, he had been 'perked up by cooking'. He comments, in particular, on the embodied process of chopping vegetables and kneading dough which he had found to be particularly therapeutic. Another research participant (Azam Habib, aged 35) reports similar feelings about food, having turned to cooking as a way of helping him through a period of severe depression following the break-up of his marriage. 'Cooking gives me good karma', he confirmed: 'It makes me feel better, especially when I'm eating [and] sharing with people.'

In other households, research participants had very different experiences of food. For example, Mary Green (aged 67) grew up in Ireland in a poor family with six other children and was sent into service as a young girl. Her childhood memories are of a family that was 'very, very poor financially, but very, very rich in every other way'. Her family had half an acre of land on which her father grew vegetables and her mother kept chickens. They also hunted and fished, had an orchard, and traded fruit and vegetables with their neighbours, only rarely buying food from the local shops. When she got married and went to live in Birmingham, Mary's experience of food and eating changed dramatically as she was subjected to domestic violence from her abusive husband who would 'just pick up the plate and chuck it . . . because he didn't fancy that at that particular time'. Family meal-times became a source of conflict and contestation, described by Mary as 'an ordeal'. Later, with her second husband Roy, meals became a source of pleasure once more, an opportunity not just to share food but to share yourself: 'You were sharing your lives round the table'.[3]

Food-related anxieties can often be located within a particular family dynamic. For example, Ted's daughter-in-law Polly spoke of her trepidation at meeting the Anderson family for the first time, feeling the need to 'hold her own' in relation to what she judged to be their more sophisticated culinary tastes. She recalls the moment when she was presented with a fish and bean stew, prompting the panic-stricken thought that 'I can't eat that!'. Her food-related anxieties were exacerbated while she was pregnant, taking on board dietary advice about the consumption of soft cheese, nuts and soft-boiled eggs. She took a similarly disciplined approach to childcare when her son William was born, following the highly structured routine-based Gina Ford method, reducing her level of maternal anxiety by imposing strict controls over her domestic environment. In this case, negotiating her own anxieties became a source of anxiety for others with Ted's wife Laura commenting on the stress of feeding their grandson who she describes as a 'fussy' toddler. When Laura and Ted are baby-sitting, they weigh up the 'easy option' of giving William what they know he will eat versus the pressure they feel from their daughter to feed him more nutritious or more adventurous food. In this case, food-related anxieties circulate among family members, with Ted and Laura occasionally feeling the need to lie to their daughter about what her son has eaten during the course of the day. It is this kind of subtlety that ethnographic research can reveal about the way food-related anxieties are negotiated within the practices of everyday life, the theoretical basis for which will now be outlined.

Ethnography and theories of practice

This chapter and the following one deploy a 'theories of practice' approach as summarized by Reckwitz (2002) and as applied to consumer research by Warde (2005). Theories of practice encompass a wide range of work, with diverse intellectual roots, the rationale for which is outlined by Schatzki et al. (2001). In everyday language, 'practice' refers to the repetitive doing of something in order to get better at it (Watson 2013: 157). But theories of practice go beyond the actions and motivations of individuals, focusing on their routinized and conventional character. Cooking practices, for example, are often habitual, accomplished with a minimum of conscious reflection, involving the coordination of ingredients, implements and appliances as well as less tangible things such as (socially acquired) skills, time and energy.[4] They may also involve coordination with the routines and rhythms of other household members and with the public and private infrastructure of food retailing and distribution, including the multiple technologies and institutions on which such everyday practices rely. Shopping, cooking and eating practices are also frequently organized in terms of fairly predictable repertoires, reproduced through socially and culturally embedded tastes and preferences. The exercise of 'consumer choice', much lauded in neoliberal rhetoric, is often highly constrained in practice, with de Certeau et al. suggesting that family meals and their associated practices frequently follow 'a pre-existing canonical order' (1998: 85).

Theories of practice also attend to the importance of tacit and embodied knowledge as well as to the more formal rules and regulations that govern consumers' experience of food. Learning to cook, for example, often involves a process of trial and error, using practices that have been handed on informally within families. Cooking is a practical accomplishment or competence involving a balance of routine and improvisation as well as the kind of prescriptive knowledge and advice that is encoded in recipes and cookbooks. Indeed, it can be difficult to articulate what 'cooking' involves in practical terms and to identify the precise nature of the skills involved. For example, does opening and heating a can of soup qualify as 'cooking' or should the term be restricted to more elaborate practices, involving raw ingredients, cooked 'from scratch'? (cf. Short 2006).

For Theodore Schatzki, practices are at the very centre of the social world: the 'site of the social', providing a conceptual middle ground between individual action and social order (Schatzki 2002). In formal terms, Reckwitz defines practices as a form of routinized behaviour consisting of several interconnected elements including bodily and mental activities, things and their use, forms of know-how and understanding, states of emotion and motivational knowledge (2002: 249). Social practices endure in ways that transcend individual actions and, according to practice theorists, it is *practices* that should be the focus of social analysis rather than individual *practitioners* or their actions. From this perspective, people are the carriers of social practices and their individual subjectivities and intentions are secondary, with practices being the primary object of inquiry.

Putting these ideas to work in analysing the dynamics of social practice, Shove et al. (2012) examine the interplay of technologies, competencies and meanings which, in the context of food research, might encompass fridges and freezers, baking and roasting skills, and conventional ideas about what constitutes a 'family meal'. To be taken up in routine domestic use, practices must be technically feasible and culturally appropriate, based on learned behaviours that have become routinized and habitual. They must also 'make sense' in social and cultural terms, fitting in with pre-existing practices and conventions (cf. Halkier 2010).

How, then, might these ideas be applied to the analysis of consumers and their domestic practices? First, it might be suggested, research should be attuned to what Schatzki (1996: 89) describes as the 'doings and sayings' that comprise social practices, providing a rationale for ethnographic observation as well as researching people's reported behaviour and discursive practices. Many domestic practices are routinized and habitual, only rarely being subject to conscious reflection or public articulation. The direct observation of social practices through ethnographic research can, therefore, make a valuable addition to interview- or survey-based work, providing access to people's actions in context as well as to their reported behaviour.[5] This is important as there is often a telling discrepancy between people's reported behaviour and their observed practices. This is particularly important in the morally charged atmosphere surrounding cooking, eating and parenting practices where (as earlier chapters have shown) 'feeding the family' has become a highly politicized and contentious domain.

A practice-based approach focuses on the way individual actions are embedded within the routines and rhythms of everyday life, shaped by social convention and subject to a variety of institutional pressures. As such, domestic practices including those associated with food can rarely be understood in isolation from a range of other practices: context is critical to understanding social practices and their implications.

Having outlined the theoretical orientation of the chapter, it is now possible to focus on the empirical detail of the research. The rest of the chapter is structured in three sections showing how an ethnographic approach to the observation of social practice can be used to counter discourses of deficit and decline; to explore the nature of practical knowledge and embodied skill; and to address the competing logics and ethical trade-offs involved in everyday domestic practice. In each case, the evidence shows how a variety of consumer anxieties about food are negotiated into practice becoming routinized and manageable rather than requiring constant self-conscious reflection.

Countering discourses of deficit and decline

Ethnographic research on food-related domestic practices can be used to challenge the conventional wisdom of a decline in cooking skills among today's
consumers compared with earlier generations. It can also be used to question
those who take a 'deficit' approach to consumer knowledge and understanding, including assumptions about the lack of culinary or parenting skills among
contemporary families and households. Both views are widely held and give
rise to widespread public concern but neither view is readily supported by the
ethnographic data.

A discourse of decline is prevalent in the British news media where, for
example, the *Daily Mail* (22 February 2010) suggested that 'traditional cooking
skills are dying out' with modern mothers 'unable to make gravy, custard or
short-crust pastry'. The alleged decline of 'family meals', and Sunday lunch in
particular, has been a staple of popular commentary on contemporary family life
for over 30 years, as noted in Anne Murcott's pioneering studies in South Wales
(Murcott 1983a, 1983b, 2000).[6] One British newspaper, *The Independent on
Sunday*, ran a national campaign in 2006 to 'Save our Sunday lunch' with numerous contributors rallying behind the call. Chef and food writer Richard Corrigan
repeated the adage that 'families who eat together, stay together', describing
Sunday lunch as a 'sacred' institution (11 June 2006). Chef Christophe Novelli
deployed a similarly religious metaphor, saying it would be 'sacrilege' to lose this
great tradition (5 March 2006). Introducing the campaign, Jonathan Thompson
described Sunday lunch as a 'centuries-old tradition' that is now in rapid decline:
'As recently as a generation ago', he asserted, 'British families sat together for a
meal nearly every day, but today a quarter of us don't even have a dining table'.
He went on to paint a nostalgic picture of a stereotypical British mother, 'cheeks
flushed, carrying the rib of beef, leg of lamb, or joint of pork to the table as father
stands by, sharpening the carving knife' (5 March 2006).

In stark contrast to media representations of relentless decline, historical
and sociological data reveal a much more subtle picture of recent changes in
family eating patterns, especially when eating outside the home is taken into
account (cf. Warde & Martens 2000, Cheng et al. 2007), leading to the suggestion that the discourse of decline has run ahead of the available evidence.
Eating patterns in the UK have always varied by class and region, for example,
with Sunday lunch eaten together being more of an aspiration than a reality for
many families (cf. Murcott 1997). For many working-class families, throughout the nineteenth and early twentieth centuries, meal times had to be fitted in
around the demands of factory-based shift work and, for more affluent Victorian

and Edwardian families, parents would often eat separately from their children whose meals where provided by nannies or other domestic servants (Jackson et al. 2009).

A similar argument can be made about deficit discourses in relation to contemporary cooking and parenting practices. As Meah and Watson (2011) have argued, there is little sense in their research evidence of any simple distinction between an earlier generation of 'saints' in the kitchen compared to the current generation of 'slackers'. For example, Ted Anderson spoke candidly about his mother's limited culinary skills and about her low standards of domestic hygiene, describing his mother as a 'very sloppy' cook:

> She wasn't clean in the kitchen, she used to wipe the surface of the worktop with this cloth she used to be wiping the floor with . . . er, or you'd have bleach in your food or something . . . There was no real hygiene.

Ted went on to explain how his mother would drop food on the floor and then put it straight back in the pan. When asked to reflect on his mother's qualities as a cook, Ted replied that 'she didn't know how to cook': 'she wasn't a very conscientious or careful cook, and she wasn't very adventurous'. In Ted's view, 'she always over-cooked vegetables, as everyone did in those days really . . . She didn't have any er, any real feeling for many foods . . . I think she never, never had good vegetables, and indeed no-one did in those days.[7]

This extract is particularly telling in terms of the way Ted uses his personal experience to generalize about what he feels was a common experience for his own and his mother's generation. Ted's wife, Laura, also commented on her mother's narrow culinary repertoire and dislike of cooking:

> Mum didn't like cooking. She didn't like housework. Just like, it was all a duty and she . . . No, she never really enjoyed it. Erm, she did it dutifully . . . She wasn't sort of horrible about it. But, you know, it didn't feel like she was . . . You just knew that, um, that's not what she thought was the most important thing.

Like an increasing number of men of his generation, Ted clearly enjoys cooking for other people:

> Yeah, well it's nice to feed people. I think it's, erm, it's . . . I mean my mother would say . . . she was a bit more casual about it . . . but her intention was to give people a good feed and that's, I think that's a great goal in life . . . There's nothing better you can do for people than give them a nice meal . . . a decent meal every day. It's a great pleasure.

Significantly, too, Ted is referring here to routine cooking ('a decent meal every day') not to the preparation of occasional celebratory meals that are the focus of some men's involvement in cooking while the regular routine of domestic work involved in 'feeding the family' continues, in most cases, to be regarded as women's work (cf. Charles & Kerr 1988, De Vault 1991, Hollows 2003b).

Laura has less interest in cooking than Ted but she insists that her house is 'kept tidy', including the maintenance of clear boundaries regarding domestic hygiene. She maintains that she has few anxieties about germs, imposing strong hygiene standards in relation to the behaviour of their pet cat, expressing her concerns in terms of disgust rather than anxiety:

> 'Cause [the cat] sits on the dining table and it does go through my mind . . . and I always try and dry off the cloth, cause I, you know, it's like rescuing this slimy cloth from the bottom of the washing up bowl and wiping the table and I'm thinking, I don't know if I'm achieving much here really. Erm, it's more about kind of disgust really rather than anyone actually going to get ill. It's like not nice really. It doesn't feel clean and nice.[8]

Hygiene standards are frequently debated within households. In her case, Laura's daughter Polly insists on the use of an anti-bacterial spray whenever the cat has been sitting on the dining table. But this provokes fresh anxieties for Laura who is wary of spraying chemicals in places where family members eat.

Although it is unwise to base general inferences on single cases, the Andersons' experience runs counter to common understandings of the nature of intergenerational transmission, where domestic skills are conventionally thought to pass from parents (usually mothers) to children. In this case, Ted's interest in cooking was piqued while his wife was working away from home, when he was impressed by the 'simple way of cooking' of his Chinese lodgers, later developing his culinary skills by reading Mediterranean cookbooks (see Figure 8.1). Similarly, Ted's son Jonathan picked up his cooking skills and culinary interests while working at Eurocamp and later by watching television programmes such as *Ready Steady Cook*. Neither father nor son relied heavily on their mothers to teach them how to cook.

The Faulkner family provides another example that challenges the popular discourse of intergenerational decline. Kate Faulkner (aged 63) describes a childhood of culinary deprivation, even though her mother's professional training as a nurse meant that 'everything was scrubbed and clean' and that she was 'quite into hygiene . . . and disinfecting things'. Kate reports matter-of-factly on her mother's strong dislike of cooking: 'She hated cooking, she hated anything to do with food, she didn't really like food or eating.' Kate goes further, suggesting that her mother was neglectful regarding food and that, as children, she and her brother regularly went hungry (in stark opposition to the 'saintly' image of maternal care often projected onto earlier generations). School food was also

Figure 8.1 Ted Anderson's Mediterranean cookbook, © Angela Meah.

described as 'appalling'. Asked how she learnt to cook, Kate is adamant that her mother was 'a dreadful, lazy cook' who relied heavily on tins and packets and other convenience foods. Unlike the paragons of domestic virtue with whom contemporary mothers are often compared, 'she didn't believe in cooking things from scratch':

> Yeah, she would never read recipe books. She would never find out how to do anything . . . She'd just think she knew everything and she's 'Oh that's how you make a curry', I suppose.

Kate's opinion of her mother's shortcomings led her to pursue what she describes as a 'better way of living . . . a better way of bringing up children'. She had been taught to cook by her housekeeper while living in the Far East and aimed to treat her children very differently from the way she was brought up herself. In practice, however, Kate reports that her children became 'fussy eaters' and she was forced to make a series of compromises that made her feel guilty as a mother:

> I went through a phase where I just had to give them rubbish food because it was driving me mad. I was getting into such a state about it . . . feeling guilty

and so bad that they wouldn't eat, they weren't getting proper nutrition and, and one day I just thought, 'Oh I can't do this any longer, I'll just give them what they want [laughs]'.

There is evidence here of the kind of maternal anxieties that can arise over giving children 'rubbish food' as opposed to food that is considered properly nutritious. The moralized discourse of 'proper nutrition' versus 'rubbish food' tends to ignore the circumstances that Kate describes, where her good intentions were, for a time, thwarted by the demands of her 'fussy' children which she candidly describes as driving her mad. As will be discussed further in the Conclusion, campaigns that promote 'healthy eating' might pay more attention to the social conditions that shape such dietary 'choices' rather than reaching disparaging conclusions about an assumed 'deficit' of culinary or parenting skills. There are many other examples in these ethnographic data of what might be called 'good' reasons for 'bad' behaviour, where everyday practices fail to match up to the standards that food safety or health authorities recommend.[9]

While no claims can be made about the typicality of the Anderson and Faulkner families in terms of their representativeness of other British families, their experience can be used to challenge generalized claims about the intergenerational transmission of cooking skills which position an earlier generation as universally superior to the current generation whose alleged deficiencies can lead to their wholesale pathologization.[10] In Kate Faulkner's case, for example, there is no lack of concern for her children's health and Kate's inability to achieve her dietary aspirations for her children is clearly a cause of considerable anxiety. Kate's eldest daughter, Hannah (now 35 years old), does not recall the anxieties that she and her sister caused their mother. Instead, she talks vividly about the care her mother took in teaching her and her sister how to cook:

When I was a teenager my mum said that I needed to learn how to cook because I'd be living away from home . . . She would always tell me what she was doing and explain how to cook things. But then I think before I left home, maybe like the summer before I went to university . . . I remember her saying, 'Right, well you need to learn how to cook and you need to learn how to do these sorts of things and understand about, you know, how to defrost food and make sure that if you defrost it you don't freeze it again' . . . and all those sorts of things in quite a structured way.

Again, however, the pattern of intergenerational transmission is more complex than this interview extract suggests as Hannah's culinary education was temporarily interrupted when she got to university and was exposed to a range of different dietary experiences. Living with other students introduced her to eating practices that were quite alien to her previous experience, discovering, for example, that you could have crisps for breakfast. When she returned home after university, she reports that she 'really got into cooking' until she became aware that her husband and children didn't really appreciate her efforts. Becoming a mother also reduced the time she had to prepare leisurely meals and she began to make more compromises with her cooking. Later, as her children grew older, she started to enjoy cooking again, making different toppings with her daughters to put on shop-bought pizza dough. There is no simple progression here, then, from 'saint' to 'slacker' (Meah & Watson 2011) but rather a range of domestic practices that need to be explained in terms of their changing social context.

Practical knowledge and embodied skill

A common assumption in much of the food safety and public health literature is that members of the public are placing themselves at unnecessary risk because of a failure to follow official advice – a failure that is attributed to their assumed lack of knowledge and awareness of such guidance. Although now rather dated, a good example is the series of video-shorts that the UK FSA broadcast during Food Safety Week in 2009, one of which shows a fictional couple (Rita and Bob) engaging in risky food preparation behaviours including keeping refrigerated food at too high a temperature.[11] The tone of the video is patronizing and the logic highly simplistic, implying that reading a single leaflet or watching a short broadcast message will have a significant impact in reducing Listeriosis and other food-borne diseases.

The ethnographic research on which this chapter is based challenges these assumptions and its underlying logic, taking a more positive view of the practical knowledge and embodied skills of contemporary consumers while acknowledging that the gap between 'expert' knowledge and 'lay' understanding can provide fertile ground for the growth of consumer anxieties about food.[12] Many of our focus group participants and those engaged in the ethnographic work expressed their frustration at official guidelines on food safety and domestic hygiene, arguing that they went against their common-sense understanding of these issues. For example, Anne (aged 63) who cooked at a luncheon club for older people was exasperated by the food hygiene guidelines that were set out for her as part of a training course she was obliged to attend: 'You sit there and you think, ooh, you know, if they just let you [get on] with it, I mean, I've always been in cooking since I left school at fifteen and it's just getting, in my opinion, worse . . . I mean, to be honest, if you [just] use your common sense.' Other focus group participants relied on advice received from their parents and other sources close to home, regarding official guidelines and technologies such as expiry dates as just 'a starting reference point' (male house-share group). Among this group, decisions about whether or not to eat a particular food depended on participants' sensory judgements of smell, visual appearance and taste – the kind of embodied knowledge that one participant said 'you get from experience' (Steve, aged 30).

Although they were aware of current food safety guidance on issues such as reheating food, many research participants tended to disregard this kind of advice or used it selectively, trusting their own judgement and their experience of not having fallen ill despite engaging in practices that food safety authorities might regard as posing a high risk.[13] Stuart Charles (aged 41), for example, who used to work as a dairy manager, reports how he has reheated *boeuf bourgignon* many times in the past without becoming ill, though his wife will no longer allow him to do so. He whispered to the researcher: 'It's all a load of rubbish I think . . . Some people say you shouldn't heat meat more than twice – re-heat it – but I've done it three or four times [and] I'm still here. So has Sally [his wife], so have the kids.' A similar attitude was expressed by Andy (aged 24), a science teacher, regarding the risks attached to reheating rice about which he insisted: 'I've never suffered anything specifically bad from food poisoning. I've reheated rice, as I've said, enough times and I've never [been ill] . . . I'll keep doing that because it's never had any [adverse] effect.'

Food safety authorities might despair at such risky and apparently irrational behaviour but the internal logic that informs and rationalizes such behaviour with reference to people's prior experience should not be ignored. The kind of practices described above may increase people's exposure to food-borne pathogens but if their increased vulnerability does not result in specific harm this is likely to be factored into their subsequent judgements of food-related risk. The same argument applies to the way people rely on their physical senses when judging food risks, including microbiological hazards that are imperceptible to the senses.[14] For example, Mary Green reports that she likes to see the meat she's buying before she cooks it: 'I will only buy pork chops or steaks or lamb chops . . . I don't buy processed stuff that's in a pie . . . I like to see what's in there.' Most of our research participants thought carefully about food-borne risks and were far from cavalier or complacent in their approach. But they used various forms of reasoning and practical skills that do not conform with official food safety guidance. For example, one research participant, Azam Habib (aged 35), demonstrated high levels of culinary skill and domestic competence in preparing a chicken curry. Like his mother who had been observed on the previous day, however, he washed raw chicken under the tap and set it to drain in a colander in the kitchen sink while he prepared other ingredients. The FSA's current advice is not to wash chicken prior to cooking as this may lead to cross-contamination, while cooking unwashed chicken at the correct temperature will kill all relevant bacteria. Azam's reasons for washing chicken may not comply with current FSA guidance but it has its own logic:

> It comes from the shop, it's been in the fridge . . . because they handle it, for me that's an issue . . . it's all that transition, innit, bringing it from there, bringing it in the bag, getting it home. For me, you've always got to be more aware of meat as well.

In other cases, people's domestic hygiene practices are more complicated and their reported behaviour may be at odds with what was observed in participants' kitchens. Mary Green is a good example. Asked about her use of a particular chopping board, Mary explained: 'I'm very concerned about uncooked meats and chicken especially'. She talks about growing up in rural Ireland 60 years ago where 'there was no real hygiene as such' but where, she says, 'we didn't get ill so easily' which she attributes to 'our immune system and what we got used to as kids'. To manage her anxieties about uncooked meat and poultry, Mary has developed a set of practices including the use of a blue chopping board which she washes in hot water and sprays with Dettol (an anti-bacterial agent). She reports that whenever she handles meat or fish she sprays the sink and surrounding area 'to be sure', wiping it down with disposable paper towel. Observing her actual kitchen practices reveals that she does not always follow this approach in a consistent way. In one such observation, she washed a piece of fish under the tap, over the washing-up bowl, patted it dry with kitchen paper and placed it on a white chopping board which she had previously used to prepare vegetables (see Figure 8.2). After removing the skin from the fish, she wrapped it up in the packaging from the fishmonger and disposed of it. She then rinsed her hands under the tap and washed the sink down in hot soapy water. In practice, she did not follow the procedure previously described involving the use of anti-bacterial spray and disposable kitchen paper. Whether or not these practices pose a significant risk of food-borne illness from cross-contamination, they highlight a gap between reported and observed behaviour where people's actual practices differ from their stated intentions. Such instances also point to a gap between expert knowledge and lay understanding of microbiological and other food-related risks, the significance of which is amenable to further research using practice-based and related theories.[15]

Figure 8.2 Mary Green washing fish, © Angela Meah.

A final example of the gap between different kinds of knowledge concerns the way consumers approach expiry dates on food labels, with many being sceptical of the technical logic that underpins their calculation. There is ample evidence that consumers are confused by the proliferation of different kinds of expiry dates. In the UK for example, 'use by' dates are intended to provide food safety information, 'best before' dates are an indication of food quality and 'display until' labels are intended for in-store stock control. Food manufacturers and retailers have been reluctant to introduce a uniform scheme, deriving commercial advantage from the range of information that they currently provide (as discussed in more detail by Milne 2013b). While some research participants were happy to be guided by date labels, including Mary Green who said 'I tend to pretty well stick by use-by dates', others were critical of friends and family members whose reliance on labels they thought unreasonable. One member of a rural focus group (Marie, aged 42) clearly took this view, as expressed in the following reported conversation with her daughter:

My daughter [aged 11] is absolutely obsessed with sell-by dates . . . everything she eats I see her check it . . .

'Have you checked the sell-by date?'

'Yes.'

'Mum, you put some crisps in my lunch box today. They were out of date. I could have eaten some.'

Marie implies that her daughter's faith in labels is misplaced (her constant checking described as obsessive) and that date-labels should not be trusted so implicitly. Other focus group participants were even more outspoken, such as Bert (aged 85), who described food labels as 'a manufacturer's gimmick', while Carmen (aged 38) thought that date labels were a cynical ploy, 'preying on your insecurities' and designed to 'have you back in the shops' as soon as possible. Steve (aged 30) focused his reservations about date labels on the process of calculation:

> First of all, who decides? I refuse to believe that it's always exactly the same period of time from slaughter to being packaged when they presumably print the date on it. They might keep really close records of it, but I doubt it. Surely . . . different pieces of the same meat . . . from different animals, are gonna age at a different rate, and then there's all the factors of how it's stored, what temperature it's stored [at], how long it's left . . . you know, there's *so* many factors.

There is little evidence here of a deficit in consumer understanding, whatever reservations food safety authorities might have about the scientific basis of consumers' views.

Ethical tensions and trade-offs

There are many examples in our ethnographic evidence of where consumers are faced with competing ethical demands that cannot easily be resolved in abstract terms but which are routinely addressed in practice. This section considers the competing ethical claims that underpin consumers' routine practices and the trade-offs that they regularly make between such conflicting demands.[16] The discussion begins with some examples of trade-offs between ethical commitment, cost and convenience.

Some research participants expressed their inability to engage in what they defined as ethical consumption practices for reasons of cost. This could give rise to real anxieties, where matters of conscience had to be weighed against questions of affordability. According to one man in his mid-thirties, for example: 'It comes down to cost . . . your conscience is weighed up of, like, I can't afford that'. Another participant (Steve, aged 30) suggested more bluntly that: 'Morality is a privilege of the rich'. In another case, Sally (aged 40) spoke with conviction about her and her husband's support for the local butcher who reciprocated their loyalty by giving them a discount on their monthly shop. But a different logic prevailed when Sally's husband, Stuart (aged 42), spotted a bargain when on an accompanied shopping trip at a large nearby supermarket: 'Look at this!', he exclaimed enthusiastically, filling his trolley with reduced-price free-range chicken and rump steaks, the lower prices reflecting the fact that they were close to their use-by dates. The apparent inconsistency between supporting the local economy and buying bargain-priced supermarket food was rationalized by Stuart's suggestion that 'We spend far too much money on food'.

In other cases, ethical commitments were traded-off against time constraints or rationalized by reference to other family circumstances. John and Liz Elland represent a particularly good example of how these tensions are addressed in practice. John (aged 41) has a clear commitment to supporting his local shops:

> I think . . . you should support your local shops and your local community, because otherwise you're gonna end up with no choice, you know, you're just gonna end up where you've got five supermarkets to buy from and that's pretty much it, and that's kind of sad you know. We need . . . people running the local shop round the corner as well.

On the other hand, John's wife, Liz, resists her husband's principled commitment to supporting local independent shops, citing other more pressing demands on her time:

> I'm not going to work and then start fucking trawling all of the different, erm, the groceries, whatever. Whereas if I can go to Tesco, I'm sorry everybody, and . . . go and buy everything, then I do. I also use the butchers and we use the greengrocers as well, but if I'm doing a big food shop then I'm not going to trawl around . . . to get your shopping list . . . It's about convenience and cost.

The use of the phrase 'I'm sorry everybody' appeals to an imagined audience (including the researcher) and seeks their support for the practical resolution of Liz's moral dilemma. It could be described as an 'unapologetic apology' where a public expression of regret is followed by a rationalization which suggests that no apology is actually required. There are many such examples in our fieldwork where competing ethical principles are negotiated into practice and rationalized in similarly mundane ways.

The ethics of supporting local traders is not always clear-cut (as discussed by Blake et al. 2010). For example, Nazra Habib (aged 55) came across two Bangladeshi men selling fresh produce from the back of a van while she was doing her regular local shopping. Nazra did not know the men who were running the mobile shop and, on inquiring, found that most of their stock had been bought from wholesale markets in Birmingham and Bradford. She bought some goods from the van at prices that were much cheaper than at her local shop. But she continued to express her loyalty to local retailers despite the higher prices and narrower range of goods they offered (cf. Miller et al. 1998).

Other participants openly admitted the inconsistency of their practices. For Hannah Faulkner (aged 35) these inconsistencies revolved around the demands of part-time work and caring for her young children. Explaining how she some-times sacrifices her ethical principles for convenience, she admits:

> I'm really inconsistent. Yeah, I think Tesco is really bad, but I still shop with them because it's easy . . . Sometimes it's just what's quick and what's easy. Convenience comes above ethics at the moment . . . I buy organic meat, but sometimes I don't. When I have time and I think about it, but sometimes if I go to Tesco Express and they don't have it, and I need it, then I won't go somewhere else to buy it. I buy what they've got . . . I buy all sorts of things and because it's a big shop and sells everything, this means I don't have to go into town, get [her young daughter] out, find somewhere to park . . . and just the thought of taking the children out, taking the pushchair, getting the timing right and all that stuff.

The reality of such time constraints (needing something 'quick and easy') and family pressure ('all that stuff') became apparent in a subsequent shopping 'go-along' where Hannah had planned to have a leisurely trip to the supermarket, browsing the aisles and studying the packaging and product labels for informa-tion about quality and value. A very different experience occurred in practice when her young daughter became irritable and upset. Hannah has also made ethical compromises in other areas of her life. Prior to the birth of her children, she had been a vegetarian but now, as a busy working mother, felt that she no longer had time to prepare separate meals for herself and for her husband and children who were not vegetarian. As a compromise, Hannah had reintroduced chicken into her diet, provided it was organic. Acknowledging its high price, she preferred to use smaller quantities of higher quality meat, bulking it out with vegetables. She concluded: 'I would rather have better quality and feel nicer about that'.

In his ethnographic work in north London, Daniel Miller (2001) suggests that similar kinds of trade-off are typical of many households' routine practices. He uses this argument to explain how his informants commonly expressed a high-level of commitment to ethical consumption at the level of principle while engaging in much lower levels of such behaviour in practice. Rather than accus-ing his informants of hypocrisy or a lack of moral consistency, Miller suggests that more abstract ethical commitments to distant others, as may be implied in buying Fair Trade and similar goods, are traded-off against moral commitments to care for those closer to home. Miller suggests that the immediate needs of family and friends will generally prevail over a wider and more abstract sense of responsibility for 'distant strangers' (cf. Silk 1998). From this perspective, a commitment to ethical consumption at the level of public discourse is not inconsistent with the expression of moral commitments within the private sphere of the home. They operate at a different scale and involve different 'geographies of responsibility', a point which will be discussed in more detail in the Conclusion (Chapter 10).

Similar tensions and trade-offs were acknowledged by other participants, such as Dave (aged 35) who reflected on his desire to support Caribbean farmers while worrying about the possible environmental consequences of their agricultural practices. Thinking about which bananas to buy, he pondered whether to prioritize what he called 'saving the environment' or supporting Caribbean farmers:

> I can save these farmers in . . . you know, Puerto Rico or wherever . . . But they might have, yeah, they might have sort of pesticides, or I can do this organic stuff, so am I saving the environment or am I saving some little farmer who's looking after his family?

The ethnographic research shows how consumers are regularly faced with a range of competing messages that are often confusing and difficult to resolve in the abstract. For example, one group of focus group participants reflected on the trade-off between support for local farmers leading to reduced 'food miles' versus the lower carbon emissions of some imported foods, grown in direct sunlight:

Rob: I think the main problem is that there's so many contrasting messages. 'You should do this, you should do that, you should spend locally. . .'

Liz: You see that annoys me. I hate this 'you should do this, you should . . .', sorry.

Rob: People don't necessarily all know [about] the environment, and even if they do have the knowledge, do they trust it? . . . Where do they get it from, do they read it on the internet, or do they read it in a scientific journal?

John: What you've just said is exactly why people get confused. It's like . . . you're told that food has a big carbon footprint if it's shipped from the other side of the world. So you think, 'alright, I'll buy stuff that's grown locally', and then another report comes out that says 'Well actually, you know, some stuff isn't better locally, it's better if it's shipped from the other side of the world' and you're like, well, what's right?

These arguments can also be applied to the practical negotiation of other kinds of ethical commitments such as those involving animal welfare. In one focus group, for example, Bert (aged 85) felt that the public were aware of the conditions in which intensively reared chickens are kept but that they preferred not to acknowledge this in their desire for lower prices:

But we don't know where, today you don't know where your chickens have come [from]. You do really, but you prefer not to acknowledge it in a lot of cases. Because, you know, to provide chickens at the price they . . . charge today, there's got to be a kick-back somewhere along the line.

Some focus group participants acknowledged that chickens and other farm animals have a 'horrible, crap life' but questioned what effect any individual taking a stand might have: 'Everybody else is gonna buy it anyway so I might as well'. Some participants were troubled by their lack of ethical consistency. Chris (aged 28), for example, felt it was hypocritical to buy free-range eggs while having 'no qualms about buying really cheap chicken that's obviously had a really shit life'. In other cases, such compromises were freely admitted as consumers sought to balance competing commitments and reach practical solutions to their ethical dilemmas. For example, Anne Elland (aged 63), admitted that 'I make some compromises'. Buying Fair Trade tea on an accompanied shopping trip, she also purchased other goods without such accreditation when Fair Trade alternatives were available, while Gina (aged 27) preferred to pay more for better quality chicken while happily buying 'economy' eggs. Rob (aged 30) explained his apparently inconsistent behaviour in terms of the need to balance a range of competing commitments:

Yeah, I'll admit, I won't keep a secret. I will drive to the farm and buy a piece of award-winning meat, that's lovely born-and-bred, that, you know, is served in a Michelin-starred restaurant. At the same time, I'll buy economy stuff from Asda and I'll run to McDonald's and KFC 'cause it's all about balance for me.

These inconsistencies are not necessarily the result of bad faith or deliberate duplicity on behalf of careless consumers. They emerge in the give-and-take of everyday life where consumers negotiate their ethical dilemmas into practices that may not be ideal but with which they are able to get by.

Conclusion

This chapter began by suggesting that consumer surveys such as Eurobarometer, based on reported attitudes and behaviour, provide a different measure of public levels of food-related anxiety compared to those experienced by consumers on a day-to-day basis. The evidence presented here suggests that the difference may be explained in terms of the many subtle ways in which consumer anxieties are 'negotiated into practice'. While consumers express a variety of food-related anxieties over issues such as health and safety, cost and value, quality and taste, provenance and waste, animal welfare and environmental sustainability, these anxieties rarely reach the point that consumers feel overwhelmed and unable to act. The gap between reported concerns and observed behaviour is explicable ethnographically in terms of the variety of ways consumers 'manage' their anxieties through routine social practices, whether through the use of date labels and similar technologies or through reliance on their senses and embodied experience or through the adoption of various 'rules of thumb' and other coping strategies.

The ethnographic evidence also suggests that consumers engage in a variety of practices that might be considered irrational, inconsistent or even hypocritical when judged against the cool logic of economic rationality or more abstract ethical and moral principles. But, the evidence suggests, such practices often make good sense when viewed in the context of consumers' everyday lives, where complex ethical dilemmas are resolved or circumvented in routine ways, set alongside the demands of people's other ethical and practical commitments. This is the perspective that ethnographic research affords, with its characteristic reluctance to make moral judgements about the perceived deficiencies of other people's lives, their alleged 'deficit' of skills, the gaps between their attitudes, knowledge and behaviour, or their apparent ethical inconsistencies.

Drawing out the implications of her fieldwork for public health and food policy, Angela Meah (2014b) concludes that food safety authorities are right to base their advice on the best-available scientific evidence, accepting that they cannot ignore the risks that consumers take when they rely on their senses to make judgements about whether food is safe to eat. But nor, she continues, should such authorities ignore the competing logic that informs consumers' everyday practices, especially where this departs from scientific understanding. It can also be suggested that official advice on food safety and related issues might have more impact if it took greater account of consumers' practical knowledge and domestic routines, based on current levels of public understanding and common stocks of knowledge rather than assuming a 'deficit' approach to consumers' assumed lack of knowledge or culinary skills. There is growing evidence that this may be the direction in which current food safety policy in the UK is heading.[17] Starting from where consumers are, in practice, rather than where the authorities might want them to be, in principle, might provide a more effective basis on which to build future food safety advice and official guidance about 'healthy eating'. Such an approach might help avoid 'blaming the victim' for issues which are beyond their control. It might also allow interventions to be targeted more effectively at points where consumers are willing to change rather than assuming a general deficit in consumer understanding, knowledge and skills. These are all areas where theories of practice have the potential to contribute to current policy debates as will be further outlined in Chapter 10.

Notes

1. The research received ethical approval from the University of Sheffield, with participation based on the principle of informed consent. All research participants have been anonymized through the use of pseudonyms.
2. The focus groups included contributions from 37 participants and were made up as follows: a mixed pilot group; a group of young male house-sharers aged 23–30; a group of older people aged 63–89 living in a former mining village; a group of Indian and Somali women with school-age children; a group of low-income mothers aged 27–38; a group of married/cohabiting couples aged 29–41; and a group of people aged 39–79 living in rural Derbyshire.
3. Mary relates the touching story of how Roy had wooed her with food (a large sack of potatoes), saying: 'I brought these because I know you like potatoes, and can I stay for dinner?'
4. Mary Douglas (1971) provides a wonderful analysis of the defining character of social convention in her discussion of eating times and the structure of what is generally agreed to constitute a meal. Her categorical analysis of pollution taboos in *Purity and Danger* (Douglas 1966) is also germane to any discussion of consumer anxieties about food and hygiene, notably her suggestion that dirt is 'matter out of place'.
5. Lydia Martens (2012) provides a searching analysis of the epistemological basis of different kinds of research evidence concerning the 'doings and sayings' of everyday domestic practice. Her work is discussed in more detail in Chapter 10.
6. Frances Short (2006) provides a detailed account of recent debates about the alleged decline of cooking in the UK.
7. There is a similar passage at the beginning of Nigel Slater's autobiography, *Toast*, where he states that 'Mum was never much of a cook. Meals arrived on the table as much by happy accident as by domestic science. She was a chops-and-peas kind of cook, occasionally going so far as to make a rice pudding, exasperated by the highs and lows of a temperamental cream-and-black Aga [cooking range] and a finicky little son. She found it all a bit of an ordeal' (Slater 2003: 1–2).

8. Words such as 'clean', 'nice' and 'tidy' are all freighted with cultural convention and social expectations that need to be understood within specific formations of class and gender. For more on the place of pets in domestic kitchens, see the 'Kitchen Life' study, commissioned by the UK FSA (Wills et al. 2013).

9. I am indebted to Anne Murcott for this useful phrase ('good' reasons for 'bad' behaviour). See also the discussion of Tim Lobstein's work on the cost and calorific content of different kinds of food in Chapter 3 and David Evans's work on domestic food waste in Chapter 9.

10. The inferential logic of case study analysis is carefully outlined in a classic paper by Clyde Mitchell (1983).

11. The video (and others in the same campaign) can be viewed on YouTube: http://www.youtube.com/watch?v=UWlxtJQ2ODM (accessed 15 July 2014).

12. Some of the examples in this section are discussed in more detail in Meah (2014b) as part of an argument that seeks to avoid 'blaming the consumer' for contemporary food safety issues.

13. The ethnographic research reported here uncovered many examples of the selective uptake of health and safety advice. The Habib family, for example, were attempting to follow official advice about reducing their consumption of ghee (a common ingredient in South Asian cooking) but seemed quite happy to consume large amounts of salt and sugar, well above recommended dietary levels.

14. Scientists often distinguish between 'hazard' that refers to the source of potential harm and 'risk' that refers to the chance or probability that a person will be harmed by exposure to a specific hazard.

15. See, for example, Eivind Jacobsen's (2013) research on domestic food safety practices in Norway. On the basis of ethnographic observation, Jacobsen shows the very different way that food-borne pathogens are understood by microbiologists in the sterile environment of the laboratory and by consumers in their domestic kitchens. These ontological distinctions led Jacobsen to argue that scientists and experts understand kitchen life in very different ways from domestic practitioners.

16. This section draws on previously published work by Meah and Watson (2013).

17. See, for example, the conclusions of the UK FSA's 'Kitchen Life' study (Wills et al. 2013) and the Social Science Research Committee's advice paper on the public understanding of food-related risk and uncertainty (SSRC 2012).

Chapter 9

Rethinking 'convenience' and food waste

Building on the previous chapter which focused on consumer anxieties about food at the household level of everyday domestic practice, this final empirical chapter demonstrates the value of applying a similar approach to two further areas of consumer practice concerning the use of 'convenience' food (often regarded as among the least healthy and most unsustainable of dietary options) and the generation of household food waste. Using ethnographic evidence, the chapter argues that 'convenience' food is not a separate category, analytically distinct from other kinds of food. Rather, in the flow of everyday life, many consumers combine 'convenience' foods with other types of food, including those that are often regarded as their polar opposite: fresh foods, based on raw ingredients, cooked from scratch. Besides its intrinsic interest, understanding how and why convenience food has become so popular and widely used may facilitate the development of healthier and more sustainable alternatives. Similarly, in the second example, the chapter argues that an understanding of everyday domestic practice challenges the common assumption that food waste is a result of a profligate attitude to food among careless consumers. On the contrary, ethnographic evidence suggests that ordinary household practices and everyday domestic routines lead to food being wasted despite consumers' genuine desire to avoid wasting food.

The chapter demonstrates how the rise of convenience food can itself be interpreted as a response to consumer anxieties about 'feeding the family' (De Vault 1991), representing a quick and easy way of meeting the multiple and conflicting demands of modern family life via the use of commercially produced 'meal solutions'.[1] But the incorporation of convenience food within family life is not without its own anxieties as such food is frequently 'tinged with moral disapprobation' (Warde 1999: 518). The generation of food waste is also subject to moralized anxieties in a political-economic context of global food insecurity and a cultural context that values thrift. In contrast to these moralized discourses, ethnographic research suggests that food waste often results from conflicting pressures within households and as an unintended consequence of ordinary domestic routines rather than from a wasteful attitude to food, which is almost universally deplored. The chapter advocates a 'theories of practice' perspective, informed by ethnographic observation, rather than a deficit approach which contributes to a discourse of blame and recrimination.

Contesting 'convenience'

Convenience food is often regarded as among the least healthy of dietary options in terms of its nutritional value with high levels of salt, saturated fat and sugar. A recent paper in the *British Medical Journal* that tested the nutritional content of more than one hundred ready meals found that none of them fully met current WHO dietary guidelines (Howard et al. 2012). The widespread use of convenience food by contemporary households is also frequently considered to be environmentally unsustainable in terms of excess packaging, the use of energy-dense ingredients and large portion sizes, all of which contribute to high levels of food waste (DEFRA 2013). For these and other reasons (discussed in more detail below), the use of convenience food is subject to moral disapprobation, contrasted unfavourably with fresh foods, based on raw ingredients, cooked from scratch.[2] Rather than pursuing this normative agenda regarding what people should or should not eat, our current research asks how consumers incorporate ready-meals and other convenience foods as part of their diet, addressing Halkier's (2013: 126) 'open question' about how convenience food is used, appropriated and made sense of in everyday life.[3]

Before considering the ethnographic evidence, it is important to recognize that 'convenience' is a problematic term when applied to food, with multiple and contested meanings. Even within a specific domain such as food marketing and retail, 'convenience food' is a sprawling category encompassing processed foods, manufactured for mass consumption, including frozen, chilled and canned goods; confectionery, snacks and beverages; processed meat, pasta and cheese; take-away food and ready-meals. What, one might ask, do a can of soup, a packet of crisps and an oven-ready lasagne have in common that warrants their common description as 'convenience food'? Nor do convenience foods stand alone as a separate category in terms of everyday consumer practice where they are frequently combined with other kinds of food – as when consumers take a jar of pasta sauce and supplement it with additional ingredients before combining it with fresh or dried pasta or when extra toppings are added to a shop-bought pizza. Convenience food is, then, an example of what Andrew Sayer (1992: 138) calls a 'chaotic conception' which arbitrarily divides the indivisible and/or lumps together the unrelated and the inessential. As Sayer argues, such concepts are unproblematic in everyday usage and when used in scientific discourse *for descriptive purposes*, but they become problematic when explanatory weight is placed upon them.

In a previous project on food retailing, 'convenience' was one of the most frequently stated responses to a survey question about why consumers chose a particular store to do their regular grocery shopping (Jackson et al. 2006). Rather than accepting 'convenience' as an explanatory term, however, it became clear on closer inspection that respondents meant several different things in their use of the term. For some people, 'convenience' was about physical accessibility as in the phrase: 'This store is probably the most convenient one . . . because we live nearby.' For others, 'convenience' referred to the way shopping could be combined with other routine domestic activities, as in the phrase: 'I fit the shopping in, if it's convenient I fit it in with collecting my daughter from school.' In some cases, 'convenience' referred to a more complicated set of factors to do with the frequency of shopping, the range or quantity of goods, and the quality and freshness of food, as in the following phrases: 'Yes, basically it's the convenience and I just buy you know once a week'; 'I prefer to go to the butcher's . . . it's convenient because there you can have it fresh . . . you can buy the amount you want, not what's in the packet.' To use 'convenience' as an explanatory term in accounting for consumer behaviour fails to distinguish between these different uses. Alternative ways of understanding 'convenience' food are therefore required including those which adopt an ethnographic perspective (as will be illustrated shortly). First, though, a brief account of the rise of convenience food in the UK is provided, focusing on one particular category – supermarket ready-meals.

The rise of supermarket ready-meals

The advent of oven-ready meals, which consumers can take straight from the freezer or from the fridge and cook in a conventional or microwave oven, is often traced back to the invention of the TV dinner by American companies such as Swansons in the 1950s.[4] In Britain and much of the rest of Europe, chilled as opposed to frozen ready-meals now make up the biggest part of the sector, introduced in the late 1970s as a 'respectable' middle-class alternative to frozen TV dinners. There are numerous accounts of how firms such as Marks & Spencer introduced 'classic' microwave meals such as chicken kiev or chicken cordon bleu, designed to mimic the experience of restaurant eating at a fraction of the cost.[5] The growing popularity of these dishes can be related to increased female participation in the labour force, where many mothers no longer had the time to prepare conventional meals when they returned home from work. Market researchers have come to talk about providing 'meal solutions' for time-scarce consumers with busy lifestyles and hectic domestic schedules. Such foods also appeal to the increasing number of single-person households whose occupants are less concerned about 'feeding the family', including the growing number of elderly people living on their own. Indeed, it is the association of convenience food with eating alone that helps explain the negative valuation of the category. These social and economic changes were accompanied by technological developments such as the widespread availability of fridges, freezers and microwave ovens, the proliferation of processed foods, and the rise of car-based supermarket shopping.

It is the relationship between convenience food and the growing popularity of supermarket shopping that helps account for different levels of market penetration of ready-meals across Europe where the UK accounts for 42 per cent of European sales, France for 21 per cent and Germany for 20 per cent, with particularly high levels of consumption among men and among urban populations (MINTEL 2013). Chilled and frozen oven-ready meals are a well-established and popular component of the British diet, where 30 per cent of UK adults report eating ready-meals more than once a week, compared to 16 per cent in France. Most supermarket chains have numerous lines of American, British, Indian, Italian and Oriental dishes at numerous price points, with both branded and own-label options, and the UK ready-meals market is currently estimated to be worth £2.6 billion (MINTEL 2013).

Convenience food has a reputation for poor nutritional quality and wasteful packaging. Such foods are often high in salt, sugar and saturated fat. They tend to be highly processed with many artificial additives, often including a high proportion of imported ingredients (such as rice and spices). Other key ingredients like chicken and prawns may be imported from distant countries such as Brazil or Thailand. They are often also associated with excess packaging, yielding high levels of waste. Addressing these issues, the UK government's Green Food Project (DEFRA 2013) examined the potential for product reformulation, including more locally sourced ingredients with lower environmental impact and better nutritional value, less wasteful packaging and reduced portion sizes compared to conventional products such as chicken tikka masala. Food

manufacturers and retailers are also seizing opportunities for commercial innovation, introducing healthier or more sustainable options with lower calories,
reduced fat and salt, biodegradable packaging, multi-portion split packs and
re-sealable bags designed to reduce waste. These issues should all be understood within a context in which convenience food is highly moralized.

The moralization of convenience food

In their research on the eating practices of British and Australian students,
Marshall and Bell (2003: 62) conclude that 'convenience' and 'homemade' food
are part of a continuum, not two separate categories, with the former commonly
combined with the latter. Yet the two categories are frequently contrasted in popular food discourse, with one category (homemade) being culturally approved
and the other (convenience) being socially derided. The same authors suggest
that convenience and homemade food should be distinguished by *context* rather
than by *content* and that this is what leads to the moralization of convenience
food as a social rather than a purely culinary category.

In a survey of 249 Swedish mothers, Ahlgren et al. (2004) report negative
feelings being expressed towards those who make frequent use of ready meals,
while Bugge and Almås (2006) describe the way Norwegian mothers associate
the rise of convenience food with the disintegration of family life. Participants in
these and other studies refer to their sense of shame and guilt, 'confessing' to
taking shortcuts and 'cheating' by using prepared ingredients and other convenience foods, while market researchers report that more than 20 per cent of British
consumers feel guilty about serving and eating ready meals (MINTEL 2013).

Rather than treating convenience food and home-made food as separate
categories, Carrigan et al. (2006) describe how convenience food is incor-
porated into versions of home-made or 'proper' meals, allowing mothers to
use such foods without feeling the full weight of moral disapprobation than is
conventionally attached to an excessive reliance on convenience food. They
refer to a 'hierarchy of acceptability' and to the 'necessary concessions' that
enable mothers to take advantage of (some kinds of) convenience food without
compromising their sense of being a good mother. In related work, Carrigan
and Szmigin (2006: 1135) refer to the inventive manner in which the women in
their study make artful compromises, involving complex emotional negotiations,
warranting their description as 'mothers of invention' (ibid.: 1138).

Research also suggests that consumers (and mothers in particular) feel
the need to justify their use of convenience food. For example, some consumers argue that using convenience food reduces the time spent preparing and

cooking food and that, as a result, they can spend more 'quality time' with family members. The use of convenience food can also be justified by reducing food waste, as when a bag of pre-packed salad is opened, used and re-sealed for later use rather than buying a whole lettuce which perishes before it is completely consumed. The use of convenience food can enable children to fend for themselves when their parents are out, and it can help parents (usually mothers) cater for the diverse food tastes and preferences of different family members. In this sense, the use of convenience food can be seen as an expression of maternal love rather than as a sign of parental neglect. As Carrigan and Szmigin argue, 'It may be that a mother's use of convenience products is as eloquent a statement about her love and care for her family as that of the mother who does it from scratch. The use of convenience [food] may be a strategy for that mother to enhance rather than detract from her devotion to her family' (2006: 1127). Rather than speculating further on consumers' alleged motivations, the next section attempts to shed light on the use of convenience food through an ethnographic study of consumer practice.

Ethnographic perspectives

Ethnographic research explores how convenience food is 'embedded in the complex practices, processes and conditions of . . . everyday life' (Halkier 2013: 123). From such a perspective, 'convenience' is enacted through domestic routines and culinary conventions that are evaluated through notions of 'social suitability' and 'normative framing' (Halkier 2009) or in terms of its cultural 'appropriateness' (Prim et al. 2007). Halkier gives the example of a Danish mother who bought ready-made porridge for the family Christmas dessert (*ris à la mande*), provoking criticism from her daughter that 'she doesn't bother to make the porridge', noting that it 'doesn't taste good either' not having been 'stirred with love' (2009: 371). Participants in this study also talked about a lack of transparency regarding the ingredients in convenience food and the dearth of information about such food's provenance, seeking 'decent raw materials' without additives (ibid.: 371). So, too, for Norwegian mothers, 'To cook a proper dinner for one's family is an important part of a woman's understanding of her own identity and an implicit part of realizing the ideal family and the ideal home' (Bugge & Almås 2006: 210), the social recognition of these conventions being maintained through what the authors call 'mutual confirmations'.

These ideas can be further explored by reference to the ethnographic work that Angela Meah undertook with families in the north of England as part of the CONANX research project. The research included shopping 'go-alongs', kitchen visits and ethnographic observation of cooking, eating and cleaning practices as well as interviews and photographic research. In one extract from her field notes, Angela observes Ted Anderson, a retired academic and self-confessed 'foodie': 'It's 23 December and Ted, who is full of a cold, is preparing tapas for a Christmas Eve party, including little Spanish pasties.' Angela expresses surprise when Ted opens a packet of Jus-rol puff-pastry and Ted responds:

> Given my weakened state. . . one or two shortcuts, [shop-] bought pastry is very good . . . they're not even shortcuts really, they're sensible ways to [save time] . . . unless you can tell a major difference . . . you can get most ingredients from the shops.

In a shopping 'go-along', another research participant, Kate Faulkner (aged 63), talks about her purchase of certain kinds of convenience food which she describes as an acceptable alternative to the use of fresh ingredients, cooked from scratch. Kate moves over to the chilled food section and picks up a tub of humus with pesto. She says that her husband Frank likes this on his sandwiches. Angela asks why Kate doesn't make her own and she says that it's not something that she has ever made although 'I'm sure it's very easy'. Likewise she looks at the Co-op's own-brand chilled soups, stating that she will avoid any with cream because of her dairy allergy. In this case, the use of 'convenience' food enables Kate to meet her partner's culinary tastes and her own dietary needs and preferences.

During a later kitchen visit, Kate was observed scraping some raw ginger with a small knife. A discussion followed where she enthused about a range of frozen products such as lemongrass, jalapeños and lime leaves (bought from the high-end British supermarket Waitrose), small 'ice-cube' packs of basil, crushed ginger and tubes of herbs, which Kate says are as good as fresh. This example demonstrates that not all 'convenience' food is of poor quality or low nutritional value. It also shows how their use can be justified in terms of saving the labour involved in peeling and chopping, while also helping reduce waste by providing the right quantity of particular ingredients rather than larger quantities of fresh produce being left to rot in the bottom of the fridge. Kate also uses such ingredients as back-up for any unanticipated culinary 'emergencies'.

A third example is Hannah Faulkner (aged 35) who discusses the impact of having children on her cooking and eating practices including the many compromises that were involved in caring for a young family. During a kitchen visit, she says: 'Babies dominate your whole world'. Since having children she had started to use a rice cooker (inherited from her mother), allowing her to prepare perfectly cooked rice without having to watch over it. But this also meant that she and her family were now eating white rice rather than the healthier brown option that she used before. At the time of interview, she was relying on food that could be put straight into the oven or the microwave including dishes that did not need standing over while trying to breastfeed her baby or keeping an eye on a small child. She had started to batch-cook and freeze food, and to use frozen vegetables that did not require time to chop and prepare. Revisiting the household eight months later, when her elder daughter had started school and her younger daughter, now almost two, had grown more independent, Hannah felt less constrained and provided this reflection on her changing domestic circumstances:

> When you interviewed me before, I was like 'I just put things in the oven'. Because Beatrice is so much easier now, when they're about a year and they just totter around all the time, you just can't do anything.

Hannah was observed making calzone for tea, having bought ready-rolled pizza dough. She explained that she used to make her own but had recently switched to a shop-bought product to which you just add water, enjoying its ease and convenience.

In another case, Sarah Dexter (aged 87) had been brought up in a rural farmhouse which was quite isolated, served by a couple of travelling shops including a van that delivered paraffin, allowing them to cook without electricity. She also had a seriously disabled Down's syndrome child to look after. As Sarah said: 'It was very hard when the children were growing up. I couldn't do a lot of cooking then, because of him. He'd knock everything over . . . He needed a lot of attention.' This had implications for her cooking practices and, she felt, justified the use of a wide range of convenience products. As Sarah explained:

> Sometimes, if I was in a hurry, I would just open a tin of mince, because the travelling shop came round with loads of tins, there was no fridge or freezer or anything there [in rural Shropshire], so we did use a lot of tins. Tinned peas and stuff . . . so I'd open a tin of beans and mince or whatever, erm, and make a meal out of that, and I always had plenty of potatoes from the garden, we had greens, plenty of greens, always had cabbage. . . I'm trying to think what we got from the travelling shop . . . tins of Spam . . . that's really nice . . . and you could fry it as well . . . yeah, you've got to create shortcuts all the time . . . I used to make a lot of pilchard fishcakes.

This extract shows that convenience food has a long history and its use is not confined to urban areas. It also shows how foods such as tinned peas or Spam can be combined with raw ingredients such as potatoes and greens from the garden, and how the use of convenience food is rationalized as a necessary shortcut, designed to meet the needs of hard-pressed mothers with childcare responsibilities including, in this case, the additional pressure of coping with her disabled son.

Two more examples illustrate further rationalizations for the use of convenience food. Liz Elland (aged 37) buys ready-made quiches to put in the freezer, explaining that these are for her husband's use, when she 'can't be arsed to cook'. She explains that they are 'really light and tasty and if I feel like it I might stab it, put more egg in and put stuff on the top'. In this example, shop-bought products are customized with additional ingredients, providing an acceptable level of quality and taste. She continues:

> I'm not a chefy cook. I'm more of a Delia [Smith] cheat cook. I don't mind using the odd shop-bought [ingredient] . . . I don't do now, but I used to use shop-bought sauces . . . but since I've learnt about the amount of crap that goes into these sauces, the amount of salt and sugar [she no longer buys them].

During a kitchen visit, Liz went to a cupboard and found a jar of sauce, noting its high sugar content. She also talked about other forms of 'cheating' involving a packet of chilli sauce, which she says she always uses as it tastes like fresh chilli and can be combined easily with other ingredients. Her cooking practices, including these short-cuts and improvisations, are based on things she learned from her mother, a process which she recounts in the following extract:

> Erm, so I don't know where my mum's got that from, but she has passed it on to me. She was here on Sunday with my dad and you know I said, 'Oh I've just got this bit of stuffing that's old from, from last week and I'm, I'm just using this stuff' and she said, 'Do you know a real good way if you're just using packet stuff?' 'I said, yeah, add a bit of garlic, put some onion in it, put some bread crumbs in it' and I just talked it through with her and she laughed at me. I said, 'Of course I know that, you told me years ago', you know what I mean?

Recalling Carrigan and Szmigin's (2006) reference to 'mothers of invention', Liz concludes:

> She just taught me how to do things and how to pad out things and if you're gonna use a sauce then, always add to it, you know, never, never just have a sauce that's maybe from the supermarket shelves, that's proper cheating, but if you get a sauce and you look at the label, you think, oh I'll just add a few more of those ingredients and maybe a bay leaf and maybe a bit of something else, and you know, it pads it out and it makes it more your own then, so I do cheat-cook as well, quite often.

This example shows that the use of convenience food can be passed on from mother to daughter in the same way that more traditional cooking skills are subject to intergenerational transmission. It also shows how convenience foods can be used in conjunction with other kinds of food, to supplement them or pad them out, 'making them your own' rather than using them in an unadorned fashion which would be considered 'proper cheating'.

Finally, Nazra Habib (aged 55) describes how she takes advantage of convenience foods which save her time and make life easier, particularly as she has debilitating health problems. During a kitchen visit, she describes using a mortar and pestle to prepare spice mixes, as her grandmother used to do before there were electric blenders. But she has also embraced less traditional things like take-away chapattis, shop-bought naans and ready-made pastry mixes for samosas, which she justifies on the grounds of her poor health.

These examples all confirm that convenience food is not a separate category from other foods. Rather, the evidence shows how convenience foods are combined with other ingredients, customized in novel ways that make their use more socially acceptable as well as improving their perceived quality and taste. The ethnographic evidence also confirms that convenience and care are not dichotomous variables and that, in some circumstances at least, convenience food can be used to express care for loved ones.[6] It can lead to reduced food waste while catering to the diverse needs of family members, saving time that can then be diverted to more highly valued activities. The use of 'short-cuts' and 'cheating' are rationalized as a legitimate response to time pressures or health issues. But their use is almost always accompanied by an apology, designed to reduce guilt or deflect shame in what is still a highly moralized domain, especially for parents (and mothers in particular). Similar arguments can be applied to another area of domestic practice, the generation and disposal of household food waste, where ethnographic evidence can also be used to challenge conventional thinking and question received wisdom.

Food waste and the dynamics of household practice

The generation of domestic food waste is another highly moralized domain in which competing demands are negotiated into practice, where 'scientific' understanding runs up against the practical and embodied understanding of 'lay' experience, and where ethnographic evidence can help explain apparently irrational consumer behaviour. Current levels of food waste in Western societies have reached staggering levels and, at first glance, appear to defy any rational explanation, especially in the current climate of financial austerity. The Institute of Mechanical Engineers (IME) recently estimated that between 30 and 50 per cent of global food production is wasted (IME 2013), with a high proportion of food waste occurring at the household level. Using their own commercial data and industry-wide figures, Tesco recently reported that around 68 per cent of bagged salad is wasted, including around 35 per cent thrown away by consumers.[7] What explains such apparent profligacy?

One suggestion is that the generation of food waste is exacerbated by consumers' concerns about food safety. Consumers are being encouraged to reduce food waste by using leftover ingredients and reheating unused food from previous meals. Such practices are advocated by groups such as the Waste and Resources Action Programme (WRAP) in their 'Love Food, Hate Waste' campaigns.[8] But being thrifty with food can come into conflict with the perceived need to observe expiry dates in the interests of food safety, not using anything that has gone beyond its 'use-by' date. While confusion over expiry dates may be taken as a sign of ignorance, ethnographic research suggests that there may be good reasons for consumers' apparent reluctance to follow official guidance. As Ted Anderson confirmed:

> [People] don't understand what [date labels] mean . . . I say to people, 'Do you think this use-by date . . . today, it's not a problem? Is it a problem tomorrow? It will kill you, is that what you think? What do you think this use-by date is? It is the day that's set well ahead of some possible danger that it might have' . . . I generally ignore these dates, completely ignore them, and I look at them and, depending on how it looks and how it tastes, how it smells . . . it won't kill you if you have a taste, and if the taste isn't very good, you can throw it away.

While Ted's 'common sense' approach and reliance on his own sensory judge-ment has its own logic, it does not conform to official food safety guidance, as invisible pathogens and other microbiological hazards cannot be readily detected by the human eye or sense of smell. Ted asks who sets these dates and what calculation of future risks (and margin of error) they employ. Like many consum-ers, Ted uses experiential knowledge and 'rules of thumb' (Green et al. 2003) to reach his own assessment of whether or not food is safe to eat.[9] Besides its practicality, Ted's approach is rooted in an ethical judgement about the value of food as something that should not be wasted: 'This stuff's precious, it shouldn't be thrown away. It's been grown and nurtured and cooked.' His attitude derives from his childhood experience and that of his mother who grew up in the 1920s when food was in short supply. Meanwhile, Ted's son Jonathan admits that he has a completely different attitude to food waste from his parents. Admitting that 'there's not many things I would treat as worthy leftovers', he suggests that his parents would be happy to accept 'a few bits of cabbage in a bowl'. Although he says he feels guilty about wasting food, his expression is rather like the 'unapologetic apology' noted in Chapter 7:

> I mean, the one thing we're probably guilty of is . . . throwing stuff away because it is very obviously just, nothing to do with the date on the pack, it's fresh stuff that's . . . a bag of herbs that haven't got used that's black in the bag, and so it gets thrown away for that reason . . . I suppose . . . we end up umming and aahing about, things like half pots of crème fraiche, opened packs of ham where they're 'once opened eat inside three days' . . . Packs of cheap-arsed ham, and I'm usually more inclined to smell and look . . . sort of trust my senses a little bit. Things like cream I tend to be a bit funny if it's like been opened . . . it's not so much the date, it's the 'once opened consume within' . . . I'm a bit of a sucker for that.[10]

This interview extract is interesting in a number of ways. First, Jonathan expresses guilt for throwing food away and hesitates before taking such a decision ('umming and aahing'). Secondly, he distinguishes between different kinds of food in terms of his propensity to dispose of it on food-safety grounds (herbs, crème fraiche, packs of cheap ham etc.). He rejects date-labels as a legitimate reason for disposing of food, except for information about when food that has been opened might become unsafe which he takes more seriously, albeit somewhat reluctantly ('I'm a bit of a sucker for that'). In other cases, like his father, Jonathan claims to trust his senses including how food looks and smells.

Andy (aged 24) shares Jonathan's reluctance to waste food, saying: 'I don't like wasting food . . . it annoys me when I have to throw stuff away 'cause firstly, I've wasted my money on it, and second of all you've just, just . . . I don't know, I don't like wasting stuff.' Even though he finds it difficult to put his reasons into words, there is certainly no evidence of profligacy here. Several other participants spoke of their satisfaction in reusing leftovers to avoid wasting food. Carmen (aged 38) talked about 'make-do' dishes, like bubble and squeak, made from left-over cabbage and potatoes from previous meals, while Joe (aged 45) spoke of his regular Monday 'risotto nights', the precise contents of which depend on what is left over from the Sunday roast. Hannah Faulkner also talked at length about her determination not to waste food and of the compromises that she sometimes felt obliged to make:

> I compost food and I, and I try to look in the fridge to see what we've got and make meals around what we've got and use leftovers, but again because everything is so . . . there's so many compromises, when I'm trying to

compromise between doing something else for the kids, healthy food, whatever. Ideally, I would like to not waste any food but sometimes if it's, if it's
a choice between erm thinking 'Oh actually I haven't got time to cook that
particular vegetable that I've bought, I've ran out of time to do it', well actually
it'll just have to go to waste because something else is more important. So in
an ideal world I wouldn't waste anything but, I am aware that I probably waste
things because I'm trying to . . . because it's part of the compromise.

Again, there is little sign of profligacy here, even if compromises are made
which fall short of the commitments that might be followed through more
consistently 'in an ideal world'. In some cases, Hannah acknowledges, food
gets wasted because 'something else is more important'.

Similar conclusions are reached in David Evans's ethnographic work on the
generation of household food waste in Manchester which, he argues, results
from the intersection of time, tastes, conventions, family relations and domestic
divisions of labour (Evans 2012), also involving households' reliance on particular
technologies and infrastructures of provision as well as the material properties of
food itself. Rather than reflecting an uncaring or profligate attitude to food, Evans
shows how food waste is 'the fall out of everyday life' (Evans 2014: 50), whereby
ordinary domestic practices combine to configure food as surplus to household
requirements and subsequently as waste.[11]

Evans's work demonstrates a close relationship between perceptions
of freshness and waste, where food that is considered stale (and potentially
unsafe) is more readily disposed of than food that is considered fresh. Similarly,
the routines of regular food provisioning including the rhythms of weekly supermarket shopping may lead to unintended waste, whereby uneaten food that
remains in the fridge or store cupboard is liable to be displaced by new food
coming into the household. As the participants in Evans's study confirm, the
pursuit of novelty can also undermine the desire to avoid food waste ('pasta one
night, Thai the next, stir fries the next') and even the best intentions of batch-
cooking enough food for several days can be undermined when the results are
rejected as tasteless or dull.

Often, it is the disruption of domestic routine by unforeseen events that leads
to food being wasted. Evans (2014) provides multiple examples such as when
unexpected good weather encourages a family to eat outdoors or go to a local
pub rather than having the meal they had planned to eat at home; a spontaneous decision to eat out to celebrate a child's sporting success; or simply
working late or being delayed in traffic on the way home, causing a change
of plan in people's domestic routine. In other households, it is the need to

accommodate the dietary preferences of different family members that leads to unintended waste. But single-person households can face equal challenges in reducing waste. As one of Evans's participants said, 'when you're on your own, you end up buying too much and cooking too much' (2012: 50–51). So, too, where people travel away from home a lot, they may have no clear recollection of what food is in their fridge and end up buying more food ('something quick and easy from the local supermarket') or resorting to other convenient options (such as 'a cheeky takeaway').

These examples show how a range of everyday social practices and household circumstances can lead to food being wasted, despite consumers' genuine desire not to waste food (cf. Evans 2011).[12] A wide range of social and cultural factors combine with food's natural tendency to decay, resulting in what at first sight appears to be totally avoidable waste.[13] These factors include cultural constructions of freshness and novelty, the routinized nature of supermarket shopping, the desire to accommodate the dietary preferences of different household members, and the quantities in which food is typically sold. While many households try to minimize waste, including some who have resorted to batch-cooking and reusing leftovers, circumstances continue to conspire against them. Such is the power of social conventions and the complex infrastructures that support routine domestic practices that food waste can seem inescapable, even when consumers try hard to avoid or reduce it.

Conclusion

This chapter has shown how the ethnographic observation of everyday practice provides empirical data that can be used to challenge received ideas about consumer attitudes to food. Far from having a profligate attitude towards food waste, the ethnographic evidence cited here suggests that consumers have a genuine dislike of wasting food but that the way their daily practices are configured conspires to compromise or defeat their good intentions. The chapter also shows how waste, itself an object of consumer anxiety, can be a response to other pressures within ordinary domestic life such as the need to cater to the tastes and preferences of different family members or the desire to provide fresh or novel foods. A similar argument can be applied to the growing popularity of 'convenience' food which is itself a response to the anxieties and pressures of modern family life but which, in turn, gives rise to its own anxieties, in a morally charged context in which 'convenience' is often contrasted with 'care' (cf. Warde 1997).

These arguments have implications for public policy which currently focuses on changing consumer attitudes at an individual level on the assumption that changing attitudes will cause a direct change in behaviour. But if, as has been argued, individual behaviour is caught up in a web of routinized social practices, sustained by institutions and infrastructures that are beyond an individual or household's ability to control, then very different kinds of intervention, aimed at reshaping these embedded practices, will be needed in order to effect a significant reduction in food waste.

Similar conclusions apply in the case of 'convenience' food which critics regularly deplore on public health grounds or criticize for its environmental consequences. While some convenience foods may be of poor quality in dietary and nutritional terms, and while they may involve an unsustainable waste of resources through unnecessary packaging or excess portion size or lengthy supply chains, ethnographic research leads to different interpretations and potentially different kinds of intervention from those currently favoured by public health professionals and environmental groups such as WRAP. The very category of 'convenience food' as deployed in the marketing literature does not correspond well with the way consumers understand food in the practice of everyday life where so-called convenience goods are combined with other kinds of food, including those that are conventionally thought to be their culinary opposite (using raw ingredients, freshly cooked from scratch). Examining how consumers make sense of different kinds of food, how they are appropriated and used in practice, provides a radically different way of understanding people's food 'choices' and dietary decisions than approaches which rely on preconceived categories such as 'convenience food'. For example, when viewed ethnographically, via first-hand observation at the household level, 'convenience' and 'care' no longer appear to be dichotomous categories. In some circumstances at least, consumers can express caring relationships with other family members via the use of 'convenience' foods. That such foods are deeply moralized leads many consumers (particularly mothers) to adopt an apologetic tone concerning their use, feeling the need to explain and excuse themselves, expressing guilt at cutting corners and taking short-cuts. Indeed, many consumers seem anxious that such practices reflect badly on their sense of self and on how others perceive them through the enactment and social recognition of culturally approved notions of caring for the family.

Rather than pursuing a normative agenda, emphasizing what people should buy, how they should cook and what they ought to eat, resulting in the apportionment of blame at an individual level, this chapter has sought to outline an alternative ethnographic approach to the understanding of consumption as social practice. Understanding the institutionalized and socially embedded practices that lead consumers to use 'convenience' food or which contribute to the unintended generation of household waste leads to very different conclusions and to potentially different ways of framing policy responses. They would be less likely to address consumers as individuals, assuming that greater knowledge will lead to a direct change in attitudes which will in turn inform a change in behaviour, and be more likely to address the social organization of everyday domestic life and the way food consumption practices are caught up in wider practices of parenting and socializing, personal mobility and public transport, and all the other routines and rhythms of everyday life. These ideas are pursued in further detail in the concluding chapter.

Notes

1. Several food retailers describe convenience food in these terms, including the Walmart corporation: http://instoresnow.walmart.com/Meal-Solutions.aspx (accessed 7 November 2014).

2. The idea of cooking 'properly, with love, from scratch' was highlighted in *Jamie Oliver's Food Revolution*, a TV series which aired in the United States in 2010 and which is discussed above in Chapter 7. The series was criticized for its use of shaming tactics and the stigmatization of obesity, the invisibility of race, the neglect of structural inequalities, and the celebrity chef's recourse to a 'heroic' narrative, based on his individual charismatic leadership (Slocum et al. 2011).

3. This section draws on a new research project on 'Food, Convenience and Sustainability' (FOCAS), funded as part of an ERA-Net consortium on sustainable food (SUSFOOD) with colleagues in Bonn, Gothenburg and Roskilde (http://www.sheffield.ac.uk/focas). It also uses empirical material from the CONANX project, the fieldwork for which was conducted by Angela Meah.

4. On the 'domestication' of fridge, freezer and microwave technologies, see Cowan (1985), Shove and Southerton (2000), Watkins (2006) and Hand and Shove (2007).

5. See, for example, Usborne (2009), Salter (2010) and Winterman (2013). Several of these accounts suggest that, but for the persistence of Marks & Spencer's chief product developer, Cathy Chapman, chicken kiev might have gone to market without one of its key ingredients, garlic butter, for fear that it would not appeal to conservative British tastes.

6. Convenience and care comprise one of the 'culinary antinomies' in Alan Warde's study of *Consumption, Food and Taste* (1997). The others are novelty and tradition, health and indulgence, and economy and extravagance.

7. BBC News Online (21 October 2013): Tesco says almost 30,000 tonnes of food 'wasted', http://www.bbc.co.uk/news/uk-24603008 (accessed 4 February 2014).

8. For details of WRAP's campaign, see: http://www.lovefoodhatewaste.com (accessed 5 February 2014).
9. There are many other reasons for being cautious in the interpretation of food expiry dates. While their calculation may involve some margin for error concerning how food is manufactured and sold, they cannot take account of the range of practices that consumers employ beyond the point of purchase. There are, for example, wide variations in the way consumers take food home from the supermarket (including its temporary storage in car boots); whether it is stored in the approved fashion (refrigerated below 5°C); how frozen food is defrosted and cooked; and how leftovers are stored and reheated. For further examples of the diversity of domestic kitchen practices (including evidence on current refrigerator use) and their implications for food safety, see Wills et al. (2013).
10. At this point in the interview, Jonathan had just disposed of an armful of half-empty jars from the fridge, tossing them directly into the bin with little sense of guilt at his 'failure' to consume or recycle them.
11. See Evans (2014) for an extended discussion of how food 'crosses the line' to be marked out as surplus, before subsequently being routed for disposal as waste. Kevin Hetherington (2004) has also tracked this transition in domestic food waste, using the anthropological notion of first and second burial, where leftovers are first stored in the refrigerator or freezer, only later to be disposed of as waste. Nicky Gregson (2011) provides comparable evidence of the complex social practices that lead to the disposal of other (non-food) household goods.
12. Tristram Stuart (2009) examines a similar range of commercial practices in the production, distribution and retail sectors that combine to configure food as waste including routine overordering to avoid empty shelves and buyers' preference for uniformly shaped fruits and vegetables. For a wide-ranging review of current social science research on food waste, see Evans et al. (2013).
13. For more on the way the materiality of food contributes to its wastage, see the work of Emma Roe (2006) and Jane Bennett (2007).

Chapter 10

Conclusion: The routes of contemporary food anxieties

This book began by outlining a paradox concerning consumer attitudes to food in modern Western societies where high levels of public anxiety are reported despite a general agreement among official sources that food is as safe and affordable today for most consumers, most of the time, as at any previous time in human history.[1] While periodic 'food scares' undermine consumer confidence in the quality and safety of food, exposing the risks that are inherent to overextended and poorly regulated supply chains, the chances of getting ill through food-borne disease in contemporary Western societies are comparatively low.[2] Through a range of case studies, various explanations for this paradox have been sought, examining the gap between high levels of reported anxiety in consumer surveys (such as those discussed in Chapter 2) and the observational and ethnographic evidence discussed in later chapters which show much lower levels of food-related anxiety in terms of people's everyday experience and social practices.

One explanation of the paradox which is consistent with the theory of social anxiety outlined in Chapter 3 is that food-related anxieties, at the discursive level, are rendered manageable as they are 'negotiated into practice', allowing consumers to conduct their daily lives without constantly being subject to paralysing anxieties – an argument that is more fully developed in Chapters 8 and 9. The book has not sought to compare consumers' subjectively experienced or publicly expressed anxieties with any putative measure of the actual risks of contemporary food consumption. Rather, it has focused on the social consequences of consumers' expressed anxieties about food, whether or not they can be justified by any assessment of their actual exposure to food-related risks.

As the evidence reported in Chapter 2 confirms, food-related anxieties cover a wide range of concerns from fear of pesticide residues in plants and animals to concerns about the use of nanotechnology and genetically modified organisms in food and drink. They include concerns about avian influenza and BSE, worries about food security, famine and hunger, concerns about dietary health and well-being, animal welfare and environmental sustainability, and the cost, quality and freshness of food. While some of these anxieties may be incommensurable, they are frequently subject to trade-offs and compromises which are ethically complex at the level of principle but which are routinely addressed and resolved in consumers' everyday lives (as discussed in Chapter 8). Before pursuing these ideas further, tracing common themes across the chapters and drawing out the book's central argument, it is worth providing a summary of the argument of each chapter in turn.

Summarizing the argument

Building on the approach adopted in our earlier work (Jackson and the CONANX group 2013), Chapter 1 introduced the book's two key words, anxiety and appetite, exploring their ambiguities and ambivalences and historicizing the tendency to discuss the present-day as a uniquely anxious age. Chapter 2 provided a literal and metaphorical mapping of consumer anxieties about food, drawing on a variety of survey data. It questioned the reliability of reported attitudes in survey data as a guide to consumer behaviour in practice, raising epistemological issues about the nature and intensity of the anxieties that are charted in such surveys.

Chapter 3 elaborated the theoretical framing that informed the rest of the book, distinguishing between individual and social anxieties, following ideas originally outlined in Jackson and Everts (2010). The theory suggests that anxieties range in scale and scope from those that pose a mortal threat (being genuinely matters of life and death) to those that affect established ways of seeing the world, disrupting the familiar rhythms and routines of everyday life until such time as new ways of 'making sense' are firmly in place. Drawing on a 'theories of practice' approach, the chapter provides a framework for examining how anxieties wax and wane, focusing on the social experience of anxiety rather than approaching it at a purely individual level. As illustrated in Chapters 5 and 6, the theory provides a way of tracing the course of specific 'food scares' whether they are prompted by environmental concerns, health and safety issues or other food-related anxieties. The theory enables the identification of the forces that promote a particular anxiety and how it spreads and/or is contained over time and space. It encourages an analysis of how anxieties are mediated and how they circulate within society (as explored in Chapter 7). The theory also recognizes that anxiety can be creative or disabling and that it is a pervasive feature of modern life.

While the book has focused on food-related anxieties, it is also important to recall what Brillat-Savarin (1825/2009) calls 'the pleasures of the table', examining the positive and negative emotions that food inspires. Chapter 3 also recognized that consumers can be drawn into a condition of anxiety whether or not they are themselves subject to specific anxieties, as in the case of 'food scares' when particular foods are removed from public sale even though some consumers may still wish to purchase them. The theory suggests that food-related anxieties are articulated by different 'communities of practice' such as government and media, and that they tend to flourish in conditions of ambivalence and uncertainty (such as when 'lay' understandings are at variance with 'scientific' knowledge and official advice). Finally, the theory examines how food-related anxieties become moralized to varying degrees, as in debates about 'feeding the family' or advice about 'healthy eating'.

Chapter 4 sought to provide a historical context for the analysis of contemporary consumer anxieties about food, examining the intensification of agricultural production and related socio-technical innovations such as the development of the 'cold chain' which had profound implications for consumers (as illustrated in the case of the modern poultry industry). While fresh as opposed to frozen chicken became available to a mass market, consumers became more 'distanced' from sites of agricultural production, giving rise to increased anxieties about food including a growing squeamishness about touching raw meat and increasing concerns about food whose animal origins are too readily apparent.

Chapters 5 and 6 used the analytical framework outlined in Chapter 3 to examine two recent food 'incidents', one in the UK and more widely across Europe, the other in China. In each case, it was possible to identify a range of underlying forces and contributory factors as well as the specific role of particular individuals, motivated by criminal intent to engage in fraudulent activity, substituting horsemeat for beef, in one case, or adding melamine to milk, in the other. Chapter 5 examined the way the horsemeat 'incident' was framed within a crowded regulatory landscape where supply chains have extended in length and complexity to exceed the geographical boundaries and jurisdictions of individual nation-states. Chapter 6 explored the reaction of the public and the media to the 2008 infant formula scandal in China, showing how parenting practices were transformed by the incident and how food businesses sought to influence public opinion and restore consumer confidence through the mediation of science and nature in subsequent advertising campaigns.

Chapter 7 focused on the role of 'celebrity chefs' in shaping social attitudes to food, arguing that TV series such as *Jamie's Ministry of Food* exert an influence that goes far beyond the actual audiences of specific programmes, providing the public with a common resource of shared images and discourses on which to draw in discussing a wide range of food-related issues. Indeed, the chapter provided strong evidence of the argument in Chapter 3 about how consumer anxieties move between fields. What started as a concern about the causes of childhood obesity, for example, or about the quality of school meals, moved quickly to engage a range of other concerns about class and gender, regional stereotyping and the moralization of family life and domestic practice.

Chapters 8 and 9 examined a variety of consumer anxieties about food at the household level including the way consumers resolve the tensions between the conflicting practical and ethical demands that confront them on a daily basis, arguing that these complex issues are 'negotiated into practice' to the point where consumers are able to carry on their mundane activities without being constantly subject to existential dilemmas. These arguments were then applied to the reconceptualization of 'convenience' food and the generation of household food waste where ethnographic observation, informed by a 'theories of practice' approach, led to very different conclusions from conventional approaches that take a deficit approach, assuming that consumers lack the knowledge and skills required to make more 'informed choices'.

The rest of this Conclusion seeks to draw out some common themes from the analysis, reading across the individual chapters to crystallize the book's central arguments. These include the integration of political and moral economies of food, the challenges and potential of combining different theoretical and meth-odological approaches, and the disputed 'locus of responsibility' for different food-related issues, challenging the present overemphasis on individualized notions of 'consumer choice'.

Political and moral economies of food

Political and moral economies are often thought of in oppositional terms, the one concerned with narrow market considerations of profit and loss, the other with higher values that are considered to be beyond price (Jackson 2013: 139). E. P. Thompson's historical analysis of the operation of a moral economy in eighteenth-century England argued that food riots were justified as a way of resisting the imposition of a market economy which threatened to raise the price of bread beyond a level that could be afforded by the peasantry (Thompson 1971). Thompson traced the 'legitimizing notions' that underpinned popular food movements including notions of traditional rights and customary practice. It was these social norms and obligations, Thompson argued, that constituted the moral economy of the poor and which were articulated in opposition to the political-economy of the market (ibid.: 78–79). Similarly, James Scott's work on subaltern resistance in Southeast Asia uses the concept of moral economy to show how an established system of patron–client relationships was being undermined by the increasing power of the state and the operation of capitalist market forces (Scott 1976). While some authors would restrict the idea of a 'moral economy' to a particular period of industrial development or to particular parts of the world where a subsistence economy persists alongside a more capitalized market economy, others have applied the concept to a range of different economic and social formations from post-socialist Lithuania (Mincyte 2011) to contemporary Cuba (Wilson 2012).

The argument in Chapters 4, 5 and 6 suggests that moral and political economies are mutually constitutive though often acting in tension with one another. For example, the drive to meet increasing consumer demand for dairy products in China led to the adulteration of infant formula causing the 2008 scandal which threatened the commercial reputation of domestic suppliers and overseas companies such as Fonterra in New Zealand who were concerned about being tainted by their association with unscrupulous merchants and the unprincipled pursuit of financial profit. But it was the specific context of the crisis – putting children's lives at risk – that caused such moral outrage, generating widespread parental anxiety and leading the authorities to impose such draconian sentences on those found guilty of carrying out the adulteration.

The horsemeat incident in 2013 can be analysed in similar terms. Although it posed no serious threat to public health, its commercial consequences were significant for companies such as Tesco in terms of reputational damage and financial loss. Here, too, the fraudulent substitution of cheaper ingredients for more expensive ones was driven by market forces but the 'incident' raised significant moral and ethical questions about public trust, the transparency of supply chains, the accountability of food retailers and whether consumers could rely on the authenticity of food in terms of how it is labelled on the supermarket shelves.

As cases like this reveal, market economies depend on notions of reciprocity and regard among suppliers, retailers and consumers, involving notions of trust, responsibility and obligation all of which have moral implications. While these issues continue to influence the commercial operation of modern agri-food markets, ethical and moral questions are no less apparent at the household level in terms of the practical and ethical dilemmas facing contemporary consumers as reported in Chapter 8 (on domestic food practices) and in Chapter 9 (on the moralization of 'convenience food' and the generation of household food waste). Similarly, while some observers (such as Morgan et al. 2006) contrast the neoliberal logic of the market economy (associated with intensive farming and conventional food retail) with the morally-driven economy of 'alternative' food networks, the idea of a moral economy can be applied to both sectors. Indeed, the distinction between the two sectors can be quite blurred in practice. So, for example, Clare Hinrichs compares the economic logic of farmers' markets and community supported agriculture (CSA) in the United States, suggesting that farmers' markets encourage closer ties between food producers and consumers while remaining firmly rooted in commodity relations, while CSAs attempt to construct a new, ethically driven alternative to the marketplace with producers and consumers sharing the risks and rewards of each season's agricultural harvest (Hinrichs 2000). Like the 'conventionalization' of the US organic movement (Guthman 2004), however, many CSAs struggle to maintain their distinctiveness from conventional food-box schemes where consumers pay to have food delivered with no real connection to where and how it was produced. As Andrew Sayer has argued, economic activities are influenced by moral dispositions and norms, and those norms may, in turn, be compromised, overridden or reinforced by economic pressures. Markets depend on and influence moral and ethical sentiments, while social norms, moral conventions and other ethical considerations exert a powerful influence on economic behaviour (Sayer 2000).

The tensions between moral and political economies are a source of significant anxiety within the food industry where morally and ethically charged notions of purity and freshness and ideas about what is 'natural' are key criteria for contemporary consumers. These crucial attributes are now being produced on an industrial scale and through socio-technical innovations that are anything but natural.[3] As many of the foregoing examples suggest, it is the tension between morality and markets that creates some of the most profound anxieties for contemporary consumers.

Several of the preceding chapters have also demonstrated how political and media debate tends to run ahead of the available evidence, leading to a widespread moralization of food issues. This was the case, for example, in terms of media coverage of the alleged decline of family meals, the perceived deficit of cooking skills among the current generation of consumers, and popular attitudes to food waste among the examples discussed in Chapters 8 and 9. Several of these cases posit a kind of Golden Age in the not-so-distant past, where earlier generations were thought to have been more skilful, thrifty and caring than the present generation. These ideas can then be appropriated by moral campaigners and media celebrities (as discussed in Chapter 7) to press for social change and political reform, often on the basis of very slender evidence. It is therefore worth drawing together some reflections on the nature of the evidence used throughout the book and which underpins its central argument.

Theoretical and methodological reflections

At various points in the book, a 'theories of practice' approach has been advocated as a way of reframing current debates about food-related behaviour, emphasizing people's everyday 'doings and sayings' and acknowledging the routinized and conventional character of many areas of contemporary consumer practice.[4] But practice theory does not offer a blueprint for action in the way that is demanded by current 'behaviour change' advocates. The discussion in Chapters 8 and 9 suggests an alternative direction of travel, seeking to identify what might loosely be called 'good' reasons for consumers' apparently 'bad' behaviour. The emphasis in these chapters was on providing an ethnographic understanding of consumer practice, observed in its social context, rather than a normative understanding of 'consumer choice', studied in the abstract and based on an excessively individualized conception of human agency.

Methodologically, this involved a shift towards practice-based research as opposed to an overreliance on survey-based evidence of consumers' reported attitudes and behaviour. But the observation of consumer practice raises its own methodological challenges as Lydia Martens has argued in some detail (Martens 2012). Seeking to clarify the epistemological basis of different methods and different kinds of evidence, Martens dwells on the problematic status of language in researching everyday domestic practice. While practices may be rendered understandable through talk, she argues, the performative aspects of daily practices such as cooking or washing-up are less amenable to talk-based methods as these practices are only rarely subject to self-conscious verbal reflection by research participants (Martens 2012: 4.13). Other methods, such as the kind of video ethnography that Martens and Scott deployed in their work on everyday domestic practices, might be preferable for accessing such data.[5] Combining methods might add further depth and insight to the analysis, as when observational data, based on participant-generated videos, are combined with interview data, allowing participants to explain the significance they attach to certain practices and how they consider them to be meaningful. Such data are always subject to 'observer effects', of course, where participants' actions are shaped by the presence of the researcher or by their imagined presence and assumed agenda if they are not physically present. The use of ethnographic methods also points to the importance of not merely observing the *performance* of social life (such as the enactment of family routines and rituals) but also of attending to the (real or imagined) *audiences* of such displays. As Janet Finch (2007) argues, the social significance of such performative practices depends not just on their display but also on whether or not they are recognized as culturally appropriate.

Muir and Mason (2012) adopt a similar position in their work on participant-produced video as a way of recording the complex social rituals of a typical 'family Christmas'. Inviting their participants to video-record their family festivities, the authors argue that the resulting footage includes self-conscious displays of family life (performed for the camera, for the participants and for posterity) as well as largely unscripted interactions (sometimes noisily chaotic and with less sense of an intended audience). The videos range from images of elegant table settings, special food and 'best' clothes – including interactions that Muir and Mason describe as characterized by 'amiable formality' and an overall atmosphere of 'cultivated sophistication and style' (ibid.: 3.8) – to more informal displays of 'family banter, drinking, and a host of tactile engagements' (ibid.: 3.10). The authors do not pretend that their data provide unmediated access to what these family celebrations were 'really like'. Rather, Muir and Mason suggest, they draw attention to some of the knowledges and histories (including a range of sensory registers and embodied engagements) that are less readily accessible via other means of data collection. The authors also acknowledge that such methods may be socially intrusive and have the potential to compromise participants' anonymity.

A combination of survey-based data on reported attitudes and behaviour and ethnographic observation of consumer practice might therefore be the most appropriate way of understanding consumer anxieties about food. Such an approach is consistent with the theory of anxiety outlined in Chapter 3 which insisted that anxieties have an irreducibly social dimension rather than being confined to the emotional life of individual consumers. The book has also examined how social anxieties inform specific practices (such as the parenting practices outlined in Chapter 6) and how they circulate among media audiences (as outlined in Chapter 7). These chapters explore the psycho-social nature of food-related anxieties where notions of abjection, displacement and projection can be observed to occur within specific social formations of class, gender and place, rather than on a purely individual level.

In Chapter 7, for example, the sexualized language in which middle-class audiences in Tunbridge Wells expressed their enjoyment of viewing the 'disgusting' consumption practices of working-class mothers in Rotherham, sharing their guilty pleasures in conversation with similarly positioned neighbours, is just one instance of how such an approach might be taken forward. As Elspeth Probyn (2000: 131) argues, expressions of disgust are productive of community. Calling on others to witness our pulling away serves as a plea to establish common ground, while sharing a common sentiment about other people's food-related practices builds boundaries of social inclusion and exclusion.[6] A good example of this tendency is Catherine's reflections on working-class eating practices (in Chapter 7) where she describes her pleasure in watching Natasha's 'shameful' behaviour, feeding her children take-away kebabs on the kitchen floor during an episode of *Jamie's Ministry of Food*. In conversation with Catherine, another focus group participant refers to people like Natasha as 'slags' and 'dirty bitches', leading Catherine to suggest that the episode appealed to 'middle-class wankers *like us*'. These comments draw in an imagined audience who are assumed to be complicit in Catherine's guilty viewing pleasure, adding layers of interpretative complexity to the discursive analysis of social anxieties about food.

Probyn's analysis of 'anxious proximities', mentioned briefly in Chapter 4, offers another theoretical lens through which to draw together the argument of several chapters. Examining the sites of contemporary identity formation with a particular emphasis on sexuality, Probyn argues that it is 'the changing nature of relations of proximity that has become the central site of concern and intensity' (2001: 173). In particular, she suggests that a visceral reaction may accompany relations of proximity that have become 'too close' – as might, for example, be seen to occur in the case of consumer squeamishness about handling raw meat (in Chapter 4). Probyn suggests that people perform an implicit calculus concerning the distance and closeness between different social sites, producing a force field wherein different practices are ordered and classified. The adulteration of infant formula in China was a case where intimate relations between parents and babies were undermined by commercially 'distant' and morally unscrupulous traders. Attempting to repair the damage (as discussed in Chapter 6) led consumers to substitute foreign brands for distrusted domestic ones, also relying increasingly on family and friends rather than impersonal commercial sources. Here, too, one might argue, to

paraphrase Foucault (1986), that proximity breeds anxiety but also fuels reflection (Probyn 2001: 183).

Similarly, Chapter 8 shows how many consumers have come to rely on
'proximate' sources of information as a credible 'lay' alternative to official
advice that sometimes appears contradictory or inconsistent, or which seems
too remote from their everyday experience. So, too, might the horsemeat incident (in Chapter 5) be interpreted in terms of a failure of transparency where
food labels could no longer be relied on as a trustworthy guide to a product's
actual content. The argument about food waste (outlined in Chapter 9) could
be interpreted in a similar way where relations of intimacy and domestic routine
produce outcomes that are easy to criticize via a more distant and dispassion-
ate logic but which may make perfect sense when viewed from a perspective
that is 'closer to home'. Finally, Probyn refers to the moral challenges of 'caring
at a distance' (2001: 174) – an argument that is relevant to the ethical trade-offs
that consumers routinely make between meeting the needs of nearby family
members and responding to the demands of 'distant strangers' (as discussed
in Chapter 8).

The locus of responsibility

A final argument that runs throughout the book concerns what might be
called the 'locus of responsibility' for a range of contemporary food issues.
At several points in the narrative, criticisms have been raised about the notion
of 'consumer choice', arguing that it leads to a tendency to blame individuals
for their questionable dietary decisions rather than paying sufficient attention
to the institutional factors and systemic forces that constrain and shape those
choices. How, then, should the locus of responsibility for food-related issues be
identified in ways that avoid the inappropriate apportioning of blame? As argued
elsewhere (Jackson et al. 2009), Doreen Massey's analysis of the 'geographies
of responsibility' is helpful here. Consistent with her previous work on the interweaving of the 'local' and the 'global' (Massey 1991), Massey draws on the
work of feminist historians Moira Gatens and Genevieve Lloyd (1999) to make a
parallel with their argument about historical responsibility (Massey 2004). Just
as a sense of responsibility may be felt for previous events over which one has
had no direct influence, she argues, so may a sense of responsibility for other
places be exercised even where no direct connection is involved. Gatens and
Lloyd argue that the past inheres in the present and that 'we are responsible
for the past not because of what we as individuals have done, but because of

what we are' (1999: 81). So, too, Massey argues, are other times and places
implicated in our experience of the here and now, raising questions about our
ethical and political connections to sometimes distant places.

These ideas, which can readily be applied to contemporary agri-food systems,
parallel those of Iris Marion Young (2003) concerning the ethics of sweatshop
production where she distinguishes between notions of individualized *blame* (for
which legal accountability can be directly attributed) and collective notions of
political *responsibility* (where legal accountability and the potential for redress
are much harder to establish). While consumers are tied into a global market
system through their purchasing practices, Young argues, individual consumers
are not personally to blame for the low wages and poor conditions of sweatshop workers. Consumers do, however, share a sense of responsibility for the
collective outcome of their everyday purchases. In other words, people may be
responsible for injustice by virtue of their structural connection to it (however
indirectly and highly mediated that connection may be), even though they may
not be individually to blame for poor working conditions or exploitative wages
(ibid.: 40).

Earlier work on the moral economies of chicken and sugar production
(Jackson et al. 2009) shows how different actors in these agri-food systems
were keen to assert some connections to the sites and conditions of agricultural production while denying others. Connections tended to be emphasized
where commercial advantage could be established by so doing, while they
were rendered invisible in cases that might offend consumers' sensibilities.
Likewise, actors in these agri-food systems were subject to a process of selective amnesia, where some issues (such as the 'heroic' histories of the UK sugar
beet industry which kept people fed during war-time blockades) were carefully
remembered, while others (such as sugar cane's problematic links with the
history of slavery and Empire) were readily forgotten or systematically erased.

These arguments can be applied with equal force in the current context and
help explain the nature and intensity of contemporary food anxieties, where
consumers can feel that they are being held personally responsible for issues
that are beyond their control or where they are unable to identify the locus of
responsibility for issues about which they may have justifiable concerns. This
suggests that as well as tracing the historical 'roots' of contemporary food anxieties (as outlined in Chapter 1), it is equally important to understand the 'routes'
and interconnections through which consumers make sense of where their food
comes from and how it is produced.[7] While consumers may be only dimly aware
of the globalized nature of contemporary food production or the extent to which
power over its production is corporately controlled, anxieties may be provoked

by the chronic lack of transparency in such systems or, conversely, by its sudden revelation in incidents such as the 2008 Chinese infant formula scandal or the 2013 horsemeat crisis.

In policy terms (as discussed in Chapters 8 and 9) this approach would mean starting from where consumers are in terms of their existing 'stocks of knowledge' rather than where policymakers might wish them to be. It would place more emphasis on an assets-based approach rather than a deficit model of consumer understanding. It would acknowledge the gap that frequently exists between everyday 'lay' understanding and 'official' knowledge based on scientific evidence (a gap which is itself amendable to research). It would also avoid placing undue weight on the responsibility of individual consumers for the 'choices' that they make, putting more emphasis on the social forces that shape their dietary decisions. Methodologically, it would involve a creative blending of the insights that can be gained from the close observation of consumer practice in its social and historical context, with a critical analysis of reported behaviour from aggregate sources, paying due regard to the epistemological strengths and weaknesses of different kinds of evidence.

Turning the spotlight on contemporary consumer anxieties about food without ignoring the pleasures of eating and drinking, this book has sought to show how different kinds of evidence, viewed through a 'theories of practice' lens, can inform academic understanding of a range of food-related issues, also making a constructive contribution to current debates in food policy and practice. To paraphrase Kierkegaard, however, much remains to be done if we are to be 'educated by anxiety' rather than remaining enthralled by it.

Notes

1. Important caveats must again be made about high levels of inequality in accessing food in even the most affluent societies. There is, for example, disturbing evidence of increasing demand for emergency food relief in the UK and other Western economies. For a recent review of these issues, based on comparative analysis of 12 countries including the UK, United States and Canada, see Riches and Silvasti (2014).
2. For example, the UK FSA reports that around 20,000 people are admitted to hospital each year because of foodborne illnesses, contributing to around 500 deaths (FSA 2014). By comparison, UK road traffic accidents led to around 200,000 injuries in 2012, causing over 1,750 deaths (Department of Transport, 2012).
3. See, for example, Susanne Freidberg's discussion of the production of 'industrial freshness' across a range of agri-food sectors (Freidberg 2009).

4. For more discussion of practice-based alternatives to the current 'behaviour change' agenda (in the context of climate change mitigation and adaptation), see Shove (2010) and Southerton et al. (2011).
5. For details of the study, see their final report to the ESRC (Martens & Scott 2004).
6. William Miller (1997) points out how disgust is closely related to distaste, quoting Charles Darwin's assertion that 'The term "disgust" . . . means something offensive to the taste', noting that 'It is curious how readily this feeling is excited by anything unusual in the appearance, odour, or nature of our food' (1997: 1).
7. Among numerous precursors, the distinction between roots and routes was a central motif in James Clifford's (1997) work on travel and translation in the late twentieth century.

References

Abbots, E. J. (2015), 'The intimacies of industry: Consumer interactions with the "stuff" of celebrity chefs', *Food, Culture and Society*, 18: 223–43.

Abbots, E. J. and Coles, B. (2013), 'Horsemeat-gate: The discursive production of a neoliberal food scandal', *Food, Culture and Society*, 16: 535–50.

Abercrombie, N. and Longhurst, B. J. (1998), *Audiences: A Sociological Theory of Performance and Imagination*, London: Sage.

Adema, P. (2000), 'Vicarious consumption: Food, television and the ambiguity of modernity', *Journal of American and Comparative Cultures*, 23: 113–23.

Ahlgren, M. K., Gustafsson, I.-B. and Hall, G. (2004), 'Attitudes and beliefs directed towards ready-meal consumption', *Food Service Technology*, 4: 159–69.

Anderson, B. (1991), *Imagined Communities*, London: Verso.

Anderson, B. (2010), 'Preemption, precaution, preparedness: Anticipatory action and future geographies', *Progress in Human Geography*, 34: 777–98.

Andrejevic, M. (2004), *Reality TV: The Work of Being Watched*, Lanham, MD: Rowman & Littlefield.

Apple, R. D. (1987), *Mothers and Medicine: A Social History of Infant Feeding, 1890–1950*, Madison, WI: University of Wisconsin Press.

Apple, R. D. (2006), *Perfect Motherhood: Science and Childrearing in America*, New Brunswick, NJ: Rutgers University Press.

Atkins, P. (2013), 'Social history of the science of food analysis and the control of adulteration', in A. Murcott, W. Belasco and P. Jackson (eds), *The Handbook of Food Research*, London: Bloomsbury, 97–108.

Auden, W. H. (1947), *The Age of Anxiety: A Baroque Eclogue*, New York: Random House.

Bai, J., Wahl, T. I. and McCluskey, J. (2008), 'Fluid milk consumption in urban Qingdao, China', *Australian Journal of Agricultural and Resource Economics*, 52: 133–47.

Barnes, C. (2014), 'Mediating good food and moments of possibility with Jamie Oliver: Problematizing celebrity chefs as talking labels', *Geoforum*, in press.

Baron, C., Carson, D. and Bernard, M. (2014), *Appetites and Anxieties: Food, Film, and the Politics of Representation*, Detroit: Wayne State University Press.

Bauman, Z. (2006), *Liquid Fear*, Cambridge: Polity Press.

Beck, U. (1992), *Risk Society: Towards a New Modernity*, London: Sage.

Belasco, W. (2007), *Appetite for Change: How the Counterculture Took on the Food Industry* (2nd edition), Ithaca, NY: Cornell University Press.

Bell, D. and Hollows, J. (2007), 'Mobile homes', *Space and Culture*, 10: 22–39.

Bell, D., Hollows, J. and Jones, S. (2014), 'Campaigning culinary documentaries and the responsibilization of food crises', *Geoforum*, in press.

Bennett, J. (2007), 'Edible matter', *New Left Review*, 45 (May–June): 133–45.

Berik, G., Dong, X. Y. and Summerfield, G. (eds) (2007), *Gender, China and the World Trade Organization*, London: Routledge.

Berlant, L. (2007), 'Slow death (sovereignty, obesity, lateral agency)', *Critical Inquiry*, 33: 754–80.

Bevan, J. (2001), *The Rise and Fall of Marks & Spencer*, London: Profile Books.

Blake, M. K., Mellor, J. C. L. and Crane, L. (2010), 'Buying local food: Shopping practices, place, and consumption networks in defining food as "local"', *Annals of the Association of American Geographers*, 100: 409–26.

Blay-Palmer, A. (2008), *Food Fears: From Industrial to Sustainable Food Systems*, Aldershot: Ashgate.

Blythman, J. (2004), *Shopped: The Shocking Power of British Supermarkets*, London: Fourth Estate.

Bourdieu, P. (1984), *Distinction: A Social Critique of the Judgment of Taste*, trans. R. Nice, London: Routledge and Kegan Paul.

Bourke, J. (2003), 'Fear and anxiety: Writing about emotion in modern history', *History Workshop Journal*, 55: 111–33.

Bourke, J. (2005), *Fear: A Cultural History*, London: Virago.

Boyd, W. and Watts, M. (1997), 'Agro-industrial just-in-time: The chicken industry and post war American capitalism', in D. Goodman and M. Watts (eds), *Globalising Food*, London: Routledge, 192–225.

Brembeck, H. (2011), 'Preventing anxiety: A qualitative study of food and pregnancy', *Critical Public Health*, 21: 497–508.

Brennan, T. (2004), *The Transmission of Affect*, Ithaca, NY: Cornell University Press.

Brillat-Savarin, J. A. (1825/2009), *The Physiology of Taste: Or Meditations on Transcendental Gastronomy*, trans. M. F. K. Fisher, New York: Vintage Books.

Broom, D. M. and Reefmann, N. (2005), 'Chicken welfare as indicated by lesions on carcases in supermarkets', *British Poultry Science*, 46: 407–14.

Bugge, A. and Almås, R. (2006), 'Domestic dinner: Representation and practices of a proper meal among young suburban mothers', *Journal of Consumer Culture*, 6: 203–28.

Bunting, M. (2004), 'The age of anxiety', *The Guardian*, 25 October 2004.

Burnett, J. (1989), *Plenty and Want: A Social History of Diet in England from 1815 to the Present Day*, London: Routledge.

Burt, S. L., Mellahi, K., Jackson, T. P. and Sparks, L. (2002), 'Retail Internationalization and Retail Failure: Issues from the case of Marks & Spencer', *International Review of Retail, Distribution and Consumer Research*, 12: 191–219.

Buss, A. (1980), *Self Consciousness and Social Anxiety*, San Francisco, CA: W. H. Freeman & Co.

Cabinet Office (2008), *Food Matters: Towards a Strategy for the 21st Century*, London: Cabinet Office Strategy Unit.

Cai, H. and Wu, X. P. (2006), 'Social changes and occupational gender inequality', *Chinese Sociology and Anthropology*, 38: 37–53.

Caraher, M., Lang, T. and Dixon, P. (2000), 'The influence of TV and celebrity chefs on public attitudes and behaviour among the British public', *Journal for the Study of Food and Society*, 4: 27–46.

Carrigan, M. and Szmigin, I. (2006), '"Mothers of invention": Maternal empowerment and convenience consumption', *European Journal of Marketing*, 40: 1122–42.

Carrigan, M., Szmigin, I. and Leek, S. (2006), 'Managing routine food choices in UK families: The role of convenience consumption', *Appetite*, 47: 372–83.

Charles, N. and Kerr, M. (1988), *Women, Food and Families*, Manchester: Manchester University Press.

Chen, C., Zhang, J. and Delaurentis, T. (2014), 'Quality control in food supply chain management: An analytical model and case study of the adulterated milk incident in China', *International Journal of Production Economics*, 152: 188–99.

Cheng, S.-L., Olsaen, W., Southerton, D. and Warde, A. (2007), 'The changing practice of eating: Evidence from UK time diaries, 1975 and 2000', *British Journal of Sociology*, 58: 39–61.

Child, J. and Beck, S. (1961, 1970), *Mastering the Art of French Cooking*, New York: Knopf, two volumes.

Chilvers, J. (2008), 'Environmental risk, uncertainty, and participation: Mapping an emergent epistemic community', *Environment and Planning A*, 40: 2990–3008.

China Statistics Yearbook (2008), Total Population by Urban and Rural Residence and Birth Rate, Death Rate, Natural Growth Rate by Region, Basic Conditions of Urban Households. Available at: http://www.stats.gov.cn/tjsj/ndsj/2009/html/D0304e.htm and http://www.stats.gov.cn/tjsj/ndsj/2009/html/J0905e.htm (accessed 15 June 2010).

China Statistics Yearbook (2009), Total Population by Urban and Rural Residence and Birth Rate, Death Rate, Natural Growth Rate by Region, Basic Conditions of Urban Households. Available at: http://www.stats.gov.cn/tjsj/ndsj/2009/html/D0304e.htm and http://www.stats.gov.cn/tjsj/ndsj/2009/html/J0905e.htm (accessed 15 June 2010).

Clifford, J. (1997), *Routes: Travel and Translation in the Late Twentieth Century*, Cambridge, MA: Harvard University Press.

Cochrane, A. (2012), *Animal Rights without Liberation*, New York: Columbia University Press.

Cockett, R. (1995), *Thinking the Unthinkable: Think Tanks and the Economic Counter-Revolution, 1931–1983*, London: Fontana.

Cohen, P. N. and Wang, F. (2009), 'Market and gender pay equity: Have Chinese reforms narrowed the gap?' in D. Davis and F. Wang (eds), *Creating Wealth and Poverty in Post-socialist China*, Stanford, CA: Stanford University Press, 37–53.

Cohen, S. (1972), *Folk Devils and Moral Panics*, London: MacGibbon & Kee.

Collins, K. (2009), *Watching What We Eat: The Evolution of Television Cooking Shows*, London: Continuum.

Colls, R. and Evans, B. (2008), 'Embodying responsibility: Children's health and supermarket initiatives', *Environment and Planning A*, 40: 615–31.

Compassion in World Farming (2003), *The Welfare of Broiler Chickens in the European Union*, Petersfield: Compassion in World Farming Trust.

Connerton, P. (1989), *How Societies Remember*, Cambridge: Cambridge University Press.

Cooper, N. and Dumpleton, S. (2013), Walking the Breadline: The Scandal of Food Poverty in 21st Century Britain, Report by Church Action on Poverty and Oxfam. Available at: http://www.church-poverty.org.uk/walkingthebreadline/info/report/walkingthebreadlinefile (accessed 24 July 2014).

Coveney, J. (2006), *Food, Morals and Meaning: The Pleasure and Anxiety of Eating* (2nd edition), London: Routledge.

Cowan, R. S. (1985), 'How the refrigerator got its hum', in D. MacKenzie and J. Wajcman (eds), *The Social Shaping of Technology*, Milton Keynes: Open University Press, 202–18.

Crang, P. (1996), Displacement, consumption and identity', *Environment and Planning A*, 28: 47–67.

Croll, E. (1978), *Feminism and Socialism in China*, London: Routledge.

Cuordileone, K. A. (2000), '"Politics in an age of anxiety": Cold War political culture and the crisis in American masculinity, 1949–1960', *Journal of American History*, 87: 515–45.

DAFM (2013), *Equine DNA and Mislabelling of Processed Beef Investigation*, Dublin: Department of Agriculture, Food and the Marine.

David, E. (1950/1988), *A Book of Mediterranean Food* (2nd revised edition), London: Penguin.

Davis, M. (2005), *The Monster at Our Door: The Global Threat of Avian Flu*, New York: The New Press.

De Certeau, M., Giard, L. and Mayol, P. (1988), *The Practice of Everyday Life, Volume 2: Living and Cooking*, trans. T. J. Tomasik, Minneapolis: University of Minnesota Press.

DEFRA (2005), *The Validity of Food Miles as an Indicator of Sustainable Development: Final Report*, London: Department for Environment, Food and Rural Affairs.

DEFRA (2013), *Green Food Project: Curry Subgroup Report*, London: Department for Environment, Food and Rural Affairs.

Department of Transport (2012), Reported Road Casualties in Great Britain, 2012 Annual Report. Available at: https://www.gov.uk/government/uploads/system/uploads/attachment_data/file/245383/rrcgb2012-00.pdf (accessed 2 July 2014).

Devaney, L. (2013), 'Spaces of security, surveillance and food safety: Interrogating perceptions of the Food Safety Authority of Ireland's governing technologies, power and performance', *Geographical Journal*, 179: 320–30.

DeVault, M. L. (1991), *Feeding the Family: The Social Organization of Caring as Gendered Work*, Chicago: University of Chicago Press.

Dickinson, R. (2013), 'Food and the media: Production, representation, and consumption', in A. Murcott, W. Belasco and P. Jackson (eds), *The Handbook of Food Research*, London: Bloomsbury, 439–54.

Dimitri, C. and Oberholtzer, L. (2010), 'Marketing US organic foods: Recent trends from farms to consumers', *USDA Economic Information Bulletin*, 58: 1–27.

Dixon, J. (2002), *The Changing Chicken: Chooks, Cooks and Culinary Culture*, Sydney: University of New South Wales Press.

Dodds, E. R. (1991), *Pagan and Christian in an Age of Anxiety: Some Aspects of Religious Experience from Marcus Aurelius to Constantine*, Cambridge: Cambridge University Press.

Domosh, M. (2003), 'Pickles and purity: Discourses of food, Empire and work in turn-of-century USA', *Social and Cultural Geography*, 4: 7–26.

Donaldson, A. (2008), 'Biosecurity after the event: Risk politics and animal disease', *Environment and Planning A*, 40: 1552–67.

Dorling, D. (2009), 'The age of anxiety: Living in fear for our children's mental health', *Journal of Public Mental Health*, 8 (4): 4–10.

Douglas, M. (1966), *Purity and Danger: An Analysis of Concepts of Pollution and Taboo*, London: Routlege & Kegan Paul.

Douglas, M. (1971), 'Deciphering a meal', reprinted in M. Douglas (1975), *Implicit Meanings: Essays in Anthropology*, London: Routledge & Kegan Paul, 249–75.

Dunant, S. and Porter, R. (eds) (1996), *The Age of Anxiety*, London: Virago.

Durkheim, E. (1897/1951), *Suicide: A Study in Sociology*, trans. J. A. Spaulding and G. Simpson, New York: Free Press.

Earle, T. C. and Cvetkovich, G. T. (1995), *Social Trust: Towards a Cosmopolitan Society*, Westport, CT: Praeger.

EFRA (2013a), Environment, Food and Rural Affairs Committee, *Contamination of Beef Products,* London: The Stationery Office (HC946).

EFRA (2013b), Environment, Food and Rural Affairs Committee, *Contamination of Beef Products: Government Response,* London: The Stationery Office (HC1085).

EFRA (2013c), Environment, Food and Rural Affairs Committee, *Food Contamination*, London: The Stationery Office (HC141).

Elias, N. (1994), *The Civilizing Process: The History of Manners and State Formation and Civilization*, Oxford: Blackwell.

Elliott Review (2013), Review into the Integrity and Assurance of Food Supply Networks: Interim Report 2013. Available at: https://www.gov.uk/government/uploads/system/uploads/attachment_data/file/264997/pb14089-elliot-review-interim-20131212.pdf (accessed 19 December 2013).

Elliott Review (2014), Elliott Review into the Integrity and Assurance of Food Supply Networks: Final Report. Available at: https://www.gov.uk/government/uploads/system/uploads/attachment_data/file/350726/elliot-review-final-report-july2014.pdf (accessed 16 September 2014).

Ellis, H. (2007), *Planet Chicken: The Shameful Story of the Bird on Your Plate*, London: Hodder & Stoughton.

Eurobarometer (2006), *Special Eurobarometer 238: Risk Issues*, Brussels: European Commission.

Eurobarometer (2010), *Special Eurobarometer 354: Food-Related Risks*, Brussels: European Commission.

Eurobarometer (2012), *Special Eurobarometer 389: European' Attitudes towards Food Security, Food Quality and the Countryside*, Brussels: European Commission.

Evans, D. (2011), 'Blaming the consumer – once again: The social and material contexts of everyday food waste practices in some English households', *Critical Public Health*, 21: 429–40.

Evans, D. (2012), 'Beyond the throwaway society: Ordinary domestic practice and a sociology of household food waste', *Sociology*, 46: 41–56.

Evans, D. (2014), *Food Waste: Home Consumption, Material Culture and Everyday Life*, London: Bloomsbury.

Evans, D., Campbell, H. and Murcott, A. (eds) (2013), *Waste Matters: New Perspectives on Food and Society*, Oxford: Wiley-Blackwell (The Sociological Review).

Fang, Y. Q., Granrose, C. K. and Kong, R. V. (2005), 'National policy influence on women's careers in the People's Republic of China', in C. S. Granrose (ed.), *Employment of Women in Chinese Cultures*, Cheltenham: Edward Elgar, 49–83.

Farquhar, J. (2002), *Appetites: Food and Sex in Postsocialist China*, Durham, NC: Duke University Press.

Faure, O. (2008), 'Chinese society and its new emerging culture', *Journal of Contemporary China*, 17: 469–91.

Finch, J. (2007), 'Displaying families', *Sociology*, 41: 65–81.

Fischler, C. (1988), 'Food, self and identity', *Social Science Information*, 27: 275–92.

Fischler, C. (1990), *L'Homnivore*, Paris: Odile Jacob.

Foucault, M. (1986), 'Of other spaces', *Diacritics*, 16: 22–27.

Fox, R. and Smith, G. (2010), 'Sinner ladies and the gospel of good taste: Geographies of food, class and care', *Health and Place*, 17: 403–12.

Freidberg, S. (2004), *French Beans and Food Scares: Culture and Commerce in an Anxious Age*, Oxford: Oxford University Press.

Freidberg, S. (2009), *Fresh: A Perishable History*, Cambridge, MA: Harvard University Press.

Freidberg, S. (2010), 'Ambiguous appetites: A modern history', *Food, Culture and Society*, 13: 477–91.

Freud, S. (1930), *Civilization and Its Discontents*, trans. J. Riviere, London: Hogarth Press.

Freud, S. (1936), *The Problem of Anxiety*, trans. H. A. Bunker, New York: The Psychoanalytic Quarterly and W. W. Norton & Co.

FSA (2013a), *Report of the Investigation by the Food Standards Agency into Incidents of Adulteration of Comminuted Beef Products with Horsemeat and DNA*, London: Food Standards Agency.

FSA (2013b), 'Chief Scientist's Report for 2012–13'. Available at: http://multimedia.food.
gov.uk/multimedia/pdfs/publication/cstar_2013.pdf (accessed 2 July 2014).

FSA (2014), New UK Food Poisoning Figures Published. Available at: http://www.food.
gov.uk/news-updates/news/2014/jun/foodpoisoning (accessed 26 June 2014).

Fuentes, M. and Fuentes, C. (2014), 'Risk stories in the media: Food consumption, risk
and anxiety', *Food, Culture and Society*, 18: 71–87.

Furedi, F. (1997), *Culture of Fear*, London: Continuum.

Gao, L. L., Chan, S. W. C., You, L. and Li, X. (2010), 'Experiences of postpartum depression
among first-time mothers in mainland China', *Journal of Advanced Nursing*, 66: 303–12.

Gatens, M. and Lloyd, G. (1999), *Collective Imaginings: Spinoza, Past and Present*,
London: Routledge.

Gereffi, G. (1994), 'The organisation of buyer-driven global commodity chains: How U.S.
retailers shape overseas production network', in G. Gereffi, M. Korzeniewicz and
R. Korzeniewicz (eds), *Global Commodity Chains and Global Capitalism*, London:
Greenwood Press, 95–12.

Giddens, A. (1991), *Modernity and Self-Identity: Self and Society in the Late Modern Age*,
Cambridge: Polity Press.

Giddens, A. (2006), *Sociology* (5th edition), Cambridge: Polity Press.

Gill, N. (2009), 'Asylum, immigration and the circulation of unease at Lunar House', in
A. Ingram and K. Dodds (eds), *Spaces of Security and Insecurity: Geographies of the
War on Terror*, Farnham: Ashgate, 147–64.

Godley, A. and Williams, B. (2007), 'The chicken, the factory farm and the supermarket:
The emergence of the modern poultry industry in Britain', University of Reading
Business School, Working Paper No. 27.

Godley, A. and Williams, B. (2009), 'Democratizing luxury and the contentious "invention
of the technological chicken" in Britain', *Business History Review*, 83: 267–90.

Gong, Q. and Jackson, P. (2012), 'Consuming anxiety? Parenting practices in China after
the infant formula scandal', *Food, Culture and Society*, 15: 557–78.

Gong, Q. and Jackson, P. (2013), 'Mediating science and nature: Representing and
consuming infant formula advertising in China', *European Journal of Cultural Studies*,
16: 285–309.

Goodman, D. and Watts, M. J. (eds) (1997), *Globalizing Food: Agrarian Questions and
Global Restructuring*, London, Routledge.

Gottschang, S. (2000), 'A baby-friendly hospital and the science of infant feeding', in
J. Jing (ed.), *Feeding China's Little Emperors*, Stanford, CA: Stanford University
Press, 160–84.

Grant, J. (1998), *Raising Baby by the Book: The Education of American Mothers*,
New Haven, CT: Yale University Press.

Green, J., Draper, A. and Dowler, E. (2003), 'Short cuts to safety: risk and "rules of
thumb" in accounts of food choice', *Health, Risk and Society*, 5: 33–52.

Greenaway, A., Larner, W. and Le Heron, R. (2002), 'Reconstituting motherhood: Milk powder
marketing in Sri Lanka', *Environment and Planning D: Society and Space*, 20: 719–36.

Gregson, N. (2011), *Living with Things: Ridding, Accommodation, Dwelling*, Wanntage: Sean Kingston Publishing.

Griffiths, M., Chapman, M. and Christiansen, F. (2010), 'Chinese consumers: The Romantic reappraisal', *Ethnography*, 11: 331–57.

Griffiths, S. and Wallace, J. (eds) (1998), *Consuming Passions: Food in the Age of Anxiety*, Manchester: Manchester University Press.

Grunow, J. and Warde, A. (eds) (2001), *Ordinary Consumption*, London: Routledge.

Guldan, G., Zhang, M., Guo, Z., Hong, J. and Yang, Y. (1995), 'Breastfeeding practice in Chengdu, Sichuan', *China Journal of Human Lactation*, 11: 11–15.

Guo, S., Padmadas, S., Zhao, F., Brown, J. and Stone, R. (2007), 'Delivery settings and Caesarean section rates in China', *Bulletin of the World Health Organization*, 85: 733–820.

Guthman, J. (2004), *Agrarian Dreams: The Paradox of Organic Farming in California*, Berkeley: University of California Press.

Guthman, J. (2011), *Weighing In: Obesity, Food Justice, and the Limits of Capitalism*, Berkeley and Los Angeles: University of California Press.

Halbwachs, M. (1992), *On Collective Memory*, trans. L. A. Coser, Chicago: University of Chicago Press.

Halkier, B. (2009), 'Suitable cooking? Performances and positionings in cooking practices among Danish women', *Food, Culture and Society*, 12: 357–77.

Halkier, B. (2010), *Consumption Challenged: Food in Medialised Everyday Lives*, Farnham: Ashgate.

Halkier, B. (2013), 'Easy eating? Negotiating convenience food in media food practices', in L. Hansson, U. Holmberg and H. Brembeck (eds), *Making Sense of Consumption*, Gothenburg: Gothenburg University Press, 119–36.

Hand, M. and Shove, E. (2007), 'Condensing practices: Ways of living with a freezer', *Journal of Consumer Culture*, 7: 79–104.

Hansen, S. (2008), 'Society of the appetite: Celebrity chefs deliver consumers', *Food, Culture and Society*, 11: 49–67.

Haraway, D. (2008), *When Species Meet*, Minneapolis: University of Minnesota Press.

Harris Interactive (2013a), 'FSA: Consumer attitudes towards the horsemeat contamination issue'. Available at: http://multimedia.food.gov.uk/multimedia/pdfs/horse-meat-consumera.pdf (accessed 11 February 2014).

Harris Interactive (2013b), 'FSA: Horsemeat Wave 2: Changing consumer attitudes following the horsemeat contamination issue'. Available at: http://multimedia.food.gov.uk/multimedia/pdfs/board/fsa-140104b.pdf (accessed 11 February 2014).

Hausman, B. L. (2003), *Mother's Milk: Breastfeeding Controversies in American Culture*, New York: Routledge.

Heidegger, M. (1978), *Being and Time*, trans. J. Macquarrie and E. Robinson, Oxford: Blackwell.

Heldke, L.M. (1992), 'Foodmaking as a thoughtful practice', in D.W. Curtin and L.M. Heldke (eds), *Cooking, Eating, Thinking*, Bloomington: Indiana University Press, 203–29.

Heldke, L. (2003), *Exotic Appetites: Ruminations of a Food Adventurer*, London: Routledge.

Hesketh, T., Lu, L. and Xing, Z. W. (2005), 'The effect of China's one-child family policy after 25 years', *New England Journal of Medicine*, 353: 1171–76.

Hetherington, K. (2004), 'Secondhandedness: Consumption, disposal, and absent presence', *Environment and Planning D: Society and Space*, 22: 157–73.

Hier, S. P. (2003), 'Risk and panic in late modernity: Implications of the converging sites of social anxiety', *British Journal* of Sociology, 54: 3–20.

Hill, A. (2005), *Reality TV, Audiences and Popular Factual Television*, New York: Routledge.

Hilts, C. and Pelletier, L. (2008), 'Background Paper on Occurrence of Melamine in Foods and Feed', Prepared for WHO Expert Meeting on Toxicological and Health Aspects of Melamine and Cyanuric Acid, Geneva: World Health Organization.

Hinchliffe, S. and Bingham, N. (2008), 'Securing life: The emerging practices of biosecurity', *Environment and Planning A*, 40: 1534–51.

Hinrichs, C. (2000), 'Embeddedness and local food systems: Notes on two types of direct agricultural market', *Journal of Rural Studies*, 16: 295–303.

Hoggart, R. (1957), *The Uses of Literacy: Aspects of Working Class Life*, London: Chatto & Windus.

Hollander, G. (2003), 'Re-naturalizing sugar: Narratives of place, production and consumption', *Social and Cultural Geography*, 4: 59–74.

Hollows, J. (2003a), 'Feeling like a Domestic Goddess: Postfeminism and cooking', *European Journal of Cultural Studies*, 6: 179–202.

Hollows, J. (2003b), 'Oliver's Twist: Leisure, labour and domestic masculinity in The Naked Chef', *International Journal of Cultural Studies*, 6: 229–48.

Hollows, J. and Jones, S. (2010), '"At least he's doing something": Moral entrepreneurship and individual responsibility in *Jamie's Ministry of Food*', *European Journal of Cultural Studies*, 13: 307–22.

Hollway, W. and Jefferson, T. (1997), 'The risk society in an age of anxiety: Situating fear of crime', *British Journal of Sociology*, 48: 255–66.

Holroyd, P. (1986), *History of the Institute of Poultry Husbandry*, Newport: Harper Adams Agricultural College.

Hong, J. (1994), 'The resurrection of advertising in China: Developments, problems, and trends', *Asian Survey*, 34: 326–42.

Horowitz, R. (2004), 'Making the chicken of tomorrow: Reworking poultry as commodities and as creatures, 1945–1990', in S. Schrepfer and P. Scranton (eds), *Industrializing Organisms*, New York: Routledge, 215–36.

Howard, S., Adams, J. and White, M. (2012), 'Nutritional content of supermarket ready meals and recipes by television chefs in the United Kingdom: Cross sectional study', *British Medical Journal*, 345: e7607, 1–10.

Humphrey, T., O'Brien, S. and Madsen, M. (2007), 'Campylobacters as zoonotic pathogens: A food production perspective', *International Journal of Food Microbiology*, 117: 237–57.

Hunt, A. (1999), 'Anxiety and social explanation: Some anxieties about anxiety', *Journal of Social History*, 32, 509–28.

IME (2013), *Global Food: Waste Not, Want Not*, London: Institute of Mechanical Engineers.

Ingram, A. (2008), 'Domopolitics and disease: HIV/AIDS, immigration, and asylum in the UK', *Environment and Planning D: Society and Space*, 26: 875–94.

Jackson, P. (ed.) (2009), *Changing Families, Changing Food*, Basingstoke: Palgrave-Macmillan.

Jackson, P. (2013), 'Moral economy', in P. Jackson and the CONANX group, *Food Words: Essays in Culinary Culture*, London: Bloomsbury, 139–46.

Jackson, P. and Everts, J. (2010), 'Anxiety as social practice', *Environment and Planning A*, 42: 2791–806.

Jackson, P. and the CONANX group (2013), *Food Words: Essays in Culinary Culture*, London: Bloomsbury.

Jackson, P., Perez del Aguila, R., Clarke, I., Hallsworth, A., de Kervenoael, R. and Kirkup, M. (2006), 'Retail restructuring and consumer choice 2: Understanding consumer choice at the household level', *Environment and Planning A*, 38, 47–67.

Jackson, P., Russell, P. and Ward, N. (2007), 'The appropriation of "alternative" discourses by "mainstream" food retailers', in D. Maye, L. Holloway and M. Kneafsey (eds), *Alternative Food Geographies: Representation and Practice*, Amsterdam, Elsevier, 309–30.

Jackson, P., Ward, N. and Russell, P. (2009), 'Moral economies of food and geographies of responsibility', *Transactions of the Institute of British Geographers*, 34: 908–24.

Jackson, P., Ward, N. and Russell, P. (2010), 'Manufacturing meaning along the chicken supply chain: Consumer anxiety and the spaces of production', in M. K. Goodman, D. Goodman and M. Redclift (eds), *Consuming Space: Placing Consumption in Perspective*, Aldershot: Ashgate, 163–87.

Jackson, P., Watson, M. and Piper, N. (2013), 'Locating anxiety in the social: The cultural mediation of food fears', *European Journal of Cultural Studies*, 16: 24–42.

Jacobsen, E. (2013), *Dangerous Liaisons: Domestic Food Safety Practices*, PhD Thesis, Centre for Technology, Innovation and Culture, University of Oslo, Norway.

Janowitz, M. (ed.) (1966), *W.I. Thomas on Social Organization and Social Personality*, Chicago: University of Chicago Press.

Jing, J. (ed.) (2000), *Feeding China's Little Emperors: Food, Children, and Social Change*, Stanford, CA: Stanford University Press.

Johnson, H. (2006), *The Age of Anxiety: McCarthyism to Terrorism*, New York: Harcourt.

Johnson, R. (2009), 'Potential Farm Sector Effects of 2009 H1N1 "Swine Flu": Questions and answers', in Congressional Research Service, Report for Congress (4 September), http://assets.opencrs.com/rpts/R40575_20090904.pdf (accessed 9 February 2010).

Johnston, J. and Goodman, M. K. (2015), 'Spectacular foodscapes: Food celebrities and the politics of lifestyle mediation in an age of inequality', *Food, Culture and Society*, 18: 205–22.

Julian, L. J. (2011), 'Measures of anxiety', *Arthritis Care and Research*, 63: 5467–72.

Kelly, I. (2005), *Cooking for Kings: The Life of Antoine Carême, the First Celebrity Chef*, New York: Walker & Co.

Kierkegaard, S. (1980), *The Concept of Anxiety*, Princeton, NJ: Princeton University Press.

Kjaernes, U. (2013), 'Risk and trust in the food supply', in A. Murcott, W. Belasco and P. Jackson (eds), *The Handbook of Food Research*, London: Bloomsbury, 410–24.

Kjaernes, U., Harvey, M. and Warde, A. (2007), *Trust in Food: A Comparative and Institutional Analysis*, Basingstoke: Palgrave Macmillan.

Knowles, T., Moody, R. and McEachern, M. G. (2007). 'European food scares and their impact on EU food policy', *British Food Journal*, 109: 43–67.

Korsmeyer, C. (1999), *Making Sense of Taste: Food and Philosophy*, Ithaca, NY: Cornell University Press.

Korsmeyer, C. (2002), 'Delightful, delicious, disgusting', *Journal of Aesthetics and Art Criticism*, 60: 217–25.

Korsmeyer, C. (ed.) (2005), *The Taste Culture Reader*, Oxford: Berg.

Korsmeyer, C. (2011), *Savoring Disgust: The Foul and the Fair in Aesthetics*, Oxford: Oxford University Press.

Kusenbach, M. (2003), 'Street phenomenology: The go-along as ethnographic research tool', *Ethnography*, 4: 445–85.

Lai, B. (2003), School Milk Programme – the Economic Dimension: A Study of the Economic Impact of China School Milk Programme (CSMP). Available at: http://www.fao.org/es/esc/common/ecg/188/en/The_Economic_Dimension_of_the_China_School_Milk_Progr.pdf (accessed 24 November 2010).

Lambie-Mumford, H., Crossley, D., Jensen, E., Verbeke, M. and Dowler, E. (2014), *Household Food Security in the UK: A Review of Food Aid* (Final Report), London: Department for Environment, Food and Rural Affairs.

Latham, K. (2006), 'Introduction: Consumption and cultural change in contemporary China', in K. Latham, S. Thompson and J. Klein (eds), *Consuming China: Approaches to Cultural Changes in Contemporary China*, Oxford and New York: Routledge, 1–21.

Lave, J. and Wenger, E. (1991), *Situated Learning: Legitimate Peripheral Participation*, Cambridge: Cambridge University Press.

Lavin, C. (2013), *Eating Anxiety: The Perils of Food Politics*, Minneapolis: University of Minnesota Press.

Lawrence, F. (2004), *Not on the Label: What Really Goes into the Food on Your Plate*, London: Penguin Books.

Lawson, N. (2003), *How to be a Domestic Goddess: Baking and the Art of Comfort Cooking*, London: Chatto & Windus.

Lee, M. and Farrell, S. (2008), *Fear of Crime: Critical Voices in an Age of Anxiety*, London: Routledge.

Leer, J. and Kjaer, K. M. (2015), 'Strange culinary encounters: Stranger fetishism in *Jamie's Italian Escape* and *Gordon's Great Escape*', *Food, Culture and Society*, 18: 309–27.

Levenstein, H. (1993), *Paradox of Plenty: A Social History of Eating in Modern America*, New York: Oxford University Press.

Levenstein, H. (2012), *Fear of Food: A History of Why We Worry about What We Eat*, Chicago: University of Chicago Press.

Lewis, T. (2010), 'Branding, celebritization and the lifestyle expert', *Cultural Studies*, 2: 580–98.

Lewis, T. and Huber, A. (2015), 'A revolution in an eggcup? Supermarket wars, celebrity chefs, and ethical consumption', *Food, Culture and Society*, 18: 289–307.

Li, H. B., Zhang, J. S., Sin, L. T. and Zhao, Y. H. (2006), 'Relative earnings of husbands and wives in urban China', *China Economic Review*, 17: 412–31.

Luhmann, N. (1979), *Trust and Power*, trans. H. Davis, J. Raffan and K. Rooney, Chichester: Wiley.

MAFF (1991), *Fifty Years of the National Food Survey*, London: Ministry of Agriculture, Fisheries and Food.

Marsden, T., Flynn, A. and Harrison, M. (2000), *Consuming Interests: The Social Provision of Foods*, London: UCL Press.

Marshall, D. and Bell, R. (2003), 'Meal construction: Exploring the relationship between eating occasion and location', *Food Quality and Preference*, 14: 53–64.

Marshall, J., Godfrey, M. and Renfrew, M. J. (2007), 'Being a "good mother": managing breastfeeding and merging identities', *Social Science and Medicine*, 65: 2147–59.

Martens, L. (2012), 'Practice "in talk" and talk "as practice": Dish washing and the reach of language', *Sociological Research Online*, 17 (3): 22.

Martens, L. and Scott, S. (2004), *Domestic Kitchen Practices: Routines, Risks and Reflexivity*, ESRC End of Award Report.

Massey, D. (2004), 'Geographies of responsibility', *Geografiska Annaler*, 86B: 5–18.

May, R. (1950), *The Meaning of Anxiety*, New York: The Ronald Press Co.

McGee, H. (2004), *On Food and Cooking: An Encyclopedia of Kitchen Science, History and Culture*, London: Hodder & Stoughton.

McRobbie, A. (1994). 'Folk devils fight back', *New Left Review*, 203: 107–16.

Meah, A. (2014a), 'Reconceptualizing power and gendered subjectivities in domestic cooking spaces', *Progress in Human Geography*, 38: 671–90.

Meah, A. (2014b), 'Still blaming the consumer? Geographies of responsibility in domestic food safety practices', *Critical Public Health*, 24: 88–103.

Meah, A. and Jackson, P. (2013), 'Crowded kitchens: The "democratisation" of domesticity?', *Gender, Place and Culture*, 20: 578–96.

Meah, A. and Watson, M. (2011), 'Saints and slackers: Challenging discourses about the decline of domestic cooking', *Sociological Research Online*, 16 (2): 6.

Meah, A. and Watson, M. (2013), 'Cooking up consumer anxieties about "provenance" and "ethics": Why it sometimes matters where food comes from in domestic provisioning', *Food, Culture and Society*, 16: 495–512.

Mellahi, K., Jackson, P. and Sparks, L. (2002), 'An exploratory study into failure in successful organizations: The case of Marks & Spencer', *British Journal of Management*, 13: 15–29.

Mennell, S. (1996), *All Manners of Food: eating and taste in England and France from the Middle Ages to the Present* (2nd edition), Urbana-Champaign: University of Illinois Press.

Miele, M. (2011), 'The taste of happiness: Free-range chicken', *Environment and Planning A*, 43: 2076–90.

Miller, D. (1999), 'Risk, science and policy: Definitional struggles, information management, the media and BSE', *Social Science and Medicine*, 49: 1239–45.

Miller, D. (2001), *The Dialectics of Shopping*, Chicago: University of Chicago Press.

Miller, D., Jackson, P., Thrift, N., Holbrook, B. and Rowlands, M. (1998), *Shopping, Place and Identity*, London: Routledge.

Miller, D. and Reilly, J. (1994), *Food Scares in the Media*, Glasgow: Glasgow University Media Unit.

Miller, W. I. (1997), *The Anatomy of Disgust*, Cambridge, MA: Harvard University Press.

Millstone, E. (2009), 'Science, risk and governance: Radical rhetorics and the realities of reform in food safety governance', *Research Policy*, 38: 624–36.

Milne, R. J. (2013a), 'Trust', in P. Jackson and the CONANX group, *Food Words: Essays in Culinary Culture*, London: Bloomsbury, 230–37.

Milne, R. J. (2013b), 'Arbiters of waste: Date labels, the consumer and knowing good, safe food', in D. Evans, H. Cambell and A. Murcott (eds), *Waste Matters: New Perspectives on Food and Society*, Oxford: John Wiley & Sons (Sociological Review Monographs), 84–101.

Milne, R. J., Wenzer, J., Brembeck, H. and Brodin, M. (2011), 'Fraught cuisine: Food scares and the modulation of anxieties', *Distinktion: Scandinavian Journal of Social Theory*, 12: 177–92.

Mincyte, D. (2014), 'Homogenizing Europe: Raw milk, risk politics, and moral economies in Europeanizing Lithuania', in Y. Jung, J. A. Klein and M. L. Caldwell (eds), *Ethical Eating in the Postsocialist and Socialist World*, Berkeley, CA: University of California Press, 25–43.

MINTEL (2013), *Prepared Meals*, London: Mintel Group.

Mitchell, J. C. (1983), 'Case and situation analysis', *Sociological Review*, 31: 187–211.

Muir, S. and Mason, J. (2012), 'Capturing Christmas: The sensory potential of data from participant produced video', *Sociological Research Online*, 17 (1): 5.

Murcott, A. (1983a), 'Cooking and the cooked: A note on the domestic preparation of meals', in A. Murcott (ed.), *The Sociology of Food and Eating*, Aldershot: Gower, 178–93.

Murcott, A. (1983b), '"It's a pleasure to cook for him": Food, mealtimes and gender in some South Wales households', in E. Gamarnikow, D. Morgan, J. Purvis and D. Taylorson (eds), *The Public and the Private*, London: Heinemann, 78–90.

Murcott, A. (1997), 'Family meals: A thing of the past?' in P. Caplan (ed.), *Food, Health and Identity*, London: Routledge, 32–49.

Murcott, A. (2000), 'Is it still a pleasure to cook for him? Social changes in the household and the family', *Journal of Consumer Culture*, 24: 78–84.

Murcott, A. (2013), 'A burgeoning field: Introduction to *The Handbook of Food Research*', in A. Murcott, W. Belasco and P. Jackson (eds), *The Handbook of Food Research*, London: Bloomsbury, 1–25.

Nelson, M. (2010), *Parenting Out of Control: Anxious Parents in Uncertain Times*, New York and London: New York University Press.

Nestle, M. (2002), *Food Politics: How the Food Industry Influences Nutrition and Health*, Berkeley, CA: University of California Press.

Nietzsche, F. (1883/1961), *Thus Spoke Zarathustra: A Book for Everyone and No One*, trans. R. J. Hollingdale, London: Penguin.

Orwell, G. (1937), *The Road to Wigan Pier*, London: Victor Gollancz.

Pain, R. and Smith, S. (2008), 'Fear: Critical geopolitics and everyday life', in R. Pain and S. Smith, (eds), *Fear: Critical Geopolitics and Everyday Life*, Aldershot: Ashgate, 1–19.

Parasecoli, F. (2008), *Bite Me: Food in Popular Culture*, Oxford: Berg.

Patel, R. (2007), *Stuffed and Starved: Markets, Power and the Hidden Battle for the World's Food System*, London: Portobello Books.

Paterson, M. (2006), *Consumption and Everyday Life*, London and New York: Routledge.

Pei, X., Tandon, A., Alldrick, A., Giorgi, L., Huang, W. and Yang, R. (2011), 'The China melamine milk scandal and its implications for food safety regulation', *Food Policy*, 36: 412–20.

Pillsbury, B. (1982), '"Doing the month": Confinement and convalescence of Chinese women after childbirth', *Social Science and Medicine*, 12: 11–22.

Piper, N. (2013a), 'Audiencing Jamie Oliver: Embarrassment, voyeurism and reflexive positioning', *Geoforum*, 45: 346–55.

Piper, N. (2013b), 'Celebrity chefs', in P. Jackson and the CONANX group, *Food Words: Essays in Culinary Culture*, London: Bloomsbury, 40–43.

Piper, N. (2015), 'Jamie Oliver and cultural intermediation', *Food, Culture and Society*, 18: 245–64.

Policy Commission on the Future of Farming and Food (2002), *Farming and Food: A Sustainable Future* (The Curry Commission), London: Cabinet Office.

Pollan, M. (2006), *The Omnivore's Dilemma: A Natural History of Four Meals*, New York: Penguin.

Poppendieck, J. (2011), *Free for All: Fixing School Food in America*, Berkeley and Los Angeles: University of California Press.

Potts, A. (2012), *Chicken*, London: Reaktion Books.

Powell, H. and Prasad, S. (2010), 'As seen on TV: The celebrity expert: How taste is shaped by lifestyle media', *Cultural Politics*, 6: 111–24.

Prim, M. K., Gustafsson, I. and Hall, G. (2007), 'The appropriateness of ready meals for dinner', *Journal of Foodservice*, 18: 238–50.

Probyn, E. (2000), *Carnal Appetites: Food Sex Identities*, London: Routledge.

Probyn, E. (2001), 'Anxious proximities: The space-time of concepts', in J. May and N. J. Thrift (eds), *Timespace: Geographies of Temporality*, London: Routledge, 171–86.

Qiao, G., Guo, T. and Klein, K. (2010), 'Melamine in Chinese milk products and consumer confidence', *Appetite*, 55: 190–95.

Reckwitz, A. (2002), 'Toward a theory of social practices: A development in culturalist theorizing', *European Journal of Social Theory*, 5: 243–63.

Rich, E. (2011), '"I see her being obesed!": Public pedagogy, reality media and the obesity crisis', *Health*, 15: 3–21.

Riches, G. and Silvasti, T. (eds) (2014), *First World Hunger Revisited: Food Charity or the Right to Food?* (2nd edition), Basingstoke: Palgrave Macmillan.

Roe, E. J. (2006), 'Things becoming food and the embodied material practices of an organic food consumer', *Sociologia Ruralis*, 46: 104–21.

Rojek, C. (2001), *Celebrity*, London: Reaktion Books.

Rousseau, S. (2012), *Food Media: Celebrity Chefs and the Politics of Everyday Interference*, London: Bloomsbury.

Rousseau, S. (2015), 'The celebrity quick-fix: when good food meets bad science', *Food, Culture and Society*, 18: 265–87.

Rowe, G. (2010), *Assessment of the COT Uncertainty Framework from a Social Science Perspective: A Theoretical Evaluation*, London: Food Standards Agency.

Rozin, P. (1976), 'The selection of foods by rats, humans and other animals', in J. S. Rosenblatt, R. A. Hindle, E. Shaw and C. Beer (eds), *Advances in the Study of Behavior*, vol. 6, London and New York: Academic Press, 21–76.

RSPCA (2001), *Behind Closed Doors: Chickens Bred for Meat*, Horsham: Royal Society for the Prevention of Cruelty to Animals.

RSPCA (2005), *Paying the Price: The Facts about Chickens Reared for Their Meat*, Horsham: Royal Society for the Prevention of Cruelty to Animals.

Ruark, J. (1999), 'A place at the table', *The Chronicle of Higher Education* (9 July), A17–A19.

Salecl, R. (2004), *On Anxiety*, London: Routledge.

Salter, K. (2010), 'Cathy Chapman: The woman who changed the way we eat', *Daily Telegraph* (10 October).

Samuel, R. and Thompson, P. (eds) (1990), *The Myths We Live By*, London: Routledge.

Sayer, A. (1992), *Method in Social Science: A Realist Approach* (2nd edition), London: Routledge.

Sayer, A. (2000), 'Moral economy and political economy', *Studies in Political Economy*, Spring: 79–103.

Schatzki, T. (1996), *Social Practices: A Wittgensteinian Approach to Human Activity and the Social*, Cambridge: Cambridge University Press.

Schatzki, T. (2002), *The Site of the Social: A Philosophical Account of the Constitution of Social Life and Change*, University Park: Penn State University Press.

Schatzki, T. R., Knorr Cetina, K. and von Savigny, E. (eds) (2001), *The Practice Turn in Contemporary Theory*, London: Routledge.

Schinckel, R. (2000), *Intimate Strangers: The Culture of Celebrity in America*, Chicago: Ivan Dee.

Scott, J. C. (1976), *The Moral Economy of the Peasant: Rebellion and Subsistence in Southeast Asia*, New Haven, CT: Yale University Press.

Scott, S. (2004), 'The shell, the stranger and the competent other: Towards a sociology of shyness', *Sociology*, 38: 121–37.

Seth, A. and Randall, G. (1999), *The Grocers: The Rise and Rise of the Supermarket Chains*, London: Kogan Page.

Sheppard, A. (2004), *The Structure and Economics of Broiler Production in England*, University of Exeter, Centre for Rural Research.

Shi, L., Zhang, J., Wang, Y. and Guyer, B. (2008), 'Breastfeeding in rural China: Association between knowledge, attitudes and practice', *Journal of Human Lactation*, 24: 377–85.

Shi, X. H. (2009), 'A comparative analysis of systematic management of infant physical development in 1995 and 2005', *Maternal and Child Health Care of China*, 24: 1316–17.

Short, F. (2006), *Kitchen Secrets: The Meaning of Cooking in Everyday Life*, Oxford: Berg.

Shove, E. (2010), 'Beyond the ABC: Climate change policy and theories of social change', *Environment and Planning A*, 42: 1273–85.

Shove, E. and Southerton, D. (2000), 'Defrosting the freezer: From novelty to convenience', *Journal of Consumer Culture*, 5: 301–19.

Shove, E., Pantzar, M. and Watson, M. (eds) (2012), *The Dynamics of Social Practice*, London: Sage.

Silk, J. (1998), 'Caring at a distance', *Philosophy and Geography*, 1: 165–82.

Silver, J. J. and Hawkins, R. (2014), '"I'm not trying to save fish, I'm trying to save dinner": Media, celebrity and sustainable seafood as a solution to environmental limits', *Geoforum*, in press.

Simmel, G. (1903/1971), 'The metropolis and mental life', in D. N. Levine (ed.), *Georg Simmel on Individuality and Social Forms*, Chicago: University of Chicago Press, 324–39.

Simmel, G. (1910/1994), 'The sociology of the meal', trans. M. Symons, *Food and Foodways*, 5: 345–50.

Singer, P. (ed.) (1985), *In Defense of Animals*, New York: Basil Blackwell.

Skeggs, B. (1997), *Formations of Class and Gender: Becoming Respectable*, London: Sage.

Skeggs, B. and Wood, H. (2008), 'The labour of transformation and circuits of value "around" reality television', *Continuum*, 22: 559–72.

Slater, N. (2000), *Appetite*, London: Fourth Estate.

Slater, N. (2003), *Toast*, London: Fourth Estate.

Slocum, R., Shannon, J., Valentine Cadieux, K. and Beckman, M. (2011), '"Properly, with love, from scratch": Jamie Oliver's Food Revolution', *Radical History Review*, 110: 178–91.

Smith, P. and Daniel, C. (1982), *The Chicken Book*, San Francisco: North Point Press.

Southerton, D., McMeekin, A. and Evans, D. (2011), International Review of Behaviour
    Change Initiatives, Report to the Scottish Government. Available at: http://www.
    scotland.gov.uk/Publications/2011/02/01104638/0 (accessed 1 September 2014).
Spiegel, J. E. (2012), 'Truly food for thought', *New York Times*, 13 April.
SSRC (2012), 'Making sense of risk and uncertainty: Public engagement,
    communication and risk assessment policy', Social Science Research Committee
    advice paper presented to the Food Standards' Agency General Advisory Committee
    on Science. Available at: http://multimedia.food.gov.uk/multimedia/pdfs/riskuncert
    (accessed 1 September 2014).
Stassart, P. and Whatmore, S. (2003), 'Metabolising risk: Food scares and the un/
    re-making of Belgian beef', *Environment and Planning A*, 35: 449–62.
Stearns, P. (2003), *Anxious Parents: A History of Modern Childrearing in America*,
    New York: New York University Press.
Striffler, S. (2005), *Chicken: The Dangerous Transformation of America's Favorite Food*,
    New Haven, CT: Yale University Press.
Stringfellow, L., MacLaren, A., Maclean, M. and O'Gorman, K. (2013), 'Conceptualizing
    taste: Food, culture and celebrities', *Tourism Management*, 37: 77–85.
Stuart, T. (2009), *Waste: Uncovering the Global Food Scandal*, London: Penguin.
Stull, D. D. and Broadway, M. J. (2004), *Slaughterhouse Blues: The Meat and Poultry
    Industry in North America*, Belmont, CA: Wadsworth.
Sustain (1999), *Fowl Deeds: The Impact of Chicken Production and Consumption
    on People and the Environment*, Bristol: Sustain – the alliance for better food and
    farming.
Sykes, G. (1963), *Poultry: A Modern Agribusiness*, London: Sykes, Crosby, Lockwood &
    Sons.
Tannahill, R. (1973), *Food in History*, Harmondsworth: Penguin.
Thompson, E. P. (1971), 'The moral economy of the English crowd in the eighteenth
    century', *Past and Present*, 50: 76–136.
Trentmann, F. (ed.) (2006), *The Making of the Consumer*, Oxford: Berg.
Troop, P. (2013), Independent Review of the Food Standards Agency's Response to the
    Contamination of Beef Products with Horse and Pork Meat and DNA. Available at:
    http://www.food.gov.uk/multimedia/pdfs/board/board-papers-2013/fsa-130704-prof-
    troop-report.pdf (accessed 11 December 2013).
Trubek, A. (2000), *Haute Cuisine: How the French Invented the Culinary Profession*,
    Philadelphia: University of Pennsylvania Press.
Turner, G. (2004), *Understanding Celebrity*, London: Sage.
Twenge, J. M. (2000), 'The age of anxiety? Birth cohort change in anxiety and
    neuroticism, 1952–1993', *Journal of Personality and Social Psychiatry*, 79: 1007–21.
Tyler, I. and Bennett, B. (2010), '"Celebrity chav": Fame, femininity and social class',
    European Journal of Cultural Studies, 13: 375–93.
Tyrer, P. (1999), *Anxiety: A Multidisciplinary Review*, London: Imperial College Press.

Ungar, S. (2001), 'Moral panic versus the risk society: The implications of the changing sites of social anxiety', *British Journal of Sociology*, 52: 271–91.

Usborne, S. (2009), 'Ready happy returns: The instant meal celebrates its 30th birthday', *The Independent* (23 July).

Van Zwanenberg, P. and Millstone, E. (2003), 'BSE: A paradigm of policy failure', *Political Quarterly*, 74: 27–38.

Vialles, N. (1994), *Animal to Edible*, trans. J. A. Underwood, Cambridge: Cambridge University Press.

Visser, M. (1999), *Much Depends on Dinner: The Extraordinary History and Mythology, Allure and Obsessions, Perils and Taboos of an Ordinary Meal*, New York: Grove Press.

Wallace, J. (1998), 'Introduction', in S. Griffiths and J. Wallace (eds), *Consuming Passions: Food in an Age of Anxiety*, Manchester, New York and Vancouver, BC: Mandolin, 1–13.

Ward, N., Donaldson, A. and Lowe, P. (2004), 'Policy framing and learning the lessons from the UK's Foot and Mouth Disease crisis', *Environment and Planning C: Government and Policy*, 22: 291–306.

Warde, A. (1994), 'Consumption, identity-formation and uncertainty', *Sociology*, 28: 877–98.

Warde, A. (1997), *Consumption, Food and Taste*, London: Sage.

Warde, A. (1999), 'Convenience food: Space and timing', *British Food Journal*, 101: 518–27.

Warde, A. (2005), 'Consumption and theories of practice', *Journal of Consumer Culture*, 5: 131–53.

Warde, A. and Martens, L. (2000), *Eating Out: Social Differentiation, Consumption and Pleasure*, Cambridge: Cambridge University Press.

Warde, A., Cheng, S.-L., Olsen, W. and Southerton, D. (2007), 'Changes in the practice of eating: A comparative analysis of time-use', *Acta Sociologica*, 50: 363–85.

Watkins, H. (2006), 'Beauty queen, bulletin board and browser: Rescripting the refrigerator', *Gender, Place and Culture*, 13: 143–52.

Watson, M. (2013), 'Practices', in P. Jackson and the CONANX group, *Food Words: Essays in Culinary Culture*, London: Bloomsbury, 157–60.

Watson, M. and Meah, A. (2013), 'Food, waste and safety: Negotiating conflicting social anxieties into the practices of domestic provisioning', in D. Evans, H. Cambell and A. Murcott (eds), *Waste Matters: New Perspectives on Food and Society*, Oxford: John Wiley & Sons (Sociological Review Monographs), 102–20.

Watts, M. J. (2014), 'Commodities', in P. Cloke, P. Crang and M. Goodwin (eds), *Introducing Human Geographies* (3rd edition), London: Routledge, 391–412.

Wenger, E. (1998), *Communities of Practice: Learning, Meaning and Identity*, Cambridge: Cambridge University Press.

WHO (1999), *Obesity: Preventing and Managing the Global Epidemic*, Report of a WHO Consultation on Obesity, Geneva: World Health Organization.

WHO (2009), H5N1 Avian Influenza: Timeline of Major Events, http://www.who.int/csr/
    disease/avian_influenza/Timeline_09_03_23.pdf (accessed 23 March 2009).
Wilkinson, I. (1999), 'Where is the novelty in our current "age of anxiety"?' *European
    Journal of Social Theory*, 2: 445–67.
Wilkinson, I. (2001), *Anxiety in a Risk Society*, London: Routledge.
Wills, W., Meah, A., Dickinson, A. and Short, F. (2013), *Domestic Kitchen Practices:
    Findings from the 'Kitchen Life' Study*, London: Food Standards Agency.
Wilson, M. (2012), 'Moral economies of food in Cuba', *Food, Culture and Society*, 15:
    277–91.
Winterman, D. (2014), 'The rise of the ready meal', *BBC News magazine,* 16 February.
Woolgar, S. (1998), *Science, the Very Idea*, Chichester: Ellis Horwood.
Wu, Y. R. (1999), *China's Consumer Revolution*, Cheltenham and Northampton, MA:
    Edward Elgar.
Xin, H. and Stone, R. (2008), 'Chinese probe unmasks high-tech adulteration with
    melamine', *Science*, 322 (5906): 1310–11.
Xinhua News Agency (2009), Sanlu Criminals Zhang Yujun and Gen Jinping Executed.
    Available at: http://news.xinhuanet.com/legal/2009–11/24/content_12532123.htm
    (accessed 27 September 2010).
Xiu, C. and Klein, K. K. (2010), 'Melamine in milk products in China: Examining the
    factors that led to deliberate use of the contaminant', *Food Policy*, 35: 463–70.
Yakovleva, N. and Flynn, A. (2004a), 'Innovation and sustainability in the food system:
    A case of chicken production and consumption in the UK', *Journal for Environmental
    Policy and Planning*, 6: 227–50.
Yakovleva, N. and Flynn, A. (2004b), 'Innovation and the food supply chain: A case study
    of chicken', Centre for Business Relationships, Accountability, Sustainability and
    Society, Working Paper Series No. 20, University of Cardiff.
Young, I. M. (2003), 'From guilt to solidarity: Sweatshops and political responsibility',
    Dissent, 39–44.
Zhang, H. L. and Song, S. F. (2003), 'Rural-urban migration and urbanization in China:
    Evidence from time-series and cross-section analyses', *China Economic Review*, 14:
    386–400.
Zhou, X. (2008), 'Eat, drink and sing, and be modern and global: Food karaoke and
    "middle class" consumers in China', in C. Jaffrelot and P. Van der Veer (eds), *Patterns
    of Middle Class Consumption in India and China*, London: Sage, 170–85.

Index